On The Run
Around Manchester

Acknowledgements

To all countryside organisations and agencies, all waterways agencies and societies and all individuals who helped provide research information. To the family members who I am not in touch with but helped in their own way and, of course, my Mum for providing an ear to listen and a hand to help a writer suffer a little less for her art.

Disclaimer

This book has been researched thoroughly and the author has taken all reasonable care to ensure that the information contained in this book is accurate at the time of publication.

First published in Great Britain in 2012 by The Derby Books Publishing Company Limited, 3 The Parker Centre, Derby, DE21 4SZ.

© Caroline Oldfield, 2012

ISBN 978-1-78091-004-8
Printed and bound by DZS Grafik, Slovenia.

On The Run
Around Manchester
Caroline Oldfield

A guide giving the layout, landmarks and history of running routes
around a vibrant city with a love for sport but edged with an almost
forgotten rural beauty.

Contents

Introduction

Sport, particularly running, is both fun and beneficial. The endorphins make you feel confident and happy, the cardio vascular work keeps your body fit and helps keep your weight down and running is free. If you know where to run it can introduce you to some stunning places around this sporting city whose beauty is hidden under a bushel.

Some misinformed people think Manchester is all about Moss Side and murders, armed robberies and angry riots. However, Manchester is a fantastic city. The soulful metropolis-wide love of music and performance; the civic pride of events from Remembrance Day to Gay Pride; everything from the 10k to Saturday buskers lining Market Street has spirit, a life about it. Manchester's bravery in rebuilding itself after the IRA bombings in 1996, to the extent that for most the matter is now a small scar also proves you cannot dent the spirit here.

But that spirit can be harnessed too in the vast array of sportsmanship that this city is known for: giant Premier League Football Clubs, the cycling Velodrome, the Manchester Aquatic Centre and rugby teams such as Sale Sharks, now based in Stockport. There is Lancashire Cricket Club and many well-known boxers notably Ricky Hatton and Amir Khan. There are also the athletics talents of clubs like Sale Harriers who became British League Champions for the third time in August 2011 and Stockport Harriers who have a membership age ranging from 8 to 80.

We are *On The Run Around Manchester* but if you thought this book helped you lose the law after a riot of felonies, you'd be wrong! This book is to open up a new world to runners and joggers in the Manchester area and places around the city in the Cheshire, Derbyshire and Lancashire areas.

Manchester has numerous swimming pools and fitness centres, not to mention the dedication to sport from hungover Sunday morning football teams and rugby clubs, to the athletics tracks buzzing with sprinters.

Within a few miles of the centre of this great city there are beautiful landscapes and stunning escape spots: from the wilderness of the Peak District, areas of the Pennines themselves, to the wind-covered grasses of summer evenings overlooking the Cheshire Plains. Moorland areas such as Saddleworth and Castleshaw are challenging but give such a re-introduction to the elements that they could bring a soul back to life, especially in testing seasons.

There are multiple rivers in the flowing forms of the Goyt, Tame, Mersey, Etherow, Medlock, and Bollin, and lesser known rivers like the Beal, Spodden and Roch after which Rochdale was named. There is also the Irk – because it is bound to niggle someone if we don't include all the rivers in the area.

There are canals aplenty with the Bridgewater being the first ever built in this country. There are also the Peak Forest, Huddersfield Narrow, Ashton, Manchester and Ashton-under-Lyne Canal and its tributaries Hollinwood Branch Canal and Fairbottom Branch Canal; Manchester, Bolton and Bury Canal, Rochdale, and Manchester Ship Canal, all created to ferry goods and materials for industry or to power machinery but now stand, though some a little neglected especially branch canals and are mostly used for leisure, like a privileged secret to the runners, walkers and occasional barge users who grace them.

Runners all want different things. Some just want to grab their trainers and donning a pair of shorts and a T-shirt, whatever the weather, run freely near home. Others want to run really long routes that take more organisation and maybe transport to reach the starting line. Some

Peak Polo: Holmfirth Road near Dove Stones.

people love the individuality of running where they can push themselves to the limit unhindered by life, rules, infrastructure or others. Some like to run in pairs, gassing as they thrash the distance. Lots of people love concrete running. Others don't count it as running unless they feel the mud and grass under their trainers, or even seeping through their trainers, and need to see fields, moors, rocks, grasses, waters and endless landscapes to invigorate the soul and mind – not just the heartbeat.

And you thought running was simple! But we are lucky in Manchester. The city, its suburbs and its peripheries have many stately homes or parks for those who like grass running but don't want the challenge of navigating moorland such as Tatton Park, Heaton Park and Dunham Massey. There is Lyme Park (where they filmed *Pride and Prejudice*) or Moses Gate Country Park (that looks like Eden in the right season and weather). There is Vernon Park in Stockport and Woodbank Memorial Park nearby, both gracing the River Goyt. The borough of Stockport alone boasts of 35 parks on its websites; so considering this is one of the biggest cities in the UK we are having a picnic where green or open land is concerned.

There are the numerous canals with towpaths that pull the runner along and we have enormous set routes which touch the city, which you can choose sections of and increase your distance as you improve in ability. There is the Irwell Valley Sculpture Trail at 30 miles or the Trans Pennine Trail. This crosses from one side of the north of England to the other so you could end up covering 215 miles if you were keen enough. In fact, if you are mad enough it was designated as the English part of the European Long Distance Walk Routes in 1996, so keep on running!

Most of all, I am a runner myself and I know Manchester has some beautiful spots that many people, including natives either don't have the time to explore or have forgotten the existence or the beauty of. Maybe you live in north east Manchester and know of top routes there but none in south Manchester or vice versa. This book could help runners find new routes and swap ideas to find new areas and with it new motivation to run.

On The Run Around Manchester also provides you with some of the history and tradition of the places you tread. Running along canal towpaths, riversides and fields can feel physically magical but is even more inspirational if you know you just ran past 'Oliver Cromwell's Castle' or that a Lowry painting of the parkland in front of you sold for £3.7 million in 2007. Sometimes it is even more amazing to know the breathtaking scenery before you was once wasteland or industrial land and is now stunning countryside so close to city chaos. It makes you glad this heritage is on your doorstep as you discover that the mud paths you pound helped transit deliveries in the embarking of the Industrial Revolution or that 500 soldiers once lived in a Roman Fort where you run a near solitary session today.

This book provides summaries to choose your next route when you are under pressure timewise and websites and contact details for useful organisations, information sources and clubs.

This is a city framed by hills and mountains, veined with canals and rivers with a vast quantity of greenery and parkland many a metropolis could only dream of. As for those who think Manchester is just an industrial city of reprobates maybe we should let them believe it; it means there is more beautiful, captivating, inspirational space for us to enjoy being *On The Run Around Manchester*.

Alkrington Wood
(via Heaton Park)

Rural visitors, naturally

After getting the Metrolink on the Bury line to Heaton Park you can alight and enter the park where a billboard offers a map of the public space. (See Heaton Park route.)

Once you have warmed up and run towards the boating lake, avoiding the park's internal tramline you can enjoy views of the water before exiting the park near Victoria Avenue (or the A6104). After being surrounded by dog walkers, calmness and a slower pace of life the sudden mass of traffic heading up Middleton Road's incline seems very urban but you are about to head in the same direction.

If you turn left and then carefully cross Middleton Road you should pass Heaton Park Road West and the entrance to supermarket grounds and retail outlets. Avoid the temptation to bend your credit card into contorted shapes and instead roll your feet a bit more, up the incline and past the Three Arrows pub on the other side of the road. Here you should see a sign for a public footpath leading down from the pavement on your side of the road just before you reach the M60. Thankfully saving you from a run no one wants!

Run down the slope and follow the path round as it skirts the River Irk. You should pass a quaint little fishing pond on your right and then go under the M60 motorway on sandy terrain.

Although you will see (and perhaps smell sometimes) industrial units and a sewage works on the other side of the river, keep running (not that you'd wish to stop for long) and you will come upon a reservoir filled with swans and ducks on the edge of Alkrington Wood.

This wooded area, though quite small when compared to somewhere forested, is packed full of flora and fauna. There were many squirrels around and although there is no obvious sign of a building that acts as an aviary there is a bird sanctuary here and the sounds in this woodland, even during a very cold January showed that our feathered friends love the area. Runners too seem to pack the pathways even on cold weekday lunchtimes.

The browns, oranges and greens alongside the River Irk, which continues to flow through the area, make Alkrington Wood a very pretty running ground, with some laid pathways to run on or if you prefer there is more rough terrain to challenge you.

There are many points where you can leave the wood to head back to Heaton Park and the Metrolink. You could find Woodfield Road, which is a residential street accessed through a gate off high ground in the woodland. From there turn right, onto Dingle Road, left onto Alkrington Hall Road South and then right onto Manchester New Road. You can then cross the motorway on this A-road before going right onto Victoria Avenue and down the hill to Heaton Park.

Alternatively if you are having difficulty finding Woodfield Road or want a quicker, though less established route back to the park, there is another public footpath on the southern edge of Alkrington Wood, on the border of Rochdale and Manchester, near Nutbank Lane. It will take you along a narrow, muddy path with one building on your left, higher up the hill. Keep climbing and you will hit a gravel area where you are tempted to turn back thinking you would have to run across the M60 itself – too challenging even for us! But don't worry as runners we never give in until we are at the finish line and there is an open footbridge crossing the M60 closer to Heaton Park than the above mentioned Manchester New Road crossing.

Next you will find yourself at the residential junction of Charnwood Road and Kilburn Avenue. Go straight on from Charnwood towards Cooper Road and keep running past the Chain Road and Alworth Road junctions down Cooper Road until you reach Victoria Avenue.

Turn right here and head along a residential A-road filled with shops. Running during a Wednesday lunchtime in January this area may seem a little like a parallel universe and perhaps one where you are better off taking a photocopy of a map rather than ask for directions. I was repeatedly followed by a car full of girl-racers and saw three men together pushing babies in prams. Good for equality when the drivers have swapped vehicles – and it does make you run a bit faster if you're being tailed!

On Victoria Avenue you have about 0.75 miles to the Heaton Park entrance you left earlier and much of this end section is downhill. A joy to run, or chance to play catch up with speeds before re-entering the park, running past the boating lake and café and back to the billboard area to stretch off and get the Metrolink.

It does sometimes seem a bit quiet along Victoria Avenue considering it is such a big road, although rural paths were busy. But as with some other areas, don't let the atmosphere of some urban or industrial landscapes put you off running to the beautiful spots like Alkrington Wood or Heaton Park. Solitude can be good. It just may not be a good idea for everyone to have their first taster of this route on a dark night while running alone.

Advantages:
- You cover every terrain here; park, tarmac, muddied riverside, gravelled paths, motorway bridges and residential areas. It is good for cross-country lovers or stamina building.
- There are some beautiful areas of countryside in the woodland and when viewing the waterways.
- There are some inclines to test you.

Disadvantages:
- Some areas might seem intimidating on a dark night if you were new to the area and the riverside paths were not lit.
- Crossing an open motorway bridge isn't for everyone.
- Some people might dislike navigating the residential sections.

Summary:
A multi-terrain intermediate circuit that offers cultivated land, rustic countryside and urban stretches with a convenient finish for the Metrolink.

Mileage:
4.5 miles.

History:
Sir Ashton Lever started collecting seashells in 1760. He opened a museum showing natural finds in 1766 and moved it to his home of Alkrington Hall in 1771. It proved very popular but it is said after footfall of over 1,000 people a day he restricted visitor numbers.

Captain James Cook was impressed enough with Lever's displays to donate finds after the natural history lover moved to London in 1774 and exhibited his 'Holophusicon' also known as the Leverian Museum in Leicester Square.

Lever lived from 1729 to 1788 but when his collection reached 28,000 items he went bankrupt and it is said both the British Museum and Russian royalty declined to buy the contents. They were then offered up as a lottery and the winner put the items up for auction in 1806.

Lever is said to have got tired of the insolence of working class visitors and made rules that they could only enter with a ticket issued by a lady or gentleman that he knew and if they arrived on a beast of burden. Luckily for us runners now we don't need royal consent nor a pony and trap to visit the beautiful woodland.

In the last century James Lees of Biddulph is said to have wanted to sell off the 700 acres of land he had for development. The *Architectural Review Magazine* said it would have been a 'great calamity' as there was 'scarcely any timber in the district'. Luckily the 70 acres of the woodland was saved for Middleton residents by the corporation in 1936.

Useful Websites:

www.rochdale.gov.uk

The local government website can give you information about places such as Alkrington Wood but also dates of events such as Teddy Bears' Picnics. If you run down to the woods today who knows what surprises you will see.

Contacts:

Alkrington Wood

Manchester Old Road

Middleton

Rhodes

M24 1WF

Tel: 01706 350459

Email: healey.dell@rochdale.gov.uk

Ashley Road, Hale

Cultured agriculture

Get off the bus, train, metro, taxi – who knows, perhaps it will be gondolas soon – at Altrincham Interchange and after finding a useful spot to stretch, run left, straight up the main thoroughfare of the town named Stamford New Road and continue as it becomes Railway Street. Run past Lloyd Street and yes, already you are on the open road which is going to take you several miles around the Cheshire countryside.

Keep running as the B5163 Ashley Road becomes the B5357 Ashley Road, the busy thoroughfare of the genteel Main Street of the wealthy village of Hale. This place is much smaller than other nearby towns but you can see from the range and size of shops here how well-off its inhabitants are.

If you can keep your credit card caged, run onwards over the level crossing near Hale Station – I would recommend not continuing when the barriers are down however – and keep on running along Ashley Road.

The next 0.75 miles or so is rather residential but then you reach Ashley Bridge and cross the River Bollin. Almost straight afterwards the road bends round to the left but there is a footpath straight on past Ashley Hall, which lets you continue along Ashley Road at the other side and also displays some beautiful scenery along the way.

Unfortunately for some this path isn't accessible for cars, bikes or even horses and the hall itself is not open to the public. However, this path will allow those of us on foot to see the red brick buildings and cobbled lanes of Cheshire. Some strange looking concrete triangular objects at the end are no doubt in place to stop vehicles heading through but once you have passed them you begin to see a more covered running area as the next stretch is forested on your right and holds some lovely scenes including ivy-covered logs in the dancing light.

Unfortunately, coming up, is also a bridge over the M56. One minute you are looking at a lane with a tiny display of light at the end under the shade of the forest, the next you are dangled over several lanes of traffic just before Junction 7. You shouldn't feel in danger but some people afraid of heights might feel queasy. If so, you could cut out the Ashley Hall detour and stick to the main road which changes to Cow Lane and goes under the motorway instead and takes you to the village of Ashley.

If you do take the Ashley Hall route, however, you should now pop-out back on Ashley Road just after Ashley village. For both options, once past the village, run to your right, in a westerly direction past Birkin Farm. Along these roads you should see wide open fields, glorious with the tones of wheat in late summer or green grasses of Cheshire's largely flat land.

Soon afterwards you should reach Birkinheath Covert, which though by the roadside is like a glimpse of a major area of forested land with its stunning sized trunks reaching to the sky and its beautiful shades and branches draped in foliage.

After the distraction of its beauty you should then turn right up Birkinheath Lane, a country lane which has some wonderful views and is about as far south as this route goes. The road becomes Dirty Lane after about 0.5 miles and gives you a strong view over Rostherne Mere. Afterwards you plod north-westerly and the rest of what was Dirty Lane is now named Cherry Tree Lane, for most of the way at least.

Near the end of Cherry Tree Lane, if you run here in the evening, you can enjoy the last sun of the day and the last view of the Mere before you start pounding on concrete again. This road brings you out near Junction 8 of the M56 and not far from Dunham Roundabout. Turn right,

Blanket of beauty, Sinderland Road.

run up Chester Road and over the other side of the roundabout to Dunham Road and cross the River Bollin once more.

After all that time without seeing people or shops there is a very handy petrol station here for a well-earned energy drink or two. If you are strong enough to continue without extra sugar though, run left onto Farm Walk and through Dunham Park to then see Dunham Massey Hall, itself at the junction of many pathways.

Next, in the deer park, head immediately right, where Farm Walk becomes more of a footpath, to head north eastwards and join the end of Main Drive. Then turn left onto Charcoal Lane and right onto Charcoal Road to join School Lane. Or you could continue straight on along Farm Walk and then head north, past the Fish Ponds, crossing Main Drive and joining the junction of Woodhouse Lane, Woodhouse Road and Smithy Lane. Beware because the similar names can cause confusion – you want to head along Woodhouse Road or Charcoal Road in the direction of Dunham Town.

Run onto School Lane as the road crosses the Bridgewater Canal, a sign you are definitely back on turf, albeit waterside turf, with a city centre connection. At night you can see city centre landmarks from here like the lights of Beetham Tower.

For those of us still out running no matter what the time, continue along School Lane until it becomes Whitehouse Lane and run past Altrincham Crematorium, battling, though you might feel close to giving up yourself. Then turn right (eastwards) onto Sinderland Lane and keep running as it becomes Sinderland Road, taking care and watching these country lanes because of the lack of footpaths, or lighting at night. Someone also saw fit to put two similar named Sinderland Roads and two Manchester Roads in this vicinity but those road names in the direction of Carrington are not the ones you want. Head east for almost 1.5 miles and Sinderland Road becomes more populated and residential as you get closer and closer to the A56 Manchester Road.

From here things become very urban once more and you can run on pavements up to Timperley Metrolink Station by heading north eastwards (city bound) on Manchester Road and then turning right up Park Road to reach Timperley Metrolink Station and get back into the city centre via the trams. Or you could simply get a bus in from Manchester Road.

Those not wanting to quit yet, however, could make a full loop of the run by turning right (or southwards) down Manchester Road and running onto Barrington Road, then finishing back at Altrincham Interchange.

If you want a shorter route, after buying your energy drink near Dunham Roundabout instead of turning off at Farm Walk and running through Dunham Park just keep running up Dunham Road. Next, turn right off Dunham Road down Regent Road to then head left along Stamford New Road and back to Altrincham Interchange where you started, very glad to see several transport methods to take you the rest of the way home! You would miss the Massey and lonely roads near Sinderland Lane but if you only have so much time to squeeze in a quick run it is a better route choice.

Advantages:
- Some beautiful, lonely country lanes and views.
- Switch your phone off; no one can reach your level of solitude.
- It is a good, long route to train for something like a 10k or even a 10-miler.

Disadvantages:
- It can get a bit too lonely if you pull something or flake out.
- Public transport doesn't cover much of the route once past Altrincham and before Timperley.
- There is not much elevation to test your muscles on this flat land.
- Dunham Massey estate is not always open and if you made a long trek especially to see it you would be narked, so it is best to check online first.

Summary:
A long route along Cheshire lanes and villages past lovely agricultural countryside and native large houses for a genteel yet taxing, isolated run which particularly seems to suit summer evenings.

Mileage:
Timperley 8 miles, Altrincham 8.25 miles, via Dunham 6.75 miles.

History:
The Bollin Valley made up of the River Bollin is 30 miles long and runs from Macclesfield Forest to the Manchester Ship Canal at Bollin Point near Lymm. The area is well loved by birdwatchers, wildlife enthusiasts and lovers of natural plants such as fungi. The 169sq-mile catchment area is also a favourite with local historians and industrial archaeologists.

Ashley Hall dates from the late 16th to the early 17th century and the Cheshire gentry met on the site in 1715 to decide whether to support the Hanoverians or the Stuarts. They backed the Hanoverians. English Heritage rate it as a Grade II listed building and even the carriage forecourt, kitchen garden wall, stable block and gate piers are listed Grade II in their own right.

The village of Ashley has one single public house, The Greyhound Inn, and a cricket club founded in 1888. Some residents fight for a soda but the village post office closed so they can send you an overarm ball or a pina colada but no postcards!

The Georgian house of Dunham Massey is set in 300 acres of a stately deer park but one of its past owners, the 7th Earl of Stamford, preferred women who liked other animals it seems. Natives claim he married Catherine Cocks a former circus bareback rider. The 2nd Earl of Warrington, who was once a resident, loved his wife so much he wrote a book anonymously about the desirability of divorce. The grounds house Britain's largest Winter Gardens and they allow dogs into the estate on leads, so you could bring other visitors with you too, or have to leap over somebody else's Labradors en route.

Useful Websites:
www.bollinvalley.org.uk
Here you can download maps of Bollin Way routes and check for footpath closures. Map 4 of 5 covers much of this *OTRAM* route.
www.cheshireeast.gov.uk
Find out which parks to run in and download leaflets for Ranger Service trails, many are in deepest Cheshire. Alderley Edge and Wilmslow are the ones closest to Manchester itself.
www.nationaltrust.org.uk/main/w-dunhammassey
Get information, prices and contact details about the stately home of Dunham Massey.

Contacts:
Cheshire East Council
Tel: 01625 374790
Email: bollin@cheshireeast.gov.uk

Dunham Massey
Woodhouse Lane
Dunham
WA14 4SJ
Tel: 0161 941 1025
Email: dunhammassey@nationaltrust.org.uk

Ashton Canal at Guide Bridge, Peak Forest Canal and Fairfield

Take your hat off to them

Guide Bridge is a major junction in railway terms but you have to admit, it is a small place on the edge of Audenshaw in other terms. But if you get a train from Piccadilly out to Guide Bridge Station you will only have to journey about three stops from the city centre.

Immediately, you will see the Ashton Canal. However, it is best, after warming up, to leave the station via Guide Lane, turn right onto Stockport Road and then right up Pottinger Street about four streets ahead.

Although you are running past industrial buildings and past the top of industrial streets here, it is the best place for getting onto the canal as a short bridge at the end of the street allows you to cross the waterway pedestrian-style and get onto the towpath.

The alternative from Guide Bridge Station would be to turn left heading around Audenshaw Road and then right onto Moss Way getting onto the canal west of the train station to then run east.

The towpath has some pretty greenery alongside and to the right you can see the River Tame flowing underneath and around the canal. After about 0.75 miles on the waterway you reach an area filled with old barges. There are several bridges over what reveal themselves to be different waterways and a sign that states you have reached the Peak Forest Canal. However, before you turn right onto this different canal, the buildings of the Portland Basin on the other side of the Ashton Canal house an interesting museum which reveals the area's past. A museum you may wish to visit on a less laboured, time-pressured occasion.

The museum includes lifelike scenes of schools, shops and pubs in historical eras; it has information on hat making in Tameside, the Industrial Revolution and the beginnings of the railway network. It has a mock barge to drive, sail, or steer; a café, toilets and this museum gives knowledge of east Manchester's heritage. Being realistic, most people out running and covered in sweat don't want to interrupt proceedings to see a local history museum, not at that precise moment anyway but it can be a good idea to start from here sometimes instead of Guide Bridge or leave family here as you head off for a run.

As mentioned above, Portland Basin introduces the Ashton Canal to the Peak Forest Canal and the River Tame flows underneath them. The restored Huddersfield Narrow Canal also meets up here. It was closed in about 1944, saw restoration projects begin in about 1974 and it was finally reopened in 2001 by Prince Charles. (See other routes.) Portland Basin is a good place to embark if you drive to the start of your run. It would then give you somewhere to leave your car and let you avoid the industrial stretch from Guide Bridge before hitting the Peak Forest Canal itself.

But whether you visit the museum or not, afterwards head back over the bridge and onto the right hand towpath of the Peak Forest Canal crossing the River Tame over an aqueduct as you do so. Not long after heating your muscles along this stretch you will see Dukinfield Lift Bridge: a black and white structure which, if your timing is right, you might be lucky enough to see rise to allow a barge through.

It has to be said the minute your feet reach this part of the Peak Forest Canal the towpath seems more stately, better kept, with trees in military alignment and more foliage beside the towpath. Some of that may be due to visible construction work taking place alongside the Ashton Canal, as part of the forthcoming Ashton line of the Metrolink, which takes away some of the peace and rustic nature of the waterway. Aside from the building work things do usually seem more rural on the Peak Forest Canal.

Almost 0.5 miles after the lift or swing bridge you will see a road crossing the canal and towpath. This is where Astley Street meets Ashton Street and where you will leave the more relaxed and solitudinous aspect of your run and rejoin concrete roads and civilisation. Turn right onto Ashton Street this B6169 becoming Shepley Road. Carry straight on at the crossroads with Denton Road and Guide Lane to Stamford Road, where you are not far from the Guide Bridge Station starting point. After another 0.5 miles the land starts to open up offering you views of Audenshaw Reservoirs to the immediate west and of several miles to the east towards the Hyde and Hadfield areas. There is also a roundabout on which to turn left onto Audenshaw Road.

If you had been hoping to be able to run around paths surrounding the Audenshaw Reservoir you are unlikely to be lucky as the footpath is shut off to the public, though it is tempting to try and sneak in if you are thirsty, as once, before they were trimmed back somewhat to make way for the M60 motorway, it is said these three reservoirs held 1.44 billion gallons of water. Well, if you've been running for hours…Now though, run instead across the bridge over the eight lanes of the M60 – but it is perhaps best if you don't dangle your feet off the side for a breather!

Continue down Audenshaw Road and then left onto Manchester Road and you should soon see a little residential street on your left named Booth Road, with new houses nearby. Though there is no sign, Fairfield Train Station is here and those who travelled to the start on public transport can get a train back to the city centre from here roughly every 30 minutes. However, there is also a bus stop nearby where Booth Road meets Manchester Road.

If you left a vehicle at Guide Bridge Station you could turn right along Audenshaw Road, then right along Guide Lane or you could turn right up Manchester Road for 0.75 miles and then right again down Moss Way towards the station. Alternatively, run on a canal loop if you wanted by crossing Manchester Road after Audenshaw Road and heading up Ashton Hill Lane. Not long up the road you could then turn right onto the Ashton Canal towpath and go full circle back to Guide Bridge, or even Portland Basin in Ashton. Beware of there being several Manchester Roads near here though it is the A635 which is relevant to this run.

This route is short and quite urban for most of the way but the canal stretches give a picturesque break from the daily concrete grind and there is a definite flavour of water with three canals, a peek at a river and a set of reservoirs to make you thirsty for both more fluids and more running.

Advantages:
- It is mixed in both terrain and scenery.
- You see three or four different waterways on quite a short route.
- If you do visit the museum it gives an interesting backdrop to the route and gives you more knowledge about a less well-known part of the city.
- Portland Basin is now designated a conservation area and part of the city's heritage.

Angels Hide on Ashton Canal.

Disadvantages:
- During rainy weeks the towpaths can be swamp-like running routes.
- You might be disappointed by the urban sections of the route if you travelled a long way to run this one.
- Some maps do not provide clear information where canal towpaths, bridges and marinas are concerned so you might have to allow extra time for your first few runs of waterside routes.
- Towpath closures can give you the run around. If the way is closed off for work it can mean a detour a mile long, or even more, trying to find the right streets or footpaths.

Summary:
A short route which covers urban terrain but allows you to run along two canals, see another canal and a river before heading back to the residential world via a set of reservoirs; dripping with industrial conservation and urban fluidity.

Mileage:
3.25 miles to Fairfield or 4.25 to Guide Bridge via Moss Way or via Ashton Canal.

History:
Donkey stones were an old method of cleaning doorsteps, especially ones fronting textile mills and industrial buildings, which the Manchester area supplied in volumes. It was a name used by a company called Read and Son and the name stuck for longer than the doorstep shine as no matter what other emblems and animal trademarks were used the tag was asinine.

The stones were made from cement, bleach powder and pulverised stone and were used a lot until the 1960s, often by housewives and they were swapped for things by rag-and-bone-men. The last company to make them was Eli Whalley based in Ashton-under-Lyne. It was founded in 1890 and it died out in 1979. That is why on one of the canals sits Donkey Stone Wharf, named to remember the heritage.

Liking to race away, like us runners, a wheel that once powered a hoist system at Ashton Canal Warehouse was powered with a 'head race' (tipped at the top) by the canal and a 'tailrace' (had its feet pushed from under it) by the River Tame, 32 feet or 10 metres beneath. It was said to have cost over £1,000 when it was constructed in 1841 and had a 24ft or 7.3m diameter and a 3ft or 0.91m wide wheel.

Ashton, thought to have been named by Anglo-Saxons — with an origin of meeting near the Ash Trees — expanded its name to Ashton-under-Lyne, seemingly because of the exasperation of being confused with other Ashtons. The natives wanted to underline who they were!

Even today Ashton-under-Lyne has one of the largest outdoor markets in the country and once had the tallest IKEA store nationwide, we are told, but it seems someone somewhere has knocked something taller together since.

It also has a 210ft high or 64m octagonal chimney which was built in 1867 and serves as a local landmark. It is all that remains of the mills that once stood to the west of Portland Basin, such as Junction Mills. One of them was named Banquet Mill after the feast that took place when it was opened. Samuel Heginbottom and Sons owned the company and all its industrial buildings and ran a fabric weaving business. The mills, first built in 1831, costing an initial outlay of £5,000, housed 1,004 looms, weaving devices and other machines and employed 700 people. They kept weaving until the firm closed in 1930, sadly just missing the centenary but stood for another 57 years until they were demolished in 1987, leaving only the chimney as a reminder.

All around this area canal boats are filled with character as the Wooden Canal Boat Society (WCBS) is registered in Ashton and has connections to Portland Basin. Many volunteers have also spent time creating a heritage boatyard in Stalybridge.

The last wooden working narrow boat was not launched until 1958. Oak was used for the main frame and elm for the base. Iron, steel and diesel engines came along and less original boats were used for industry, than those of the previous 200 years. The UK railway network and later motorway network meant the death of much of the canal boat haulage industry and today only around 200 wooden working boats survive, most in a poor condition.

However, the society restores the boats and wishes to let people see them at work showing the history of how canal life worked. A boat named Hazel is a favourite from 1914. It, or 'she', spent many years transporting salt and coal between Lancashire and Cheshire and at the time of writing was awaiting restoration by the society.

In 1987, the then Wooden Canal Craft Trust (now WCBS) used a donated boat named Lilith to take musicians and entertainers on tour to get publicity about reforestation projects.

The society has restored boats for canal holidays for those recovering from depression and some are used in the Droylsden area to collect unwanted clothes and goods to help raise funds and keep the environment tidy. The heritage of the society also lets even us runners get to see 'butties' sometimes, as we are told that was the name for towed barges in days of old.

Useful Websites:

www.canaljunction.com/canal/ashton.htm
To find information about the heritage of Ashton Canal and also the Peak Forest Canal, where the waterways join and about industrial usage of the canals in the past.

www.huddersfieldcanal.com/society/boattrips.htm
For information about boat trip services at Portland Basin, Ashton-under-Lyne, and others trips attached to different canals and routes such as the Standedge Tunnel.

www.penninewaterways.co.uk/peak/pf4.htm
See pictures of both the Ashton and Peak Forest Canals and features such as the Dukinfield Lift Bridge in action.

www.tameside.gov.uk
For information about Portland Basin Museum, Tameside Canal Boat Trust and the history of the area in general.

www.wcbs.org.uk
Hear about the Wooden Canal Boat Society's latest projects and heritage.

Contacts:

Huddersfield Canal Society
Transhipment Warehouse
Wool Road
Dobcross
Oldham
OL3 5QR
Tel: 01457 871800

Portland Basin Museum
1 Portland Place
Ashton-under-Lyne
OL7 0QA
Tel: 0161 343 2878

Tameside Canal Boat Trust
Tel: 07807 262170 or 07966 212902
The trust offers 40-minute trips around Portland Basin on Sundays and Bank Holidays, Easter to October, and can be chartered for groups. It also offers trips to Standedge Tunnel further into the Peak District and it caters for wheelchair users.

Wooden Canal Boat Society
173 Stamford Street
Ashton-under-Lyne
OL6 7PS
Tel: 0161 330 8422
Email: wcbs@care2.com

Bridgewater Canal and River Mersey Circuit

Channel along England's first canal

Find your feet at the Bridgewater Canal for a waterside run that keeps you pounding footpaths and towpaths. You can start anywhere along the Bridgewater but it is a good idea to go where there is an accompanying Metrolink stop. (Having said that Brooklands is a particularly good stop for warming up).

For this route head towards Stretford along the canal (towards the landmark water tower). If you did start from Brooklands you will run along a pretty stretch of canal with houses backing onto the towpath and, not unusually, anglers using the stretch, then you will pass the King's Ransom pub with picnic benches overlooking the canal and Sale Waterside, a modern-design glass library and council building.

Run on as the towpath bends towards Dane Road and the large water tower. It hits wider running areas and what was once a little parallel country road but is now more of a cycle route. Unfortunately it also heads past more industrial buildings. The route then runs under a motorway bridge but after this the path becomes more scenic again and there is more foliage to the left of the towpath.

Ahead you will see the little white, old, cottage-style building which is the Watch House Cruising Club. Many barge owners like to park up at this place so jokes about onion 'bargees'

Do it the Bridgewater Way, Bridgewater Canal near Sale.

aside, you may have to 'barge' past crowds on busy, warm, summer evenings when the place is open for a pint. Most of the time, however, you can flee at a faster speed and not merely cruise past.

In recent years lottery funds have meant the rustic, muddy canal towpath has been tagged Bridgewater Way and restored with widened paths, coated in a sort of glazed gravel and new signs and barriers have been placed alongside the waterway. It also ties the towpath in more neatly with routes such as the National Cycle Network Route 62 and the Trans Pennine Trail but it does mean, in my view, that some of the charm of the route has disappeared.

It also means the route is now filled with people. Even on a wet Monday lunchtime the once solitary area is packed with cyclists, barge users and walkers. Part of the route between Brooklands and Sale is best avoided at school run times as children are now encouraged to cycle to and from a school which backs onto the canal. There are barriers in place to guide them on journeys but of the sort that could sandwich a lone runner between a tide of children wanting to rush home to their PlayStations.

It is good for the area and the canal that it now has such popularity. Disused canals often become unloved and can eventually become watery wastelands in many towns. Now, however, you will have to battle for your place along the towpath. The tidying of the path and designation of exact areas for people to walk or cycle on has widened the leisure space at the side of the canal in some parts: especially on the Stretford Metrolink station side of the Watch House Cruising Club.

It looked beautiful before, especially the more rural stretches. Now it looks very beautiful showing the country's first built canal in its bluest tones and best light but it has changed the feel to something more urban to the eye and the ground is too hard underfoot for us runners. Incidentally, we runners, as in many other places, don't get a mention in all the signs for walkers and cyclists and the websites even mention anglers and boating so perhaps we have to remind them we exist by reaching top speeds near them.

Turn left just before the cruising club (as approached from the south) and then right to run in an upside-down horseshoe shape, under the canal and Metrolink bridges before you reach the signpost for Stretford Ees. You could turn right here but I have found it best to run concrete for a little while longer along the rural, often picturesque Hawthorn Lane which is just to the left of the Stretford Ees sign.

After pounding hard ground you should soon join the almost lawn-like banks of the River Mersey to the right hand side. Lovely as it is to be back on grassland the riverside paths can get rather bogged-down after rainy spells but wet, muddy feet add to the endorphins and sense of achievement we runners get when we reach home later.

Where there is an option to either carry straight on or turn right, take the right turn to pass a sign for Chorlton Nature Reserve and follow the snaking line of the River Mersey to see the tranquil, pool-like water surface of Sale Water Park at some points and the rippling, coursing flow of the river at others.

On a sunny, summer day this is a massively popular route for dog walkers, runners, families, kids on bikes, most of whom park on Rifle Road near Jackson's Boat public house which you are heading towards.

To the left of the riverside path Chorlton Ees has some stunning woodland areas which you should visit in the autumn time. A 'Healthwalk' route before your right turn to the Mersey path, gives a good leg in the shade for this run. However, going back to flow with the river, if you continue along the path you will see a multi-green shaded bridge that takes you across the Mersey, no ferries needed at this point and you could stop here for a drink in the very large beer garden area of the aforementioned pub.

To finish your loop back to a Metrolink station run up Rifle Road, a delightful, leafy country lane with dancing shadows. The cooler air is much welcomed if you have been running alongside the Mersey with the water attracting the sun in the summertime.

At the end of Rifle Road, using caution, turn right over the slightly dangerous motorway access and exit roads and run up Old Hall Road. You can then either turn right up Dane Road, to head for the Metrolink station of the same name about 0.75 miles away, or continue along Old Hall Road and take the Broad Road turning and run about 0.75 miles up the road to Sale Metrolink station. There's always another 0.5 miles back from Sale Metrolink Station to the start at Brooklands after that, running along the towpath or parallel Hope Road if you want a full loop or more of a challenge and all three of those Metrolink stations sit aside the towpath for more mileage.

This is a very flat run. The scenery is beautiful and though the terrain is not as easy as it used to be on the now Bridgewater Way there is at least very little chance of spraining an ankle on uneven ground. Therefore, to make it a good run with regard to pushing yourself you have to travel further and make it about speed and stamina rather than a massive challenge on the exertion to tackle steep gradients. The advanced runner might be better starting earlier on the Bridgewater or running farther along the Mersey but would then encounter different transport needs at the start or finish.

It is a good run to have as a regular route if you live nearby and as said above, Chorlton Ees really is delightful with the golden hues of shedding trees in the woodland in the autumn time – so perhaps should be planned as part of a separate route or regular alternative.

Advantages:
• It is a beautiful waterside route covering both the man-made Bridgewater Canal, the Bridgewater Way towpath along it and nature's River Mersey.
• Though you are running along a footpath the land opens up alongside the Mersey and the woodlands of Chorlton Ees provide more nature.
• It is a good, regular route to use to clock-up mileage.

Disadvantages:
• If you like to go running to think or find solitude this isn't always one of the best routes. A lot of people congregate here at weekends and in the summer.
• The land may be too flat and the route not demanding enough for some runners who love testing inclines.
• You could get lost along the Mersey section on your first run with the choice of so many paths that cut through Chorlton and Stretford Ees but it will become familiar after running the route once or twice and you can take a lightweight photocopy of a map on any route.

Summary:
An improving beginner or intermediate running route. Flat and easy terrain, with a little road running but largely made up of towpaths and country lanes. It can be a beautiful summer or autumnal route and it offers a choice of finishes convenient to the Metrolink.

Mileage:
3 miles via Dane Road, 3.5 miles via Broad Road and 4.25 miles via Hope Road.

History:
The Bridgewater Canal

The Bridgewater Canal opened on 17 July 1761 and was the first canal built in England that did not follow an existing waterway. It was built as a cheap way of transporting coal for the Industrial Revolution from the Duke of Bridgewater's mines in Worsley. In 1974 it ceased to be used as a transport route for freight and began to be used by barge owners on holidays and for leisure. The 39-mile waterway forms part of the Cheshire Ring canal system surrounding the area. Some say the now 250-year-old waterway is affectionately known as the 'Duke's Cut' because of the coal heritage.

The Bridgewater's creation required the building of an aqueduct to cross the River Irwell and sparked canal mania in Britain for about 70 years in the late 18th and early 19th centuries. Packet boat steps exist on the canal near Stockton Heath and Worsley and once acted as kind of watery bus stops when roads were unusable. As with many waterways around Manchester 'turnover bridges' where the towpath swirls from one side of the canal to the other, with both ends facing the same direction, took tow horses safely across the water. They now add character to the canals and fun to the run. The Bridgewater connects with the Rochdale, Trent and Mersey, and Leeds and Liverpool Canals at various points – if you want to run that far by teatime.

The Watch House Cruising Club, the white building on both Hawthorn Lane and the canal towpath, was the residence of the foreman who watched for flooding at the nearby Barfoot Bridge and placed timber baulks across the canal so the bridge had less liquid to deal with. Barfoot is still standing now after over a century of floods and today it carries the Metrolink system out to Altrincham. These days in times of flood, sluice gates open near Jackson's Boat and send waters to Sale Water Park and then onwards to rejoin the River Mersey downstream.

The Watch House Cruising Club cottage actually pre-dates the canal and is the oldest building is Stretford. It has been used as a stables, coffin store and saddle-makers. In more recent years the club members have extended into the stable block to build a concert room.

The towpath improvements and changes made along the Bridgewater Canal itself and named the Bridgewater Way, first opened in 2010 after backing from various charities and trusts and the canal owners. The work has increased access for those with disabilities.

As this book was written, work was continuing on the Bridgewater Way scheme, which plans to regenerate the entire 39-mile canal towpath for walkers, cyclists, runners and schoolchildren. The regeneration already covers the towpath included in this route but will head northwards towards the Trafford Centre, Worsley and Leigh and south to Preston Brook in full. However, all this concrete is not always best for the 'sole' of a runner.

The River Mersey

The River Mersey, which starts in Stockport, is about 70 miles long and ventures off to Liverpool. The water is formed by the tributaries of the River Goyt, River Etherow and River Tame. The name Mersey in Anglo Saxon was said to have meant boundary and much work was done in the 1970s to improve boundaries and stop flooding around the river.

The Mersey Valley Countryside Warden Service started in 1978 making Trafford, Stockport and Manchester councils work together to improve the surroundings and in time sewage works became nature reserves and gravel pits became water parks. The dry weir at

Hawthorn Lane was begun in 1841 after the failings of a previous structure to stop flooding downstream at Barfoot Bridge. The weir was last used in 1915.

Jackson's Boat is in a timeless location for a public house but it was called the Greyhound or the Bridge Inn in the past and as well as changing its name it has changed its provenance. It was considered to be part of the City of Manchester and thus Lancashire under old boundary guidelines and on the river's south side and thus in Cheshire under other rules.

It was a place loved by Jacobite royalists and cock fighters in the past and it is thought that the drinking spot was named Jackson's Boat after a farmer from there started charging to ferry people across the Mersey. Cue the music! When it was put up for sale in 1814 the title 'Jackson's of the Boat' stuck. After an 1815 footbridge was washed away by flooding it was replaced with an iron girder bridge which charged a toll from its opening in 1881 to the end of the 1940s.

There is debate about the actual source of the river with information from the John Stockdale Map going back to 1784 saying the River Mersey starts at Mottram-in-Longdendale and forms the county boundary between Cheshire and Derbyshire. The Encyclopaedia Britannica stated in 1911 that it began a few miles up, at what we today would call the junction of the Rivers Goyt and Etherow, in Marple. Now it is widely accepted that it starts in central Stockport with the junction of the River Tame as well as the Goyt and Etherow. The river then journeys through a large part of south Manchester before joining the Manchester Ship Canal at Irwell and heading away from the Manchester landscapes and scenery and off towards the Irish Sea.

Useful Websites:

www.bridgewatercanal.co.uk
Information about the history of the earliest of the country's canals and the activities that take part along its 39-mile path.

www.merseyvalley.org.uk
Information on wildlife sightings, mapping and general information on the area.

www.sustrans.org
Information on cycleways and walking routes to save our environment and get healthier.

www.visitsalford.info/bridgewater.htm
Find information and read of Salford's pride in its industrial heritage and the earlier life of the Bridgewater Canal.

www.whccstretford.com
Find out the opening times of the bar and membership details of the Watch House Cruising Club.

Contacts:

Bridgewater Canal Company Limited
Peel Dome
The Trafford Centre
Manchester
M17 8PL
Tel: 0161 629 8266
Email: mwebb@peel.co.uk

Mersey Valley Countryside Warden Service
Tel: 0161 881 5639
Email: info@merseyvalley.org.uk

Mersey Valley Visitors' Centre
Rifle Road
Sale Water Park
Sale
M33 2LX
Tel: 0161 905 1100
Email: info@merseyvalley.org.uk

Watch House Cruising Club
1–3 Hawthorn Road
Stretford
M32 8WE
Email: whcc@whccstretford.com

Bury and Rochdale Old Road

Steeped in cliff faces

Maybe Rochdale is your native turf and you are looking for extra routes around the area, or maybe you are from the footballers' wives territory of south Manchester or Cheshire. Either way some of the shop names and so on give away the fact that there are some characters in the town. 'The Butty Shop' tells you the seasoning of these sarnies won't be all spin…and that's before we even get to 'Mi Julie's Baps'.

If you are starting from Rochdale town centre, it might be an idea to make a stop from the bus station at the Town Hall first. This large old building has a garden area with a fountain to the rear and it is a great place for you to warm-up (and stretch off later). After all who wants to stick their rear into a native's face outside M&S when stretching calf muscles with folk as direct as this to contend with?

Once you have pushed and pulled every muscle and sinew (or close enough) head past the Town Hall in the direction away from the bus station, along South Parade and over the roundabout to The Esplanade. Continue along Dane Street and Mellor Street and eventually you will turn left and hit the long Bury Road.

You may be tempted, especially if you are not the sort of runner who prefers concrete underfoot, to run alongside the River Roch at Dane/Mellor but this path runs alongside a sewage works and can be quite dangerous with old bricks sunk into the mud and no lighting. Some parts of the path become sunken bogs further along the way too, so even if concrete is not your favoured underfoot fibre it is best to stick to it for this run.

Run along Bury Road past Rochdale Cemetery, the Dog and Partridge public house and a petrol station; handy to stop at for a high priced energy drink if you need to. Much of this route starts off residential and becomes more and more open. Some of the views along this road later look like a backdrop for a film about Henry VIII. There are such vastly open fields and spaces to inspire that you can imagine Greensleeves playing in the background.

After running the inclines and dips of this road for just over 1 mile you will see the road becomes Bury and Rochdale Old Road. Just under 1 mile further on you will encounter the private road entrance to Bamford Hall. Don't take it, obviously, it being a private road. However, it is a hint that you are nearly at your turning. For us mere mortals the rather industrial looking initial greeting of Ashworth Road should not put you off running up there. Steamy paper mill type buildings sit in the dip and you must skirt round them before you begin to reach a lovely, open, country lane with testing inclines.

There are signs everywhere warning of dangerous cliffs in the area so although you are likely to see many hikers along the lane heading for the river bank, even on a wet Monday, it may be best to stick to the road, at least until you know the area well.

This route gives you an insight into Gelder Wood Country Park as Ashworth Road travels over it, without you having to risk battling the cliffs. The winding lane crosses over the river and at some times of the year, just off a stone bridge, you can see icicles hanging off the rocky crags and even hear them dripping water. It is a stunning view and well worth stopping for a water-break! Once you have been distracted for long enough climb up the lane, past a cattery, follow the lane and then turn right onto School Lane and past some cottages. You will then reach Waterloo Farm and land will not only become more residential but also open up again after the surrounding trees of Carr Wood and Gelder Wood in the country park around Ashworth Road.

Old Age meets Space Age as Manchester
Velodrome and a viaduct abut at Philips Park.

Continue left up Rake and then Furbarn Lane, avoiding Lower Jowkin Lane (jokes about Jowkin aside). Then turn right along Clay Lane where you are sorry once again to hit civilization. Run along Clay Lane to its end and then you can either continue straight on along Bagslate Moor Road and right onto Edenfield Road to head back to Rochdale town centre that way. However, you can instead turn right onto Bagslate Moor Road and very soon, on your left, you should see a public footpath that crosses Rochdale Golf Course and gives your feet a break from concrete to run on grass again for a while.

However, be wary after the muddy path runs past people's conservatories it gets very brambly for a while and if your feet get caught in that at speed, I speak from experience when I say you could be somersaulting not running this stretch. Once craggy buildings are past (and the brambles avoided), this part of Bagslate Moor passes Rochdale Rugby Union Club and you head onto Broadhalgh Avenue. Turn right onto Fieldhead Avenue and left where you will once again find yourself pounding old faithful Bury Road for about 1 mile back to Rochdale Town Hall to stretch off by the fountain.

Advantages:
- You get to see some beautiful country sights without having to fear you will get lost in the woodland.
- It is a great test for different gradients and inclines.
- The distance at about 5.5 miles is great training for a 10k race.
- It is easy to get a bus back from most places on the run if you tire out or get injured…but who likes to quit?

Disadvantages:
- It is nearly all concrete and tarmac underfoot. Lovers of grass running, pounding on moss and moorland have more solid ground beneath them than they prefer.
- Things can seem monotonous and leave you checking maps after Clay Lane with the residential part all looking very similar.
- You may want to head off the country lane and run through the Gelder Wood Country Park land but navigating this with dangerous cliffs has obstacles.

Summary:
A long run with many residential stretches but one that acts as a gateway to the beauty of the countryside and offers testing uphill running as well as some distance building.

Mileage:
5.5 or 5.75 miles.

History:
Rochdale was amongst the first industrialised towns in the country, initially through its woollen mills and then through its textile mills during the Industrial Revolution. Perhaps this explains why the entrance to Ashworth Road near the fields looks the way it does, being well-located to take wool from sheep and process it near the big old road to then transport it to the large towns of Rochdale and Bury.

Rochdale Town Hall is a Grade I listed building built in 1871 in Victorian Gothic revival architectural style. The town is also the birthplace of the Co-operative Movement after the

Rochdale Equitable Pioneers' Society began there in 1844. A group of 28 idealist workers, many of whom were in the textile industry, formed the society to bring about a better social order.

William Cooper was the cashier and Samuel Ashworth the salesman of the shop they initially opened for just two days a week. They met at the Weaver's Arms public house for weekly meetings and took £710 in the first year, despite hard financial times. They became world renown and a book was even written about them entitled *Self Help By The People* in 1858.

The museum dedicated to this movement in Rochdale has undergone refurbishment work and was due to re-open in 2012.

Useful Websites:
www.co-op.ac.uk/our-heritage
Search the history of the famous society.
www.rochdale.gov.uk
Search for information about parks, leisure and opening times throughout the borough.

Contacts:
Rochdale Metropolitan Borough Council
Tel: 01706 647474
Email: council@rochdale.gov.uk

Rochdale Pioneers' Museum
31 Toad Lane
Rochdale
Lancashire
OL12 0NU
Tel: 01706 524920
Email: museum@co-op.ac.uk

Castlefield, Manchester to Salford Quays

A tale of two cities

For this route you get off the Metrolink at Deansgate-Castlefield. (Incidentally, the stop once known as G-Mex.) Walk through the bizarre polytunnel structure, reminiscent of something gardeners keep plants in, not yet feeling like a wilted begonia and out through the train station exit at Deansgate. You walk past what at first appears to be a glass office come bar, only to keep looking up…and up. This is Beetham Tower, part of which houses the Hilton Hotel in Manchester and it's now the tallest building in the city at around 554ft (169m) high.

Obviously one must never jump to conclusions, but I'd guess as you're going running you are not dressed for such an establishment, so fittingly, you should turn left down the less salubrious Liverpool Road. (I know, but I am a Mancunian.)

Down here you will see something I'm sure a lot of Manchester doesn't know about. Here is the Roman Fort replica that resembles the North Wall that helped protect the city in around AD200. (See Medlock Valley Way for more fort history.) Strangely enough sitting there

Beat-Them-All, near Beetham Tower, Deansgate.

admiring the view now are concrete sheep. Yes, bizarre (bah!) but it's not the only location where urban Manchester wants farm animals. If you travel on the Altrincham or Eccles lines near Deansgate-Castlefield you will see more glass offices surrounding a green, grass verge housing plastic cows. If people are that desperate for the countryside they should go running!

Anyway, behind the recreated Roman fortification you may see graffiti images of men charging forward on white horses. This is a reference to the political Peterloo Massacre, not Roman Legions but after warming up near here hopefully you too will be charging away from restrictions.

Continue along Liverpool Road and turn right onto Water Street. Here you pass the entrance to the famous Granada Studios Tours. Again you're not dressed for even the Rovers Return but it is interesting to see the exterior of buildings like this one and Granada Television.

In fact, this route does tour some of Manchester's most well-known sights and the day I last ran this route they were holding auditions for the *X-Factor*. Having a camera pointed at yourself while warming up with your rear in the air doesn't really appeal to most people, so, keep on running, up New Quay Street, Irwell Street, briefly on to Trinity Way and then turn left on to Chapel Street which becomes The Crescent. You never know what you may have to outrun!

Officially speaking you are in Salford and because it has its own cathedral apparently that makes it a city in its own right and that status is often symbolised in logos and on giant signs for buildings. The University of Salford's motto is 'Let Us Seek Higher Things', but we've already covered that on this run passing Beetham Tower in a neighbouring city!

Although this is very much a concrete run and one involving a lot of road crossing around Salford, it is often where the number of other runners seems to increase, with many favouring inner city canal circuits. For this route, however, go left off The Crescent and down Albion Way. This can be busy with traffic and the pavements vary in accessibility and width. Though the central reservation is large enough to run on it does make you uncomfortable jogging down the middle of the A5063. You could instead run down Cross Lane but then you would have to join the roundabout at the end of Albion Way, which isn't actually that long anyway.

At the giant roundabout, or junction 3 of the M602 if you prefer – well, this is urban running – head over to Trafford Road. After a short distance turn right on to Broadway. Those *X-Factor* audition kids would have loved it here no doubt (on Broadway!) – but for us it is a short stretch to the real glamour of running here at Salford Quays.

At the end of Broadway, dodge the final curtain and run on to the road named The Quays as you enter Salford Quays and marvel at the number of unused bicycles apparently contemplating suicide from the posh new high rise apartment balconies. Run past Harbour City Metrolink stop, ignoring Anchorage Metrolink stop if you see it out of the corner of your eye. You could get the Metrolink to Harbour City initially but Deansgate/Castlefield is accessible to more tramlines and you would miss many Manchester sites if you got off at Harbour City.

After bridging the gap between Manchester and Salford you will now cross lots of bridges, starting with the red and blue one. After admiring the architecture and design of the Lowry Museum then step onto the white bridge, which leaves you spoilt for choice where views are concerned.

Many red Mancunians will look left to their spiritual home of Old Trafford; people nostalgic for bread or battle can look towards the Hovis Bread Factory or the Imperial War Museum North and looking straight over the bridge you will see MediaCityUK or Quay West, a kind of golden glittering tin foil structure on the edge of these man-made waters.

This is where navigation may get tricky. If you want Salford Quays Metrolink stop it may be best to ignore some of the existing direction pointers. Turn left and keep running, though you may encounter rough smells on a rainy day as you notice the iron-like smells of the old steel wheels parked at the side of the path.

Keep on watching Old Trafford in the distance, head around the Norseman and keep going towards a marshy bit of ground which houses a spiral, metal staircase and run back on to Trafford Road, crossing yet another bridge but this time one which is part of the actual road. From here you should see Salford Quays Metrolink Station set back from the traffic.

The spiral staircase does look a bit disused and if you want the Altrincham line anyway it might be a good idea to cut off and head towards Manchester United's ground but then carry on down Trafford Road, over White City Circle and down White City Way before heading left briefly, along Talbot Road to Trafford Bar Metrolink. This is, all said and done, a very nostalgic run for natives covering a site where Romans once lived. After that it's a 'Roman Bath' for almost everyone.

Advantages:

- You get to see lots of sights around Manchester without having to fight old ladies with hatboxes on Deansgate or Piccadilly Approach.
- You don't need major travelling time and spells on trains to reach the start line in a rural outpost.
- You get to imagine life in many eras covering a reconstructed Roman fort and the modern MediaCityUK and Beetham Tower.

Disadvantages:

- It is all concrete. Though they may try and pull the wool over your eyes with manufactured sheep there is no greenery on this route and no leaves or mud underfoot for cross-country lovers.
- The traffic and road systems could prove disruptive if you are doing time trials.

Summary:

An inner city concrete run that gives you a good look at Manchester's city centre and can be added to or adapted as stamina improves. A regular route to clock up weekly mileage, or a semi-regular visit to see the city sights.

Mileage:

Salford Quays Metrolink 2.5 miles, Trafford Bar Metrolink 3 miles.

History:

The Peterloo Massacre was an uprising which took place in August 1819 in St Peter's Field, Manchester. The lack of suffrage, hunger and the introduction of the Corn Laws brought about a rebellion headed by Henry Hunt. Cavalry charged into a crowd of between 60,000 and 80,000 to arrest the man and stop the revolt. Between 400 and 700 people were injured and 15 killed and it was given its name as a play on the Battle of Waterloo which took place in 1815.

Salford Docks and Pomona Docks together made up Manchester Docks and Queen Victoria sailed in to open them in 1894. It was once the third busiest dockyard in the country but restrictions on ship sizes because of the canal and changes in loads meant the 120 acres of water and 1,000 acres of land closed.

Salford City Council bought the Quays and thus began the regeneration project in 1985. The Lowry theatre and gallery originally known as the Salford Quays Project For The Performing Arts changed its name in 1994 and was named instead after the well-known stickman painter L.S. Lowry who brush-stroked his canvases with scenes from around these parts. The Lowry was designed by James Stirling and Michael Wilford in the late 1980s but Stirling died abruptly in 1992 leaving Wilford to finish the task as architect. Lottery funding was secured and building began in 1997. The iconic tourist magnet of a building, which includes theatres, exhibition areas and eateries opened its curtains in April 2000 at a cost of £106 million.

Lowry himself started at art college when he was 15. He went to evening classes in 1905, studying at both the Manchester Academy of Fine Art and Salford Royal Technical College. It is said he still attended classes for his art in the 1920s. He originally lived in Victoria Park but money shortages forced his family to move to Station Road, Pendlebury which surrounded him with the sights that he was to make his name painting. At first he detested the scenes of mills and chimneys but with time, looked on sights like the Acme Company's Spinning Mill with an artist's eye, with rapture.

The former rent collector painted in his suits, wiping paint on the sleeves and lapels, living and breathing his work. Salford Museum and Art Gallery began collecting his works in 1936. He had his first London exhibition in 1939. He died aged 88 in 1976 just months before a retrospective exhibition of his work opened at the Royal Academy which broke attendance records for a 20th-century artist. In his later years he went to live out in the suburb of Mottram-in-Longdendale. In 2011 two of Lowry's paintings sold, each for £5.6 million. One of them was of a football pitch, perhaps appropriate in that his museum today sits in sight of Old Trafford.

The Dockyards at the end of the Manchester Ship Canal closed in 1982 and went on to be one of the biggest and earliest regeneration projects in the country, so much so that the BBC began decentralising and moving to MediaCityUK in 2010, with the first real filming taking place in February 2011. The BBC's Sport, Children's, and Research divisions are moving and Radio Five Live is getting its boots on to join us on Salford Quays' Pier Nine, next door to The Lowry.

Oddly enough, rivals Granada, the North West's ITV station is also said to be planning a move to MediaCityUK in 2012 and closing Granada Studios in 2013 but strictly speaking its base will be on the other side of the Manchester Ship Canal in Trafford Wharf, giving it a Trafford, Manchester rather than a Salford address. Channel Four are thought to want a place at the development as well so, addresses aside, the pace of movement and competition are not just at the front of runners' minds here.

Back to a more sporting theme, a water sports centre was opened in 2001 giving training in canoeing, sailing, rowing and windsurfing backed by the Royal Yachting Association.

In 2003 the first International Triathlon Union World Cup in the UK was held at the quays and the Great Salford Swim was held in September 2010, getting the whole city to jump in and doggie-paddle – but we runners can train here all year round.

The Deansgate-Castlefield Metrolink stop was once known as the G-Mex stop, named after the nearby exhibition centre's old name. Today the exhibitors' centre is called Manchester Central.

Useful Websites:

Imperial War Museum North

north.iwm.org.uk

Learn about the latest exhibitions and attractions at the museum.

MediaCity UK

www.mediacityuk.co.uk

Learn about studios, apartments, commercial buildings in the vicinity of the Quays.

The Lowry

www.thelowry.com

Book tickets or read about the history of the building and the artist it was named after.

Contacts:

Imperial War Museum North

General Enquiries

Tel: 0161 836 4000

Email: iwmnorth@iwm.org.uk

MediaCity UK

Tel: 0161 886 5300

Email: hello@mediacityuk.co.uk

The Lowry

Box Office

Tel: 0843 208 6000

Administration

Tel: 0843 208 6001

Chat Moss and Irlam

Make hay while the sun shines

Take what is only a 20-minute train ride out from Manchester's Oxford Road Station and once you alight at Irlam Station run to your left up Liverpool Road. Not long afterwards you will pass a road which vehicles use to access the railway line to your left and then head onwards past shops and a public house on the other side of the road. Then head past a church on your left and then turn left immediately and run up Astley Road in Lower Irlam.

You will initially pass a bowling green and houses on your right but you will barely notice because out of seemingly nowhere the world opens up and in the late summer or autumn time especially you are greeted with fields of gold and yellows, browns and bronzes. The flat Cheshire landscape reaching out forever and you are running along what can only be described as eternally long country lanes.

This area is on something akin to a grid system and there are private roads to farms and houses but mainly it is just these endless, concreted but rickety lanes; no twists, no corners, just ever onwards or right and east and ever onwards as the west is not very accessible from here.

You will pass Rose Farm and then run across a bridge over the M62, which is the sad thing about this route: the constant murmur of motorway traffic in the background. Immediately after the motorway the field on the right of the lane near Woodstock Farm is almost neon in its green radiance in September time.

Do not turn right here after Woodstock Farm to go to try to find Hephzibah but continue on. Head past Landhill Farm and Larkhill House on the right with the entrance road which you are tempted to take with a sentry line of very tall trees along its left side. Head past Hope Cottage on the left – with the little pond outside used by somebody with a little boat – and past Ebenezer Farm.

Head onwards to Four Lane Ends Farm where you turn right up Twelve Yards Road. Here the road becomes even rockier or lumpier with changes to the camber as well as the potholes and cracks you encountered in Astley Road earlier.

Keep on running and you will see to your left at harvest time roll after roll of wound hay, like a field full of cotton spools. Chat Moss (the one north of Irlam Station rather than to the west of it) is the border between Salford and Wigan and you can see trees in the distance but no real urban existence. This countryside is just metres away from the metropolis' Manchester Ship Canal and the M62.

After the turning for Woodbarn and Birch View Farms continue onwards. Unfortunately this Thomas Hardy-esque country vista doesn't last forever. You can continue on to Barton Moss Farm and run along the quaintly named Raspberry Lane over the M62 and turn right down Liverpool Road to reach Irlam Station. However, you can turn off before that and run right, down Cutnook Lane. The lane, lined with rhododendrons, looks more cultivated than the hawthorn and lime tree edgings of earlier lanes. It takes you past the Moss Farm Kennels and Catteries, the Moss Farm Fisheries, the pond area with anglers and a café; all of which greet you out of nowhere.

Sadly, this is where the beauty starts to end. Perhaps you have the energy or a mileage quota to fill, to run onwards to see the Manchester Ship Canal and the River Mersey joining it, these being well-known Manchester waterways, yet if you want to leave with only bucolic sights uppermost in your mind perhaps it is best to head back to the station at this point.

Roll On at Chat Moss.

Cutnook Lane next takes you right, over the motorway and then left over the other side of the motorway and back into Irlam proper and a residential landscape. Beware that the motorway crossing country lane is accessible for cars going to the Moss Farm Fisheries. Along Cutnook Lane you pass the Tiger Moth public house on your left and St Joseph's Primary School. You can run from here, onto Moorfield or finish Cutnook Lane as they both take you to Liverpool Road to then turn right and head back to the station.

If, however, you want to see Irlam Locks and the weir, turn left up Ferry Road from Liverpool Road, heading onwards towards Cadishead Way. On your left near the Boat House public house you will see some open land and be tempted to think it leads to the water but it does not. On your right after the pub, you will see what is described on many maps as the old course of the River Irwell. Now it is like a branch canal, a strip of water travelling no distance.

Take care as you step out from Ferry Road onto Cadishead Way, not so much because of traffic, though it is a fast road but because of the cycleway immediately in front of you that is well used.

Run onwards around the grey railings on the left hand side of the road, next to a Manchester Ship Canal Company sign stating access is only to cross the locks. You are greeted by grey, industrial views here and the stagnant smell of the canal. Once you've seen the locks run further along Cadishead Way to the roundabout and beyond, looking back at the sight of the locks here, for what is perhaps a better perspective. Run past the tempting right hand turn for Fairhills Road and onwards past the weir where the River Mersey joins the man-made waterway. Head past Irlam Wharf Road and right onto Excalibur Way which will lead you right back to Irlam Station and trains to Manchester's Oxford Road.

Advantages:
- Stunning plains like those of Cheshire but closer to the city centre.
- See special land and habitat, yards from shops and services.
- There is very little traffic, though you have to move aside for the 4x4s when you do see them.

Disadvantages:
- The continual hum of speeding motorway traffic, like a bee buzzing down your ear, interrupts the peace of the place.
- The state of the country lanes' surfacing which may discourage running at night.
- There are few turn offs and no buses if you have an accident or wish to quit early. You have to finish the rural end of this route on the lanes, with peat bogs over 20ft (6m) deep as possible challenges if you try otherwise.
- There are no road names and not all farms have name signs in the rural stretch so that can hinder navigation even though it is on a grid system.

Summary:
Unexpectedly beautiful land of open, flat fields and farmed countryside like that of the Cheshire plains in a Manchester suburb standing only metres from the realities and necessities of urban life.

Mileage:
Via Cutnook Lane 4 miles, Irlam Locks 4.5 miles and Bartonmoss Farm and Raspberry Lane 5 miles.

History:
Chat Moss, the area beyond Twelve Yards Road, is thought to make up 30 per cent of the land mass of Salford. It covers an area of over 10 sq miles (26sq km) and the peat can be between 24ft (7m) and 30ft (9m) deep.

Some people believe peat development there dates back 10,000 years to the Ice Age. By the beginning of the 19th century they had still not conquered the nature of the place with drainage ditches and the tiny roads built to deliver lime, clay and marl in an attempt to try and dry out the vast bog which was once a giant lake or pond surrounded by trees. They know this from the wood residue in the depths of the peat.

The Liverpool and Manchester Railway Company was concerned they would not be able to get a train line through the bog and felt their project might be in jeopardy. In 1829, however, George Stephenson floated a line through the area and the train line was built. In 1976 the M62 was constructed, crossing the land parallel to Twelve Yards Road.

Manchester's population went up around 150 per cent between 1831 and 1851. The opening of Irlam's Train Station in 1873 brought people and business to the town which had been very isolated. In 1894 the waters of the Irwell were re-directed into the Manchester Ship Canal giving the Irlam area business as a sort of inland port.

If you run onwards at Four Lane Ends Farm instead of taking the Twelve Yards Road turning, you reach Astley and Bedford Mosses which were designated as a Site of Special Scientific Interest in 1989. This area, also including Holcroft Moss and Risley Moss is cited as a European Union Special Area Of Conservation known as the Manchester Mosses.

There is some upset in the area that peat is being ripped up and used to make compost to sell in major quantities to big companies, which is leaving the land like a desert or dust bowl.

The Salford MP Barbara Keeley has described parts of the area as a moonscape in the wake of the peat removal and in 2010 the council removed planning permission for the peat to be extracted but the peat industry wants the decision overturned. Residents want to see surface peat harvesting processes as used in the past rather than the deep extraction methods used recently, or they want the extraction stopped altogether.

In 1958, a skull was found near the eastern edge of the moss near Worsley. It was thought to be that of a sacrificed Romano-British Celt. The name Chat Moss is thought to either be named after St Chad a seventh-century bishop of Mercia, or to have a partially Celtic origin with Ced once meaning wood and Moss being local tongue for peat bog.

The area is said by some to have the largest farming community in Greater Manchester and on land north of the Moss, Botany Bay Woods is the largest woodland area in Manchester. The area is known to wildlife lovers as a home to merlins, owls and many other bird species.

Useful Websites:
www.manchesterbirding.com/chatmosssiteguide
If you are a birdwatcher get tips on what to see north of Irlam and see pictures of the landscape.

Contacts:
Moss Farm Fisheries
Cutnook Lane
Irlam
Tel: 0161 775 1655

Moss Farm Kennels And Catteries
Cutnook Lane
Irlam
Tel: 0161 775 5777 or 0161 775 9465

Crompton Moor

Taming the wilds

As the Friends Of Crompton Moor say 'Crompton Moor is a precious and unique place. It's a breath of fresh air which lifts us above the urban sprawl that seeks to smother us all.' Whether you drive or take public transport to first reach the bustle and buoyancy of Oldham Town Centre, at present especially, it feels the antithesis of what you are expecting at the moorland destination you are heading for.

The Metrolink service is building a new line out to Oldham and Oldham Mumps. It is set to open in 2012 and should reach Oldham Town Centre in 2014. It means the town is alive with change but the moorland, the tops you are heading for, which have stood there for eons, seem to defy time.

For this run you can head directly north out of Oldham Town Centre on Shaw Road for about 2.5 miles or you can tackle the moorland from the southern edge by getting a bus to Shaw, or from the eastern edge by getting a bus to Denshaw. However, if you decide to get the bus to Denshaw and run onto the tops from there, public transport is much less frequent, every hour as opposed to every 15 minutes to Shaw.

If you go via the Shaw route, turn off Milnrow Road and onto Buckstones Road and not far up the road, maybe even less than 0.25 miles, you will see signs for public footpaths off to your left: for instance Oldham Way and Crompton Circuit. If you head up the side of a little cottage, the path takes you to Pingot Quarry and a small car park area.

The pathway passes ever more rural housing and the climb gets steeper as you slog it past the fabric of heather which coats the hills in summer and autumn time. Oldham Council have worked to put very visible signs around to direct cyclists, walkers, runners and dog walkers to places such as Pingot Quarry but that can be one of the things which makes this moorland area different from others on the Manchester edge of the Pennines.

Castleshaw Moor for instance or Running Hill Head, both under Oldham's jurisdiction, are untamed. You can run for miles through sloppy bogs and not see a soul but here on Crompton you slog it up this lane-come-footpath, lined with the odd cottage, to reach the top and see an area with a little car park which is a beautiful viewpoint. You see other visitors even on weekday afternoons when you would have thought most people would be stuck behind a desk. In short, every time you think you have left the civilisation of Manchester and Oldham as part of a distant metropolis under the shimmering sun, civilisation jumps out.

The area with a little stream and a towering, curving wall of rocks gives you a little wooden bridge to cross the water and climb up the steps to the very top for an amazing view of Oldham and Manchester and to Rochdale and Bury behind you. Instead for this route you can keep on running at the same level as the stream and follow the set, rocky, sandy footpath, ground out of the heather and moorland peat gradually to your left and upwards, looking down over Brushes Clough Reservoir car park and running alongside Old Brook's waterfall on your right and pine forests on your left.

Even though some parts of the Pennines once served an industrial purpose that has then just drifted away into the sands of time, such as quarrying or the housing of reservoirs, these hills still feel untouched: timeless. Be it Saddleworth or Castleshaw Moor, be it Hobson Moor in Tameside, the rolling, natural whale-like humps, line followed by line, never seem to end. You run to the end of one hill, to see others and in many parts that is a very solitary and stress-relieving experience; to have the wind blow the cobwebs from you and just look upon nature and nothing else for hours.

Pining for purple at Crompton Moor.

But strangely enough Crompton Moor has been so well signposted and laid out with paths and cultivated for leisure activities that many people want to visit its beauty, especially during the summertime. One weekday afternoon in August there were more dog walkers visiting here than at a rehearsal for Crufts' Dog Show!

There is also a now well-established and signposted Mountain Bike Trail and some of the area's water in the form of the Old Brook, dancing down the concrete steps into the quarry seems to sweep youths towards it in the school holidays, as they sunbathe and dip in the cooling liquid.

But the higher your altitude and the further the runner gets up the hill, past the waterfall's summit and the pine forests, alongside the telecommunications mast at Crow Knowl the lonelier and more like moorland things get.

The mast itself has fencing around it but you can run up alongside it to see an even higher view, akin to the one you would have seen if you mounted the steps across the little stream near the curving wall earlier. If this level and its open moorland is high enough for now and you want to pound more open expanses and peat, head along the path you are already on swirling under the TV mast and past moorland fields often packed with sheep.

The path then widens and a wooden signpost hints at directions to Shaw and Denshaw, as to your right you see Crompton Moor itself, beautiful, vast and free of numerous pedestrians and more akin to the moorland regular fell runners are used to. To your left you see a handful of scattered farms and houses and to your right the village of Denshaw. The longer you stare the more you can make out the light bouncing off the glass and metal of cars as you see a road, the A640 Huddersfield or Rochdale Road, which hides itself at points under the camber of the surrounding moorland and hills. You can see both how stunning this area can be but also how man is overtaking it from all sides.

If you run towards the road and Highland House, which sells various farm products, or the Alpine Restaurant, which was closed and up for sale as this was written, the road has dangerous paving in places and no paving in others. It also has cars travelling at lethal speeds, so it is one for high visibility clothing and because of the camber of the roads, you should run cautiously and towards oncoming traffic, especially if you stay on it for long.

The road itself has permanent signs warning about things like ice, which motorists don't tend to see on everyday roads, showing how wild this road is but it is an occupied road nevertheless. You could run to your right towards Denshaw or jump back on the path towards Crompton Moor. Tempting as it is to run over the central part of Crompton Moor by heading onto it behind Cherry Clough and Ogden Edge in order to avoid such set tracks as those you encountered on the way out, parts of this route can get a little too rustic; the peat bogs can suck off and steal your trainers and the barbed wire fences can leave their mark long after the calf strain has faded, not to mention the ankle risks you take running off set footpaths on uneven land such as this.

There is, however, a set footpath south if you can find it, which begins behind Cherry Clough but moves to run parallel with Oldham Road which will take you across the moor with less risk. However, it may be best to return along the path you headed out on, perhaps veering off onto other paths once along the return footpath.

If you ran this route from only Shaw or Denshaw it is not a massive run distance-wise and though it is taxing in stamina up the hills to Pingot Quarry and Brushes Clough, it is not really taxing in other respects. This might make you want to pound such beautiful earth and explore still further from the city you call home. You may end up running onwards towards Rochdale or even further north.

Advantages:
- Stunning beauty.
- Quite a quickie for a moorland run so would particularly suit someone running on moorland for the first time or a native of Oldham wanting a change from urban concrete.
- Brilliant for the mind and soul – not just the body.

Disadvantages:
- A bit too short for some fell runners' taste.
- A bit too cultivated for moorland.
- Despite being cultivated for moorland it is still rocky and uneven enough to put your ankles at risk away from the footpaths.
- A bit too popular with others, including dog walkers, especially on summer weekends.

Summary:
A beautiful taste of the Pennine moorland with views towards numerous places including Manchester, Ashton, Rochdale and Bury. A challenge for concrete runners but a light one for fell runners. Crompton Moor has an almost meadow-like cultivated feel in the summertime.

Mileage:
Denshaw 3.5 miles, Shaw 5.5 miles, Oldham and back about 8 miles.

History:
Crompton Moor was once said to be known as High Moor, though there is a High Moor further south towards Saddleworth today.

Crompton Moor's highest point of Crow Knowl sits at 1,281ft or 391m above sea level and thus is higher than Werneth Low in Hyde and a little higher than the Pots and Pans Memorial over towards Greenfield (see other routes). It was made a site of biological importance in 2003 for much of the wildlife including Red Grouse and Golden Plover that sit atop its summits.

Dry stonewalls still exist from 18th-century farmsteads, and palstave axes or chisel-like implements from 1,500BC or 2,000BC have been discovered proving that man lived in these hills in the Bronze Age.

Crow Knowl houses a telecommunications mast but also the Ordnance Survey Triangulation Station, the stone pillar, letting people navigate and discover exactly where they are as they look north west to Rochdale or south west to the city landmarks like Beetham Tower, which is now the most obvious landmark in Manchester from a distance.

Coal and sandstone were once quarried from the Crompton Moor area but it came to an end in the 1970s and now a tributary of the River Beal trickles down into the Pingot Quarry over steps, creating a waterfall as it steps and speeds.

The Crompton Moor Mountain Bike Trail was built with £30,000 of National Lottery money awarded in 2007. Oldham Council planned to change existing spoil heaps left over from the quarries for new materials but following a public meeting decided to simply make the site more family friendly and the 1km (0.6 mile) trail sits near Brushes Clough.

Now as the edges of the moor become more touched by the tools of man and we see the Crompton Waterfall, the Mountain Bike Trail and the planted pine forests it is a shame that the ruggedness of this spectacular beauty seems to be if not disappearing, then being subtly frayed at the edges. At least the changes allow people fearful of open moorland to have a taster of such a spot and it encourages more people to use the land as they did in times long past but have forgotten to in recent years.

Useful Websites:

www.friendsofcromptonmoor.org.uk
A website about safeguarding the moor's nature and wildlife and about trying to stop the city life and its motorised madness from taking over the moors.

www.oldham.gov.uk
Look up Crompton Moor on the council website for information on the users group, nature and habitat.

Contacts:

Crompton Moor Project and User Group
Tel: 01706 663631
Email: cllr.john.hall@live.co.uk

Crompton Moor Users Group
Email: contact@cmug.org.uk

Daisy Nook Country Park

Nook 'em beyond their Waterloo

This park is on the boundary of the areas of Oldham and Tameside so you can run 1 mile from Ashton-under-Lyne centre or about 1.75 miles from Oldham to reach it.

If you decide to go from Ashton, from the bus station turn left along Wellington Road and then go right up Oldham Road, past the IKEA warehouse which is the size of an airport hangar. Run this Roman-like road, which sometimes rises and dips but is very straight nevertheless and head past several schools (so best avoided at school-run time) and run through an area called Waterloo. This has an Astroturf five-a-side pitch and sports facilities. Don't worry though, it might be called Waterloo but it is not that great a battle to get down to the park!

Keep running past residential turnings you should see Bardsley Bridge approaching in a dip, with a hill at the other side like the North face of the Eiger. Again, don't worry (unless you want the climb) because to run in the quaintly named Daisy Nook Country Park turn left, avoiding the hill and run along a path called Riversvale Lane which is sited just before a car park. Run a tree-lined walkway if not avenue, Riversvale Arboretum, which is a delight in the autumn time.

The path is easy to follow but has a lot of steps and slopes and would be a nightmare for someone trying it for the first time in the dark. There is not enough lighting really to run this one at night but you would miss the beauty of the River Medlock and all the nature here if you ran it past dusk-time anyway.

Once you have swept along the path, past fen-like marshland or pond areas and wildlife (don't try and take squirrels on: it's de-motivating) you should see the imposing Waterhouses

Aqueduct curves over the River Medlock at Daisy Nook Country Park.

Aqueduct that you can run towards. Once here turn left to run to the Rangers' or Visitors' Centre or right (northwards) to run the Hollinwood Branch of the Manchester and Ashton-under-Lyne Canal (not to be confused with the Ashton Canal nearer Ashton town centre).

The Visitors' Centre is ideal for those who want to stop for a drink but for most runners it is a bit of a distraction from an almost circular route. Once treading the canal towpath on the Hollinwood Branch you then head over the 80ft (24m) high aqueduct until you reach a junction where the canal to the right is the Fairbottom Branch Canal but turn to the left, a continuation of the Hollinwood Branch Canal and head towards Sammy's Basin, a pond made by the canal and run under a wrought iron footbridge on your way past Pinch Farm.

You will cover staircase-style locks on the canalside part of the run, unusual locks which as the canals are now closed won't see barges trying to grapple with them but are nevertheless interesting sights. You will also see other pond-like areas made by the widening canal – and many lethargic fishermen.

Keep pounding the path onwards to Crime Lake. This is as far west as you will head on this route and it would be good to be able to circle the lake to head back towards Ashton Road via the other side of the canal but it is not possible on this canal. So you make your own furthest point but with this the residential houses and the sight of East Cutler Hill Road will be the last point at which to turn round and cover the towpath in the opposite direction. Make sure you edge left as you go around Sammy's Basin and stay on course along the towpath otherwise you may still pass Sammy's Basin but veer away from the canal slightly.

From then on you cover about 0.5 miles more towpath pounding straight ahead and this time on the Fairbottom Branch too, which seems to pass very quickly, before you reach Bardsley Bridge and the junction of Ashton and Oldham Roads.

On the other side of the road there is a bus stop which has services that will take you back to Ashton. If that felt like just a warm-up you could climb the Eiger-like Ashton Road and run towards Oldham. Or you could repeat the original route in the other direction through Waterloo, past the IKEA hangar and back to Ashton bus station.

Advantages:
- It is adaptable for your training schedule because you can run the park, the park and canals, or to the park from either Ashton or Oldham or cover Ashton, the park and Oldham.
- You get a lovely condensed taster of part of the Medlock Valley.
- There are toilets and such facilities which moorland running for example, does not afford.
- This park is great for parents who run, as there are environmental clubs to keep the kids busy while you yourself get back in touch with nature – unless your kids are under eight and then you have to go with them!

Disadvantages:
- You can get a little boxed in inside the park if you wanted to finish early or if you run out of steam.
- The geese and ducks around Crime Lake are so friendly they may slow you down when trying to reach your personal best – as are the dogs and walkers.
- Sometimes the litter can spoil the scenery.
- The Easter Fair is a big event to keep the family happy but the masses of people won't be to every runner's taste.
- The layout and long names of the branch canals may prove confusing when route planning.

Summary:
A lovely park with a lot of history for one so young (we know the feeling!) but it is good for families. Perhaps a little too popular at times, such as Easter, for the runner that wants to sizzle the soils!

Mileage:
4 miles.

History:
It is said local writer and poet Ben Brierley wrote a short story about a day out or summer ramble entitled *A Summer Day In Daisy Nook* in 1859 and got an artist friend to draw *Daisy Nook*, then called Waterhouses. The quaint title for the area has stuck ever since.

A pub was named after Brierley in his hometown of Failsworth but it closed down and became a Citizen's Advice Bureau instead. Perhaps noteworthy as a lot of his writings concentrated on portraying Lancashire life to those far and wide who did not know a lot about it.

A different artist's talent was also shown through his connections with Daisy Nook. The most highly prized L.S. Lowry painting was of the park in celebratory mood following World War Two. A collector paid over £3.7 million for it in 2007 making it the most valuable Lowry until 2011 when two sold for £5.6 million each.

The Hollinwood Branch Canal once ran from Droylsden to Hollinwood in Oldham, after it opened in 1797 to transport coal from collieries between Ashton and Oldham. Many tramways ran from the collieries to canals including one near Crime Lake. Though the Hollinwood and Fairbottom Branch Canals stopped being used to transport goods in the 1920s and early 1930s, the Hollinwood Branch was closed north of Crime Lake in 1932 because of subsidence problems.

The canals were not filled in completely and were still used for barge sailing and leisure but the Fairbottom Branch was no longer navigable by 1948 and the Hollinwood was closed between Littlemoss and Daisy Nook in 1955. The Daisy Nook area was made into a country park with the waterways as features in the 1970s. Sadly, most of those particular canals outside of the park, towards both Droylsden and Hollinwood, have now been filled in so you cannot cover the ground the towpaths took people on over half a century ago.

The Hollinwood Branch Canal was 5 miles long and held eight locks, including the two which make up the staircase lock. On the Hollinwood Branch beyond the Visitors' Centre there was once a tunnel known as Dark Tunnel, which had an eeriness which used to scare and entertain the Victorians on their walk into Daisy Nook. The long passageway was made into a cutting in the 1920s as the roof was said to have kept caving in.

It had been planned in 1792 that an extension would be built to join the Hollinwood Branch Canal with the Rochdale Canal, said to have been less than a mile away but it never came to fruition. Slowly chugging along though, the idea to build and renew the branch canals may yet come to fruition in the 21st century. In 2008, a £100 million project in Droylsden built houses and shops around a restored canal area in a marina style refurbishment.

Useful Websites:
www.ashton-under-lyne.com
Gather information on previous walks, local monuments, heritage and photographs of Ashton's top sites.

www.visitoldham.com
Get brief information on Daisy Nook's facilities and opening times but on many other Oldham-based running locations and visitor attractions as well.
www.hollinwoodcanal.co.uk
Find out about the history of this little known branch canal.

Contacts:
Hollinwood Canal
2 Rock Bank Stamford Road
Mossley
OL5 0BD
Email: hcs@hollinwoodcanal.co.uk

John Howarth Countryside Centre
Stannybrook Road
Failsworth
Oldham
M35 9WJ
Tel: 0161 308 3909

Dove Stone Reservoir

Hope the dove provides peace

Take the Huddersfield train from Manchester Victoria to Greenfield Station, about a 25-minute journey. Jump off outside the station and in the homely, stone-clad village you should see a pub called The Railway opposite. It is filled with old pictures and lads playing pool that have probably known each other since their schooldays.

If you want to grab a sugar filled drink here you might need it for energy. Once watered, turn right and go down the hill. This might seem to contradict the map but quite a few maps send you up Shaw Hall Bank Road to go down Chapel Road when you can just get onto Chew Valley Road where you want to be by taking that right turn at The Railway pub and veering left at the bottom of the hill.

Once on the uniquely named Chew Valley Road you should cross over Huddersfield Narrow Canal towpath, which looks tempting – but not a route on this run. (See other routes). Pound past a modern-style public house called The Kingfisher before the village reverts back to its original appearance with stone terraces from light years ago. The Kingfisher looks better suited to bistro consumers, tourists and high prices than locals and real ale but it is sitting amidst good countryside and relaxing commuter-esque weekend views, with Pots and Pans Memorial on one of the visible hilltop ridges and Frenches Marina nearby.

It is best to run on the left hand side of the road here, largely because there is no pavement on the right and your running might be interrupted by Mabel sweeping her front doorstep. I know, it's concrete and you are itching for freedom, open country, fresh air and grass under your feet but you'll see it soon, just earn it first!

Running through Greenfield you will see devices like ancient petrol pumps outside an old-style garage and you will cross other pathways and routes such as Greenfield Path and Oldham Way, which, on another well-prepared day will take you over Saddleworth Moor to Diggle and the other direction to places such as Hartshead Pike and Quick.

At the end of the road you will see a pub called The Clarence Hotel as the road meets Holmfirth Road. Go left here but you might want to take a minute to look at Chew Brook on the other side, especially as you now have to run up something akin to Mount Kilimanjaro.

Holmfirth Road starts off shrouded in trees and a residential vibe then it opens right up. This is Peak District Country. Motorcyclists love this road, you can tell by the volume of them sometimes (in both noise levels and numbers) but you don't have to kill yourself running here for long.

After seeing houses and the odd stone factory in the valley you will see Bank Lane on your right after about 0.5 miles. Run down this countrified lane, over a cattle grid and then just as you look up a grass covered bank at the side of the reservoir you will really feel you are now in the Peak District. Run up that hill, that bank, it's well worth the effort.

The views of Dove Stone Reservoir are gorgeous on a nice day: especially when as a runner who has just climbed that hill, you are gagging for fluids. What better spot to take a water break? You will run in an anti-clockwise direction around the reservoir. There is a path around the waterspot but sometimes it's levelled with stones and grit, other times it's uneven and you wouldn't want to run on it in the dark as there would be too great a risk of suffering some injury.

There are toilets in the car park just before you run left past Dove Stone Sailing Club. There are ice-cream vans too but how many of us can run a personal best with a Cornetto as a baton?

Eyes meet at Dove Stones.

You could, of course, drive here and start the run from the car park but think of the fun you'd miss running up Holmfirth Road!

Just after the sailing club I saw sheep sat there nonchalantly ignoring humans. There were men planting trees, memorial gardens, children sitting on rocks, paddling in the ford. It is a place both of relaxation and beauty and one that defies time. One of the enchanting things about this route is that the further around the reservoir you run, the more isolation you earn. As you progress along the route, wooded areas appear and separate you from the water. These woods are stunning both in their colour and on hot days because of the shade they offer too.

It is almost like this reservoir is in two parts because after you veer round to a point where you can't see the start anymore it opens right up. That is the freedom that comes from the Peak District's open spaces and hills. They sit there like whales frozen in some sort of sea of slowed time, happy not to move on. Always there, they give the runner somewhere to push themselves and somewhere to gain stamina.

Just past the weir you reach Binn Green and an initially bucolic lane that will take you back to civilization, motorbikes and Holmfirth Road, then back to the train station, if you've had enough already.

However, you can run up alongside the second reservoir, the more lonely and raised Yeoman Hey Reservoir and if you have had something very special on your cereals there is another reservoir, sitting solitary from the first two, in the form of Greenfield Reservoir, after that.

But after Yeoman Hey if you want to head back it is best to retrace your steps and go back to Binn Green and the junction with Dove Stone Reservoir. Climbing up quite a short but steep hill with no paths looks easy from the side of Yeoman Hey but it is peat bog and could be dangerous on a bad day. You shouldn't try to hurdle the fences but run back to Binn Green.

At the end of that shady lane you very abruptly join Holmfirth Road and should take care getting back on pavements on a road some motorists see as a speed track. Turn left and get your speed up as you head back to Greenfield, soon passing the top of Bank Lane and retrace your steps back along Holmfirth Road, downhill this time. Then turn right, past The Clarence Hotel where travellers alight buses from Manchester, or indeed Oldham, to the reservoirs.

Run past the ancient petrol station – if you are not out of petrol yourself – before an intense but very short right turn at the end of Chew Valley Road back to the train station. Beware that the trains can be unpredictable here, every 30 minutes some days, none at all at certain times of the year. This is one to call National Rail Enquiries about first.

Advantages:
- Stunning scenery.
- A loop that you can adapt for different abilities, on different days, for different stamina. You could cover three reservoirs, one reservoir. There is a lot of choice.

Disadvantages:
- Don't go alone on a dark night! Whether you are a strong and confident runner or nervous alone, there is no lighting and the paths aren't always ditch-free.
- Not a short 2-miler to clock-up distance for the week. This one wants stamina and preparation to visit first.
- Despite the need for stamina on a sunny Saturday you might be trying to outrun Great Auntie Freda and her walking stick! It is tourist heavy in the sunshine.
- Dove Stones, Dove Stone, Dovestone – when researching this place it has more names than a bigamist on the run but everyone locally calls it Dovestones, regardless of how it is written.
- It is quite some journey from the city centre and will take up a lot of time before you even get running.

Summary:
Yet another beautiful gem of a man-made lake to run around just outside Manchester. The sights, hills and open air are fantastic but it would be advisable to plan for it. Don't get stuck here in winter, miles from the station after the last train has gone.

Mileage:
4.25 miles.

History:
The reservoirs were built in 1967 to supply water to the people of the nearby towns and city. It is thought the Dove Stones reservoir got its name from a cluster of stones that looked like a dove, which you can still see today on the hillside from the corner of the dam wall. It is also suggested it may come from a dialect word of Celtic origin as 'dubh' meant black and Black Stone Edge is nearby.

Despite all the myths about why it was named as it was, initially, there had been objections by mill owners and industry to the reservoirs as the businesses thought they would lose their water supply. It meant a by-pass tunnel was fitted as a compromise so they could still access river water.

In March 2010 the Royal Society for the Protection of Birds (RSPB) told Saddleworth Council it plans to build a Visitors' Centre at Dove Stones in the coming five years to offer refreshments, toilet facilities and increased staff numbers to help those out to see the sights.

Useful Websites:

www.go4awalk.com

Information on walks, places to stay and photographs to see areas before you run there.

www.peakdistrict.gov.uk

Find details about policies, open land and freedom to roam history, and where you can go running or off-road with vehicles.

www.ukattraction.com

Information on a range of venues and locations for North West based activities, including many we runners will pass while pounding pavement and grass.

Contacts:

National Rail Enquiries

08457 484950

Peak District National Park Authority

Tel: 01629 816200

customer.service@peakdistrict.gov.uk

Dunham Massey and Bridgewater Canal

Mist and mellow fruitfulness – of divorce

This can be a beautiful route for runners. Get the Metrolink to Altrincham Interchange then when you leave the complex turn left, and then right onto the pedestrianized George Street near Marks and Spencer and continue up the side of the shop towards the market. Next turn left and onto Regent Road.

If you are warmed up then run right up Regent Road, turn left onto the busier Dunham Road at the top and run up the hill past St Margaret's Church. Then at Bradgate Road squeeze through the public gate in a little white fenced area and run through a beautiful patch of rhododendrons, trees and crisp leaves alongside Dunham Golf Course.

After heading up an incline you can then run through the Golf Course on a public footpath and run either right onto Oldfield Lane at the side of the golf course and then left on to Charcoal Lane. Alternatively run to the bottom of the golf course and straight onto Charcoal Lane where you reach the high outer wall of Dunham Massey and are sitting on the edge of the courtly and beautiful village of Dunham.

Next, dance left over the stepped gateways into Dunham Massey and run past ponds and deer in the estate. The estate's land is another Cheshire stately ground which looks like the Jurassic Park film set in summer and like a potential Keats' inspiration, for his season of mist

Blue waters run deep at Dunham Massey Deer Sanctuary.

and mellow fruitfulness poem, in autumn. There is a pond in the grounds which looks majestic on the right day and trees which are hundreds of years old. The grounds are covered with established heritage and wealth. This area is filled with visitors, even on colder days and the deer and ducks are used to you popping by. At the time of writing adult access to the House and Gardens was £10, cars £5 and a family ticket £25 but see the website for details and for opening times. Estate access was £5 for cars and £1.50 for motorbikes.

After running in the deer park you may want to head back to Altrincham not via Dunham Road and busy roads but via the Bridgewater Canal. If so, leave the Massey grounds by a north east point to head towards Dunham Town. Run over Smithy Lane, left up School Lane, Charcoal Road and past Little Heath Farm. A little further on, turn right onto the canal. You could otherside leave the Massey, run left up Woodhouse Lane and onto the canal as it crosses over the road, yet although this is a straight route it is harder to reach the waterway at this point. However, either way onto the canal will help you head east to Manchester Road and then left up Barrington Road and Stamford New Road to Altrincham and the public transport options unavailable in the rural town.

Advantages:
- It houses Britain's largest and best winter garden.
- Some of the most stunning parkland in the Manchester area to run round again…and again…and again.
- You get to watch the deer feeding or rutting.

Disadvantages:
- Once you are on the Bridgewater Canal it is a straight run but around the golf course and Massey you could lose track of exits.
- Running past all the children and tourists loose in the grounds of the Massey could interrupt timing.
- As it is parkland check opening times on the website, otherwise it could be a 'deer' night if you make the effort to visit but are locked out.

Summary:
A beautiful house owned by the National Trust filled with mists, deer, a pond and mediaeval-flavoured grounds that allow you to run through the Cheshire countryside and blow off the cobwebs.

Mileage:
4.25 miles (canal route).

History:
The 7th Earl of Stamford who once lived in the Georgian Dunham Massey married Catherine Cocks, a bare-back circus rider. Also a resident there was the 2nd Earl of Warrington, who secretly wrote a book on the desirability of divorce. Perhaps they had both just wanted to horse around!

Dunham Town itself has a population of only around 500 people and Dunham Massey was once on the main route from York to Chester, major towns in the mediaeval period of the history of this country. Indeed, the road was a boundary, separating Dunham Massey from

Bowden. The name Dunham is thought to derive from the Anglo Saxon dun which meant hill and though the area has some inclines this area is very flat in comparison to areas like the Peak District.

There was once a railway line through the largely agricultural area but the station at Dunham closed in 1962 leaving the town more isolated again. It is mainly inhabited by the wealthy who rely less on public transport.

The deer park covers almost 300 acres according to The National Trust and the Hall was used to house the injured military during World War One. It was just before that war that Dunham Town's population peaked at almost 3,000 residents and it has never been so populous since. The town has a quaint charm about it with the low, white cottages that farming families have lived in dating back many years, some of the homes facing the Massey grounds.

Massey Barons owned Dunham, hence the rest of the name of the estate and they also owned Dunham Castle, Watch Hill Castle near Bowden and Ullerwood Castle near Hale. The Massey family died out in the 14th century and the estate was bought by the Booth family.

Dunham Castle was demolished in the mediaeval period, as was the old hall. It was rebuilt in 1616. The Hall, Stables and Carriage House are Grade I listed buildings and were built by the Booths. There is an obelisk, used to mark the burial ground of a racehorse, which has a Grade II listing. The mill on the estate dates back to the 1860s but there are claims that there was a mill there as far back as 1353.

The Dunham Massey Brewing Company was set up in 2006 after former Tetley Brewery Worker, John Costello, decided to start up solo. This was about 10 years after his former place of work in Warrington closed down. His love of beer and brewing continued and The National Trust suggested that he used Big Tree Farm's barn in Dunham, which hadn't been used for seven years, as a brewery. Waste products from brewing like the spent grains can be used to feed cattle and as fertiliser so with farmlands nearby it gave another reason for John to brew his drinks, which have names like Deer Beer. So in Dunham maybe the animals are happy that he decided to continue brewing too.

Useful Websites:
www.dunhammasseybrewing.co.uk
Read about the green hop beer brewed onsite, as well as pub and eating out tips in Cheshire.
www.nationaltrust.org.uk / main / w-dunhammassey
Find the opening times and prices of admission through this website.

Contacts:
Dunham Massey
Altrincham
WA14 4SJ
Tel: 0161 941 1025
Email: dunhammassey@nationaltrust.org.uk

Emotion to Motivation

You know what it is like. The bills will not go away. Your boss makes Genghis Khan look refined. Your neighbour (who sings like a scalded cat) has just bought a karaoke machine. In short, you could burst with upset, anger or frustration at aspects of your life. But one of the fantastic things about running is it's always there. You don't have to wait for the swimming pool to open. You are not trying to tie yourself in with the schedules of five or 10 teammates on a Sunday morning. Running is always there. When you feel anger, sorrow, grief, hyperactivity or you just want to keep fit: running is forever on your doorstep.

That anger though can be one of the tools to motivate you to stop watching the 13th repeat of some cop show and make you move faster or try harder and for longer up Pennine hills that make the Pyrenees seem like a kid's drawing. Well, feel like it at least.

Having a class to go to at a set time or mates to compete with is sometimes the encouragement some people need to do exercise. But if you would rather be in control of how your body works out, running gives you choice. You can run several short routes: such as loops close to home, say, every day after work. You can do a giant run once or twice a week, coated in mud and let your body relax for the rest of the time.

A great idea though is to have a target and keep a record of achievements. Make it so you have to run say 5 or 10 miles a week; or cover it timewise, give yourself three hours running time per week.

Either way when you have to drive your arms up steep hills to help your legs reach the summit think of pounding your rival's favourite car. As you pound pavement imagine your neighbour's karaoke machine is beneath your feet. For some people the opposite philosophy works best and forgetting all financial, family and career based worries as they run drains stress away. Whatever your philosophy using exercise as a positive in your life and employing such thinking should not only make you go faster but you will be amazed when get home what with all the fresh air and freedom, all the sense of achievement and stress relief, just how good you feel.

Depression is a tough stain to shift from life but sport, especially running, is a great way to combat it. As long as you can overcome the first and largest hurdle, that of getting motivated. Running will then take the negative energy and make it positive. Endorphins – the feel good hormones you get from exercise – like opiates, have natural pain relieving qualities, so come out to play with exercise!

The feeling that you have done something, achieved something and been in control of that aspect of your life will help you gain positivity. Then, hope that things can improve should surge to other areas of your existence. Keeping busy and not 'playing the victim' are essential ways to beat stress or depression and running is a big help with this.

Of course, running is not just there to beat the blues and for some people the problem is not finding the motivation but rather the time to run, what with work, children and so on but once you love training, you can manage your time and also add other sports to your timetable to exercise the parts running doesn't work or test hard enough. Well, once you've got the bug…

Goyt Valley
(Etherow and Goyt Valley Way)

Park it before you know the way!

Right next to the roadside of New Bridge Lane in Stockport, between Stockport Road West and Carrington Road you can escape the hassles of urban life by heading through one of the entrances to Vernon Park. If you follow the left-most path it veers round to join the path to the right, meaning that many entrances lead to the bottom of some very steep stone steps. Lots of steps! What better way to warm up than running up and down these at speed? Carefully, of course.

One of the good things about this route is it starts with the very set paths of a park. Good for people on a quick nightly run after work, or a run for two or three friends. If you follow the path alongside the River Goyt it becomes more and more rural and muddy, before eventually looping back via the country scents and foot coverings of the Goyt Valley.

You can start at Vernon Park on a February day with blue skies and brilliant sunshine yet pass Stringer's Weir and the second weir alongside the adjoining Woodbank Memorial Park riverside path, to then find oneself in a snow-storm. The riverside path does not so much have testing inclines as the gentle tumbling of the pathway mimicking the water of the river to your left.

The footpath has places where mudbaths have not been dried out by the authorities. There are stretches where wooden stairs take you onto different levels of the track, up and away from the mud and there are some places where you have to climb up steep slopes without steps, which could be quite risky in the dark. Most days though if you decide not to merely loop the outskirts of the parks and decide you are going to get a thorough mud-coating along the riverside, it is well worth it and sometimes there are the beautiful golden leaves underfoot or you find a hay-covered track at some points akin to a royal visit to Caribbean roads, where no doubt walkers and leisure seekers have tried to get over the mud.

There are the weirs with beach-like pebbling on one side and the waters marching you on. You are almost offended on the river's behalf at council signs warning you not to swim in it as it is polluted because the area can look so beautiful and blue with the mill in the background. But admittedly, it can have a strong scent of soap or detergent here on some days.

March on to the second, higher layer, not seeing Woodbank Athletics Track or the Cricket Ground in the park on this particular route, but which are to your right if you are interested in visiting them. Pass through tunnels made of leaves and a skateboarding area and you should soon see a little green bridge across the water. Cross here because soon afterwards the pathway runs out.

On the other side of the river climb up a banking and head to your right then straight on and you will see some gateways and fences as the foreground to the beautiful Goyt Valley. Well, you didn't want to quit this early at only about 2 miles in. Head towards Mill Lane and Dooley Lane, which houses the massive Wyevale Garden Centre.

You will be coming back this way too so just to vary things there is the Goyt Valley path in this direction which is solid; but closer to the river, across a little gully, there is a thinner but more natural waterside path.

Run down the waterside path until you come to Chadkirk Kennels and Cattery, then get back on paved ground to run to the end of Mill Lane towards Otterspool Road and Dooley Lane, watching out for the hurrying pet-loving four-wheel drive owners as you do so.

Log with snow icing in the Goyt Valley.

Over the Otterspool Bridge at Dooley Lane is the garden centre where you can perhaps grab a drink. However, if you don't want the concrete you can avoid all this at the cattery and turn round and run back up the other side of the gully on the true Goyt Valley path through the dale.

After you have covered the area you will have already seen that the path directs you out into wider countryside with steeper paths. After about 0.5 miles you pass Goyt Hall Farm with very little navigation to worry about through the aromas of the Cheshire land and Middle Farm's farmyard.

You will see horses, chickens and cows along the way here. This is a very good stretch of run for the soul but very different to the organised after work, run-in-pairs area back at Vernon Park at the start line.

After passing through a gateway you will head along the path, past the entrance to Bredbury Hall advertising offers such as girls' champagne nights, and back out to 'civilisation'. There are many ways back to the main road, Stockport Road West, yet it is probably easiest to turn left onto Osborne Street and hope you have time to stretch off before your bus comes and your exercise and country scents enter other passengers' nostrils!

Advantages:
- Brilliant mix of scenery with the urbanised parkland greenery, such as sunken gardens, against the countrified scents and space of the Goyt Valley.
- There is very little concrete on this route. Set paths, country tracks, riverside paths but not much pavement pounding.

Disadvantages:
- A lot of dog walkers! Some lovely if holding back a canine version of Hannibal Lecter.
- It is a shame you have to loop the same stretch of the Goyt Valley after crossing the river on this route. You can cut that section out but it would shorten the route considerably or you can run a bigger loop not crossing the green bridge but turning right up Holiday Lane, left onto Marple Road and left onto Dooley Road near the garden centre but that adds concrete to the run.
- It may be easily confused with the nearby 10-mile north/south Goyt Way route.
- Park access to begin the run can be restricted at certain times. It may be best to check opening times, especially if you plan to leave a vehicle in the car park.

Summary:
A route like that of a cold safari. It starts civilised in beautiful parkland, gives you a taste of more stunning nature and then sees land open up and animals and their aromas' appear, before ending near halls and country clubs.

Mileage:
3.5 miles.

History:
Goyt Hall, which stands near the River Goyt between Otterspool Bridge and New Bridge, is a black and white structure. It was erected by Randal Davenport, originally of Henbury, Macclesfield in about 1570 and is a half-timbered structure. It is thought by some that

alterations to a wing have damaged the architectural impact of the building and there are many signs in the vicinity focusing on and relating to Goyt Hall Farm.

Information in Stockport's heritage library states the Hall was said to have gone on to have links to the Arderne family who at one time also owned Arden Hall in Bredbury.

Neolithic farmers are said to have worked their trade in the valley going back to 3,000BC, which is understandable considering the area still lends itself to farming today. But in more industrial times gunpowder was one of the products made around here and some people believe Sir Francis Drake blew his Spanish Armada opposition away with Goyt Valley's powerful dust. Well, even we runners need some launch power sometimes.

Vernon Park, Stockport's oldest park, was opened in 1858. It was built by mill workers on land donated by Lord Vernon and was sometimes referred to as Pinch Belly Park by some. Good encouragement for under motivated runners!

The last marriage of the Davenports – who owned the Hall – in the 17th century was to Sir Fulke Lucy a relative of Sir Thomas Lucy, who was said to be an acquaintance of William Shakespeare. This is said to be what led to streets near Vernon Road being named with a Shakespearean connection such as Hathaway Gardens, after Shakespeare's love Anne; Marlowe Walks and Shakespeare Road after the man himself.

More recently Vernon Park re-opened after restoration through a £1.6 million lottery grant to give it back its Edwardian and Victorian gardens. There are disabled access and baby care facilities as well as a fernery and sunken rose gardens.

In Woodbank Memorial Park Peter Marsland built a house between 1812 and 1814 with the help of architect Thomas Harrison of Chester. In 1921 Sir Thomas Rowbotham gave Woodbank Hall and 89 acres to the town as a memorial to those who died in World War One. He then gave a further £2,000 towards the refurbishment of the house, which reopened as a museum in 1931 but closed to the public in 1948 and only the café now remains. In 1953, glass houses were built to replace those lost in neighbouring Vernon Park.

Useful Websites:

www.dashathletics.co.uk
A family friendly club giving young people the chance to excel in athletics.
www.goytvalley.co.uk
A website with good photographs and ideas for leisure around the Goyt Valley.
www.stockport.gov.uk
Get information about park opening times and the history behind the land.
www.stockportharriers.com
Visit the website about the club which has over 400 members and does off-track training as well as running on the athletics track for more sprint orientated ambitions.

Contacts:

Dash Athletics
Tel: 07863 299863 (Mike Frost, Club Secretary)
Tel: 07974 743639 (Joe Frost, Head of Coaching)
Email: dashathletics@yahoo.co.uk
From six years to senior age groups. Training is held at Woodbank Memorial, Vernon Park or Hazel Grove High School.

Parks, Sport and Cemeteries
Fred Perry House
Edward Street
Stockport
SK1 3SU
Tel: 0161 217 6111
Email: parks@stockport.gov.uk

Stockport Harriers And Athletics Club
Woodbank Memorial Park
Tel: 0161 494 1604
Email: jerzygeorgesh@btinternet.com
Jerzy Matuszewski – Membership Secretary
Public Training Times:
Monday, Tuesday, Thursday: 6.30pm until 8.30pm
Sunday: 10.30am until 12.30pm

Vernon Park Museum
Vernon Park
Turncroft Lane
Offerton
SK1 4AR
Tel: 0161 474 4460
Email: parks@stockport.gov.uk

Hartshead Pike

Grab the bull by the horns!

Finding somewhere to warm up near Ashton-under-Lyne town centre could be tricky. There are plenty of car parks near the bus station and the big retail outlets and Ashton Market has pockets and corners to stretch in but who wants to be Mr Motivator against commuters and shoppers determination to buy?

Once you are ready, from Ashton centre there is a loop of roughly 4.5 miles, which you can run in either direction to Hartshead Pike. It is often wrongly assumed that the Pike is the stone building, but it is, or certainly was originally, the name of the hill upon which the stone structure stands. The stone tower rises on the landscape at about 940ft above sea level from which point you can see Jodrell Bank, the Holme Moss transmitter mast and even the Welsh mountains on a clear day.

For this route begin by running along Wellington Road and past the council offices with the conveniently placed digital clock for your timing and continue as the road becomes Penny Meadow, Crickets Lane and then opens up to become Mossley Road.

Bizarrely, even though Hartshead Pike can be seen from many places around the area and itself offers stunning views of Manchester and the edge of the Peak District National Park, for much of this road you cannot see your target, the tower, ahead. If you would rather have something visual to aim for it may be best to tackle this route in the opposite direction but there are some benefits to Mossley Road. Considering the height you are reaching this is a very mellow and gradual climb (see Joel Lane at Werneth Low if you want vertical hell).

Along the way you will see Ladysmith Barracks where military ground has stood since 1845. It was the home of the Manchester Regiment from 1881 to 1958.

Barracks soldiers were trained to fight civil unrest from the workers in the cotton towns like Ashton and nearby Stalybridge and Hyde but there is a theme here on this increasingly rural land as it was once an Anglo-Saxon law-making site.

Shortly after you pass the Heroes of Waterloo public house and start sniffing the lovely scent of Ashton-under-Lyne Golf Course's freshly cut grass, the road swirls around more, offering corners after which you keep expecting to see the tower in your sights but it remains hidden.

If you look behind you there is already an ocean of residential, manufacturing and business buildings. It is not just those that are a part of Ashton that you are leaving behind but of Manchester and its constituent parts and it shimmers on a sunny day with light bouncing off glass and heat rising to make it look like the haze shining off the sea.

But run on and eventually that hidden talisman appears. Some people claim to have seen UFOs near the Pike – and probably needed to stay off a different type of grass en route – but admittedly it is beautiful when you are slogging it up a long A-road and then the old stone building appears. It is almost as if it were a picture placed there, it seems so majestic and yet contrasts massively with the more modern surroundings you have just pounded past. It does seem to almost float and it is to see that view that I have suggested you tackle the route in this direction.

After the golf course there are public footpath signs pointing you to Hartshead Pike which now seems very much more level with your current position…well, than it did.

You can try these public footpaths but there are a cornucopia of challenges such as a brook to hurdle, irate cattle wanting you off their land and you having to squeeze through barbed wire fences to excuse yourself from the beasts.

Nature and the Pike, Hartshead Pike.

Maybe you like a real battle and would love to dampen your face in the Pennine waters of the brook on a hot day. Maybe you are just better off running a little further: then take the left turn to Broadcarr Lane and there, having more of a battle retreating from motorists trying to get to the Hartshead Inn and its picnic area, have your last little uphill stretch to the spirelet itself.

This monument looks like something from a time you daren't believe in. You can imagine Rapunzel winding down her hair here. This is where princesses wait and the imagination hurries.

A plaque here offers information about how far different places are from the beauty spot, surprisingly distant in some cases and it informs you about delightful ancient names of Pennine hills such as Pots and Pans just behind you. (See Oldham Way route.) But it is a shame that the setting isn't better looked after with some graffiti on the stonework of the Pike and nearby major tombs or stones used over a long period of time as ashtrays. You can see four counties from this spot as well as a major British city and parts of the UK's first national park.

Before the launch of an anniversary walk in 2011, Jim Dixon, the Peak District National Park Chief Executive said that 60 years ago the Peak District became Britain's first national park protecting the landscape for current and future generations to enjoy.

Here at Hartshead Pike, Druids are thought to have worshipped and lit fires in the Iron Age. It is nice to use this moment to sup your water and contemplate country versus city life matters; whether aliens have landed or if it was just an irate cow and a young smoker at sunset in 1973 when a silent UFO was thought to have been spotted here.

The views of Manchester are probably better from here than from Werneth Low and after the Werneth Low battle to reach the summit and tackling more of the elements at the top you would think the Low was higher up but it is reportedly several feet lower. Hartshead Pike does offer green views and is closer to farms but also some sort of scrapyard stashed out of the way in the hills here, so it does feel more urban in some ways.

When deciding how to get down and back to Lees Road there is a temptation to follow the half visible footpaths to the very visible long B-road you are heading for. Though the signpost for Lily Lanes seems to be taking you away from that long road in a southerly direction it is probably your best route. Other sandy paths, dead end paths and semi-swamp crossings find you trying to navigate around farms and though they have you touching on parts of the Oldham Way path make navigation much trickier.

Again the countryside flavours are rustic with stone steps and horses next to paths but you should take care with ankles and knees when bouncing down these routes. Lily Lanes the footpath heading south eastwards which becomes a roadway offers a more solid route back to Lees Road and pops out at St Damian's RC Science College where you should turn left and run about 1 mile as the road later becomes more and more urban and then changes to Queens Road. Here turn right onto Mossley Road and back to Ashton centre in another 0.5 miles.

When tackling Lees Road, you may prefer it as your up route and Mossley Road as the down (in other words you may have run the loop in the opposite direction) as it would afford you more views of the tower for quite a distance during the approach. It may also have made it easier to navigate from Lees Road up to the Pike itself but you can make this route your own. Even on a Friday lunchtime/early afternoon I saw around four other runners tackling parts of this route – one with dogs to heel.

One websites states the inscription on the tower reads: 'Look well at me before you go and see you nothing at me throw.' Well, if you gave it some welly reaching Hartshead Pike on the way up and have yet to get home you may have 'thrown' everything you have into reaching the Pike already.

Advantages:
- Taste running concrete and the countryside.
- Enjoy the scents and smells of freedom from freshly cut grass to animal aromas.
- You can make the route your own running it in either direction.
- Buses head up both Mossley and Lees Roads.

Disadvantages:
- Poorly established and fenced off public footpaths.
- Unfriendly animals glaring at you and your gall for being on their turf!
- You can get cut off from direct routes by farm buildings, especially if you don't take the Broadcarr Lane or Lily Lanes routes.

Summary:
A nice gradual climb for quite a high point in your running, to reach a landmark and see both the city you love and the countryside you adore from the same perspective. Just watch out for angry animals, barbed wire scratched escapes and access agonies on some footpaths.

Mileage:
5 miles.

History:
The earliest structure on the site is claimed to have been placed to commemorate King Canute's passing through the area, as are the road names Knott Hill and Knott Lanes. A building was built on the site of Hartshead Pike by public contributions in 1751. This was then replaced in 1863 with a building by John Eaton to commemorate the marriage of HRH Albert Edward, The Prince Of Wales, to Princess Alexandra.

In the 1930s there was a sweet shop in the tower to add further enjoyment to visits but the entrance was bricked up at the outbreak of World War II and you still can't get flying saucers there now (most people believe)!

At the time of the Crimean War in 1854/55 the Ladysmith Barracks were occupied by the 6th Royal Lancashire Militia. Gas stopped being used for lower floor lighting as the marching of the soldiers on the upper floor moved the earth until the gas mantles were broken. In 1921 the War Office granted permission for the site to be named the Ladysmith Barracks in recognition of a siege in the Boer War in which the 1st Battalion had taken part. Women were drafted into the barracks during World War Two and wore the fleur-de-lys of the 63rd Manchester Regiment above their tunic pockets. It is said some still lived in Hyde but travelled to the site seven days a week, being forced to walk on Sundays because of the lack of public transport before a days work at the Barracks. Now that's training!

Nearby Whittakers Mill was used to house the extra men drafted in from other Regiments who are said to have trained to use machine guns there. The Regimental Depot was closed in 1958 and the land sold off to developers leaving only the imposing gate facing Mossley Road today, thanks to the donation by developer Roland Bardsley to Tameside Metropolitan Borough Council in 1984.

Useful Websites:
www.ashton-under-lyne.com/history/hartshead
Background and visitor information on the monument.
www.mysteriousbritain.co.uk
One or two articles on the Pike.
www.tameside.gov.uk/museumsgalleries/mom/history/ladysmith
Information about military history in the area.

Contacts:
Hartshead Pike
Back Lane
Off Broadcarr Lane
Mossley
Tel: 0161 330 9613

Heaton Park

Beating heart

Heaton Park is said to contain 25 per cent of the city of Manchester's green space and it is a good route and one of the most convenient routes to get to if you live near a Metrolink station in the north of the city.

Along the Bury line you can depart at Heaton Park tram station and cross over the busy Bury Old Road to the entrance of the green gem – one of the biggest municipal parks in Europe – complete with warm-up space and a giant map on a billboard to plan your route. There are bigger parks around the edge of the city but this is only 4 miles from the city centre.

Even on a saturated Monday morning in December the park can be full of schoolchildren running cross-country, golfers, dog walkers and other runners. It is a popular place and it is little wonder if you see the beauty of the views toward Manchester from the Temple, the picturesque qualities of the ponds and lake and the romance of the Hall and Orangery. Children would love the farm and tiny horses here if they came on a day trip or you left them grazing there with a partner or friend while you went running.

Within the park there are concrete pathways that are great for those who find navigation a bore and a hold up. However, it can sometimes be a mentally defeating route because everything leads back to the Hall in the centre. You can run to the Horticultural Centre, the Temple, the Colonnade even the woodland up at Hazlitt Wood but sooner or later you will be running past or in sight of the Hall again. The Hall is the heart of the park and all roads lead to the heart. But don't lose heart – keep running. It is, in the scheme of things, quite a manicured park. But those who like to get their feet wet by running on real turf can run alongside the paths or across the grounds giving the route regular variation.

If you head north toward the Horticultural Centre it gives a nice start to the run, running past something akin to miniature woolly mammoths. It is best not to be tempted to include the reservoir as part of a longer route as it is fenced off to a large extent.

After passing the Horticultural Centre and reaching the Bowling Pavilion, the pathway will gently lead you past the site of the radio communications tower and if you choose onwards to the Fish Pond and Hazlitt Wood. Then run toward the Farm, Heaton Hall and the Orangery.

For those of an inquisitive nature there is a great deal to capture your attention, taking thoughts away from running rhythms and stamina building.

After browsing around the Hall, take one of many signed pathways to the Temple to enjoy a little comfort break and a scenic swig of your water as the winds blast and cool you. Initially it looks like a pavilion at the top of a slope but it is reputedly the highest point in the city of Manchester and the views toward the aforesaid area over rolling green lawns and wide skies, even on a bad day, are beautiful.

After the Temple and the amazing views, back down in the park it is tempting to run around the edge of the park via the golf course to let your feet pound some more beautiful open turf but it may merely be a recipe for getting lost and a guarantee that you will get up the noses of fanatical golfers – perhaps a bonus for some of us!

It is better to stick to the pathways after shuffling down the other side of the hill from the Temple, that way you still get to enjoy the beauty of Blackfish Pond with more concern for being hit by flying fish than flying golf balls.

After rounding back past the Hall, head towards the Tramway Museum before rounding the Boating Lake, which in the autumnal months is carpeted with leaves.

Rolling greens of Heaton Park.

If you wish to take a detour to the smaller south exit at Sheepfoot Lane you will pass under the wonderful old 1820s Colonnade, which was moved to the park in 1912 and used to be the entrance to the old Town Hall in King Street, Manchester. It gives a stately importance to the park that is somewhat contradictory in that the grounds and golf course are immaculately kept yet one wing of the Hall has boarded up windows and is going to rack and ruin. There are rumours more lottery money could be applied for to fund refurbishment, which if true would remind onlookers the Hall could be a grand sight.

Another exit before going clockwise back to Bury Old Road and Heaton Park Metrolink Station is the Grand Lodge which is available to rent as a holiday let some weeks of the year – if you get really tired!

For those who want to finish at the original entrance and want to go back up to Bury Old Road head up the set pathways from the Boating Lake near the Boating House, past the Papal Monument and back to the original exit of the park near the Metrolink station, cooling down and stretching off before inflicting your scent on your fellow travellers…again!

Advantages:

- It is difficult to get lost with so many posted maps, signs and set pathways.
- There are some lovely sights compared to pounding concrete in rundown urban areas.
- It is ideally served by the Metrolink's Bury line.

Disadvantages:

- It is a shame the route is so short. It is 3 miles at most and with all the sights you may find yourself gagging for further scenic turf to run along.
- You could quite easily find yourself fighting for solitude on routes during warm summer weekends.
- It can be mentally defeating because most of the paths lead back to the same centre point, the Hall.
- There isn't a set path circling the outskirts of the park to run the same distance each visit for time trials.

Summary:

A beginners or light intermediate route. It could also be good for regular use when a runner wants to visit the park frequently but vary the actual route within it, but it is not a stamina course.

Mileage:

2 to 3 miles depending on which landmarks you cover.

History:

Originally the Hall is thought to have belonged to the Holland family from the Middle Ages but became the property of the Egerton family through marriage in 1684 when Sir John Egerton married Elizabeth Holland.

In 1772, Sir Thomas Egerton, later the 1st Earl of Wilton commissioned James Wyatt to design the present house. It was thought to have been inspired by European travel and fashionable designs of the 18th century.

The Temple was also designed by James Wyatt and built around 1800 with the same bow frontage design as the Hall. Sir Thomas Egerton may have liked staring at the stars from the Temple as it is thought it might have been used as an observatory in 1803 when he bought a telescope from London for £18 5s: then a butler's annual salary.

In 1807, Sir Thomas employed landscape architect John Webb to make alterations to the park that William Eames had laid out for him in the late 1700s. A 4-mile long boundary wall was created and The Grand Lodge Gatehouse was designed by Lewis Wyatt and became the then main entrance to the estate.

The 2nd Earl of Witton and his wife Lady Mary were socialites and are thought to have held parties at the Hall in the early 1800s. Among the guests were the Duke Of Wellington, most famous for defeating Napoleon at the Battle of Waterloo and the renowned actress and author of the 19th century Fanny Kemble.

Manchester Corporation bought the park from the family in 1902 after Alderman Fletcher Moss campaigned that it should not be sold to developers. The council bought it from the Egerton family for £230,000 and they then extended the already existing tramway into the park with the first tram arriving on 31 May 1903. (The Metrolink wasn't that early.) A tram shelter was built where the Tramway Museum is now in 1904–05 and converted to a tram shed in 1976 for the use of the museum.

As stated above, the Colonnade originally formed the entrance to the old Town Hall in King Street, Manchester around 1822 to 1824 and was moved to Heaton Park when the Town Hall was demolished in 1912. For architecture lovers the Doric columns with Ionic scrolls atop are a majestic sight.

The 12-acre Boating Lake was once a racecourse and was constructed through hard work: reportedly, unemployed people were taken-on to dig soil and move it to other parts of the park between 1908 and 1912. The Hall is Grade I listed by English Heritage and the park is Grade II listed and it has had some improvements thanks to Heritage Lottery Grants and Manchester City Council's £10 million millennium project partnership. There are eight other listed structures within its boundaries.

Surprisingly the racecourse was there from 1827 until 1839 and illustrations in the Hall show lively meetings.

Extras:

Heaton Park has a health walk for free every Saturday and Sunday. You can meet the wardens the day before the walk but it is best to check times online.

Useful Websites:

www.heatonpark.org.uk

Information on the park from the people who run the park. A good site for information on architecture and history as well as opening times and activities.

Contacts:

Heaton Park

The Farm Centre

Manchester City Council

Manchester

M25 2SW

Email: heatonpark@manchester.gov.uk

Tel: 0161 773 1085

Hobson Moor...
or Hollingworthall Moor...
or Shaw Moor

Cloud nine route to heaven

I know, you are covered in dust from traffic on the busy road which runs through Hollingworth and Tintwistle, or 'Tinsel' as it is known to locals and you are wondering how paradise can be anywhere near here but that is one of the surprising things about many Manchester routes, the scenery changes from urban to rural very quickly.

Get off your bus either on Market Street in Hollingworth or Manchester Road in Tintwistle, which essentially is getting off on the same long road, a busy thoroughfare for traffic crossing the Pennines. If you start in Hollingworth turn up Green Lane follow the road round to Meadowbank and turn left again past Meadowbank Farm up the fairly steep country lane incline before you.

If instead you start in Tintwistle, turn up Woolley Mill Lane and follow the delightful country lane and parallel paths to Meadowbank Farm where you will join the route that starts in Hollingworth.

From the footpaths behind the farm you can already see landmarks which look high from many other spots in the area, like Mottram Church but it doesn't look quite so high up from here. It makes you wonder if there can be much more to climb. You are far from the pinnacle though. From this point you can see the Longdendale Valley and its numerous reservoirs, the Arnfield Reservoir which you ran alongside if you started at Woolley Mill Lane. On a sunny day the man-made lake shimmers like a forbidden but enticing invitation.

Don't get too comfortable yet though. Keep climbing up the tree-shaded incline and past Widowscroft Farm. Run ever upwards and at the top of this road you meet Hobson Moor Road and its ever so slightly confusing navigational hurdles. If you turn left you are greeted by a private road sign. If you do take that route you would see Hard Times (Hard Times Farm that is).

If you step around another gate but don't head as far as the private road sign there is an official sign at the bottom of a stepped slim path marking out public footpaths to various moorland areas like Shaw Moor or Hollingworthall Moor. I know. No more, no moor signs! All these moorland titles can prove confusing. But if you turn right when you reach Hobson Moor Road you can run onto a well-kept area often filled with livestock, such as gentle lambs and sunbathing cows in late spring.

After this the path sort of entices you, draws you ever onwards and upwards even if the signposts aren't clear – or even in existence in some places – so you may not know exactly which of the three moorland patches you are on but up here you may not care. With the ocean of white land you cannot help but be drawn to keep on running.

The tops here are paradise. You keep climbing. When you believe you have reached a plateau and the views around you tempt you to keep stopping for water breaks (or to be reacquainted with oxygen) and you can see Dinting Arches railway viaduct, Padfield, the Nestlé chocolate factory in Hadfield, Shire Hill, Bankswood Hill and as you climb ever higher you see more and more of the Longdendale Valley. Then you climb over a stile and see views closer to Manchester City Centre; Oldham, Stalybridge and its surrounding areas like Millbrook – its hill protruding from the ground like the hump of a whale. The views are not only spectacular but they offer reminders of running routes you may have covered already, distantly visible like old friends, from an elevation around Hollingworth Hall Moor of 1,000ft (304m), even up to 1,800ft (548m) at some points. Indeed, Wild Bank, in the centre of a triangle between Mottram Road, Hobson Moor Road and the Walkerwood, Brushes and Shineshaw Reservoirs stands at about 1,310ft (399m) and is sometimes compared with Werneth Low but as a more rural equivalent and one 400ft (121m) higher up. (See other routes.)

Here, in late spring or early summer the grasses are bleached by the sun and the land is yellow, or sometimes even white. Indeed even in late autumn the land is very light compared with other Peak District coverings. Sound seems to echo up here and as your feet pound the dried peat-filled earth it barely feels or sounds like you are making contact with the earth at all. The views, the sounds, the colours around you all make it feel like you are training on a cloud and that you could float away at any moment. It certainly doesn't feel like the squelch of moorland such as that alongside Running Hill Head (see other routes) during the wet winter months when the ground is like a monstrous vacuum.

Unfortunately, there are reminders that you haven't quite made it to heaven yet in the smell of tar which may be from the busy roads surrounding this untouched moorland. There are also vast numbers of walkers, dogs and cyclists on warm days especially during holiday seasons. To bring you back down to earth you get dusty socks, laden with Peak District soils to take home as a souvenir. It is stunning land with hilltops on the borders of four counties.

Technically, facing north, Hobson Moor is to the left behind Hobson Moor Road, Hollingworthall Moor is to the right and left beyond Hobson Moor is Shaw Moor so your endless footpath will take you up for the last section to a stone obelisk on the tops which is on Shaw Moor. Here the landscape changes dramatically as the glaring white bleached grass changes to blackened heather, the complete antithesis to the earlier colours. You can also see several electricity pylons from here and a farm with a lot of telecommunications ahead.

From here though you no longer face testing inclines and your focus tends to be away from the stunning scenery as you have to concentrate on not falling or tripping on the downhill, rocky, cobblestone paths and lanes back to civilisation.

Again it is surprising how distant normal life feels from here and yet how close it is. If you head straight on you will reach Gallowsclough Road at the Waggon and Horses at Roe Cross and you can get a bus back to Ashton or Stalybridge. However, not long after the obelisk you could head left along a 10ft (3m) long concrete strip between two pond or water-filled areas and then head upwards (again) if you are a glutton for punishment. Then turn right heading in the direction of Mottram Church to take you over the Hobson Moor, part of this moorland triangle. Then you can come down Dewsnap Lane, Rabbit Lane and Old Hall Lane to end up on concrete again near Roe Cross.

From here you could cross the busy Back Moor (a road, not moorland) and touch more urbanity out of nowhere but it may be best for those wanting buses to Hyde or Manchester to run from Back Moor towards Mottram-in-Longdendale, the village once lived in by the painter L.S. Lowry.

Head along Stalybridge Road and at the traffic burdened crossroads just before you cross over to a bus stop on Hyde Road you should see a sculpture sat on a bench of the artist enjoying his pastime even now his time is past...and so is the runner's distance for this route.

Unspoilt land around Hobson and Shaw Moors.

It is surprising how lonely, free and towering this route can be and yet no real distance from traffic jams, petrol stations and school runs. This peek at the Peak moors looking down on many of the Manchester landmarks from a wild paradise has to be seen at least once though.

Advantages:
- Stunning views not just from the moorland itself but from the lanes and parts of the villages up to the moors.
- A sense of freedom and wilderness, yet you are so close to a major city.
- It really pushes you to invest effort to see the sights that are well worth it.

Disadvantages:
- Though navigation sorts itself out on the clear footpaths of the tops it can be more tricky or hazardous going up and coming down from the moors.
- Some bus routes are infrequent and there are plans to withdraw some services altogether so check your public transport times before you go.
- If you had a fall up here in wintertime it could be a while before you saw any assistance.

Summary:
A steep and testing route which constantly lulls you into thinking you can't go higher – and then pushes you to new pinnacles, thus a good stamina tester with amazing views. A taster of a re-invigorating beauty worth investing time in but not a speedy run due to terrain not distance.

Mileage:
1.5 to 2 miles.

History:
A flint scraper from the late Neolithic/early Bronze Age was said to have been found on Hollingworthall Moor and the area is known for cairns; rock piles often used as a memorial or landmark in areas with few navigationally obvious points. The cairns are about 460ft (140m) apart but the most rounded is said to be the best preserved Bronze Age monument in Tameside and a Scheduled Ancient Monument.

Vessel now demolished Hollingworth Hall was built in 1640 and during the War of the Roses owner John Hollingworth put up Sir William Brereton and his men and horses on their march towards York. It remained in the Hollingworth family's hands until 1734 but only Hollingworth Farm still exists today.

Nearby Stalybridge was originally called Stavelegh and a stave was a stick, or sometimes a bedstaff, used to hold down bedding. The name Stalybridge thus is said to mean 'wood where the staves are got', or woodland where they gather sticks.

Stalybridge was a major town in the Industrial Revolution and textile producing world, largely because of the damp climate but was badly hit by the American Civil War in the 1860s as supplies of the raw material needed to produce fabrics and cloths dried up. Only about three or four of the town's 39 factories stayed open and as many as 7,000 people were laid off. In a town that today has around 22,000 citizens that would have had a negative effect on every dweller in Stalybridge.

The ending of textile production reduced commerce levels in the town and it is now sadly a very quiet, almost abandoned looking place at times. However, it still had firsts in the form of

Mrs Ada Summers who was Stalybridge's first female mayor and then the country's first female magistrate who was apparently sworn in on New Year's Eve 1919.

The painter L.S. Lowry spent some of his life in Mottram. He lived on 'The Elms' from 1948 until his death in 1976. The artist known for his stick figures and factory scenes of Manchester went to evening classes in antique and freehand drawing in 1905. He studied at Manchester Academy of Fine Art and Salford Royal Technical College in Peel Park and sought and found a unique way to represent his creativity and home sights.

He lived in the Victoria Park area of Manchester but his family moved to Pendlebury and the move did not sit well with him at first. Indeed, he is said to have detested it initially but like all good artists he saw the potential in what was around him and began to represent the mills and factories of home in a way considered almost timeless.

He moved to Mottram aged about 50 and he died aged 88 never having put down his paintbrush or pencil. A Royal Academy exhibition showing his work just before he died broke all visitor records for a 20th-century artist.

Actress Kathy Staff, who was Nora Batty in *Last of the Summer Wine*, and killer GP Harold Shipman both lived in the little village on the edge of both the moors and the conurbation of Manchester as well making Mottram-in-Longdendale a village with a lot of history.

St Michael and All Angels Church, better know locally as Mottram Church is a gothic style structure atop a hill which can be seen as a landmark for miles around. It dates from the late 15th century and though the interior was remodelled in 1854 the exterior remains intact as it did in the 15th and 16th centuries. Only vandals destroying the windows of the Grade II listed building have affected the exterior with cork boards being used after they hit the church in 2010.

Hobson Moor quarry area was tidied up in the 1990s and is now a favourite with outdoor sports enthusiasts like climbers but apparently some runners have encountered a growling gamekeeper around Hobson Moor and Walkerwood Reservoirs telling them footpaths are for walkers not for sport. He threatened to have someone's car towed away near Brushes, Stalybridge as they were out running on the moor, saying they were parked on private land – yet there was no signage stating so. It may be best to visit the moors, or certainly this part of them, via public transport, or to park on Hobson Moor Road itself or over the other side of the moors on Brushes Road.

Useful Websites:
www.fellrunning.org.uk
A website for those who love fell running.
www.rockfax.com
A climbers' website detailing good spots for rock lovers to grapple with.
www.thelowry.com
The museum website about the stick-figure painter behind the name.
www.traveline-northwest.co.uk
Times and route assistance on buses, trains, all sorts of transport in and around Greater Manchester and the north west.

Hollingworth Lake

Manchester's answer to the Lake District

Challenging, varied, mercurial…unforgettable. The route from Rochdale Station can be confusing and the place looks like a cross between an empty wild west watering hole and a 1970s movie set. After leaving the station go left up Durham Street, left up Oldham Road and then right along Milnrow Road. However, after pounding about 1.5 miles of concrete you are greeted by the overpowering Kiln Lane. This makes the south face of the Eiger and Mount Everest seem like the Cheshire Plains!

Anyway we exercise junkies like a challenge! After riding and mounting your muscles up the hill turn left onto Wild House Lane. Things open up here. It is no longer concrete jungle despite you still being on a roadside but with cars accelerating to well over the 50mph speed limit so can you!

The scenery here after turning onto the road and passing initial houses is magnificent, with the moving, distant, traditional wild hills of the Pennines in the background and there are many tempting public footpaths along the way.

But if you stick to the road it becomes Milnrow Road, a different Milnrow Road to the one you encountered in the centre of Rochdale. Carry on and the road again changes to become Smithy Bridge Road. After turning right here, there is a bend at the end and a pub called The Beach and you can run down a little side lane greeting the lake at last, to run around it in an anti-clockwise direction.

Around this lake you will meet other runners, even in hailstorms in the middle of August. Believe me! You will also see boathouses and little perfect white cottages; you will run on

The mist framed Hollingworth Lake.

concrete lanes and mud pathways, see ice-cream vans and brooks, hills and steps covered in cascading waters.

You will see kids in kayaks, cattle in the distance, hills of every shade of green and horse manure in seven shades of…This is a bucolic paradise interwoven with some features. Manchester's hidden answer to Lake Windermere or the Lake District.

After circuiting the lake about 1 to 1.5 miles anti-clockwise you will see Rakewood Road and Lake Back at the end of your circuit. This area is filled with Italian Restaurants and after a 4-mile run the drool-inducing scent of fish and chips! It has little cafés and tea-rooms like something from a picture postcard. There are pubs, rowing clubs (though it may be best not to tackle them in that order) and benches to sit and contemplate on. There is even a telescope to view the other side of the lake.

For a shorter finish run back to Smithy Bridge Road (continuing the end of the circuit past Rakewood Road and Lake Back) past The Beach and run down the hill towards a level crossing. Turn left without crossing the tracks and you are on the platform for Manchester. That is, of course, if you are not on your third platter of caviar and gorgonzola dips or some such novelty as the idea of food cooked by somebody else was delectably tempting at all the restaurants and cafés after covering all that mileage. Well, you've burnt so many calories maybe you deserve a treat! Then again you could run the concrete 'Dukes Of Hazard' route back to Rochdale!

Advantages:

- What a beautiful place. You could even do time trials here and repeated circuits and leave your other half on their sixth fry-up or the kids feeding ducks or learning to paddle a kayak. It would also be a great place to have Sunday dinner afterwards – but you may need a change of clothes and a dip in the lake for that!
- It can get very busy in summer and if you have the freedom and time it might be best to run the route when you know it will be quieter i.e. schooldays, weekdays, early mornings otherwise you may find times slowed by pedestrian congestion.
- There is plenty of room for warming up, cooling down, stretching off, buying water from the cafés or ice-cream vans. It is an ideal place for the runner without many other commitments!

Disadvantages:

- Getting out to Rochdale in the first place is damaging to one's sanity! With engineering works some Sundays, trains only running from Victoria Station and then frequently being cancelled, platforms changed and so on, you may have a certain amount of negative energy to burn by the time you reach Rochdale.
- If you are not a concrete fan the long route out here could be depressing and you might be better travelling by train straight to Smithy Bridge Station near the lake.
- If you are a fell runner there might be a bit too much organisation about the place and it could leave you desperate to run on hills that stretch for miles in the sight of no one, instead of pounding the same concrete loop – albeit a beautiful loop.

Summary:

A stamina testing concrete run out to a beautiful lake that is Manchester's secret answer to Windermere. Stunning scenery and a solid run even in bad weather but perhaps too set for freedom-seeking fell runners and moorland lovers.

Mileage:
4.5 miles to Smithy Bridge Station or 6.75 miles to Rochdale Station via Kiln Lane.

History:
Hollingworth Lake was completed in 1800 as a main feeder source for the then new Rochdale Canal. It covers 130 acres and the peripheral pathway is 2.5 miles long. The water is 25ft (7.6m) deep in places and it is said it was capable of holding 40 million gallons when first built – almost enough to quench a hard working runner's thirst.

Local mill owners feared the lake would drain water from streams and brooks that were vital to their business. But the waters began to make someone profits after steamers, hotels with ballrooms and pubs opened and attracted tourists in the 1850s and the area began to be served by trains from Manchester, Bradford and Leeds.

The nearby Ealees Valley was used as a training camp during World War One which affected the area's use for leisure but it was granted rights to become a country park in 1974 and has been used for leisure activities and by wildlife since.

The Hollingworth Lake Rowing Club was formed in March 1872 after an earlier club had vanished at the Hollingworth Lake Hotel. With Justices of the Peace and MPs carrying the rank of colonel among its top members the club was very well thought of around Rochdale if not at the Henley Royal Regatta (where it is reported they saw the name and thought the people were Canadian!) They won their first trophy at Agecroft Rowing Club, now based at Salford Quays, in 1902. The club's motto is 'Ready Aye Ready!' but we runners will stick to pulling on our calf muscles.

On the lake itself the *Lady Alice* passenger boat takes passengers on 25-minute trips around the waters on weekend afternoons (April to September) and it is a lovely way to keep your 'relaxing' family members busy as you get running.

Useful Websites:
www.hollingworthlakerowingclub.co.uk
See which opposition their members beat in which events – and get details of events and regattas.
www.rochdale.gov.uk
Search under Hollingworth Lake or under parks for information on activities and events.

Contacts:
Hollingworth Lake Country Park and Visitor Centre
Hollingworth Lake Country Park
Rakewood Road
Littleborough
OL15 0AQ
Email: holwac@link4life.org (Activity Centre)
hol.lakecp@rochdale.gov.uk (Country Park)
Tel: 01706 370499 (Activity Centre)
Tel: 01706 373421 (Country Park)

Hollingworth to Shineshaw

The icing on the mountainous cake

Whether you get a bus to Mottram-in-Longdendale and then run down the notorious Mottram Moor or manage to get a bus to Hollingworth itself, once you hit the small but traffic-heavy village run past several pubs including the friendly New Inn, then turn left off Market Street and onto Green Lane.

Follow Green Lane round to the right and on your left you will see a steep private road near Meadowbank Farm called Cow Lane by some natives, though unnamed on many maps. A few metres further on there is a public footpath if you wish to run on grass but the path is less defined and there are few cars on the concrete lane itself anyway.

Climb Cow Lane but almost expect to use mountaineering equipment not strong calf muscles. You can see Mottram Church on the hills to your left and open fields to your right before trees hamper the view but shelter you from the weather and a stream simpers down alongside you.

If you make it to the top (pretend you are thinking of directions as an excuse to stop and have an energy drink and admire the view – for about 30 minutes) then turn right. You should now be on Hobson Moor Road. This road is the former site of Hollingworth House. Remote as it seems, this location was used since just after the Norman Conquest as a hunting lodge and subsequently for many other uses. Keep hunting yourself and run past the sign not towards Hollingworthall Moor but onwards for Swineshaw Reservoirs.

Along this stretch you will have to open (and close of course) many large gates to keep running along the path, keeping up countryside courtesy. Then to your right you will see a large expanse of water but don't be misled, this is Arnfield Reservoir in Tintwistle, not the Shineshaw

Open up the Longdendale Valley.

Reservoirs you are eventually heading for. Though why they let something which sounds so much like a Liverpudlian football ground into the edges of Manchester one will never know!

Stunning as the scenery is here the pathway is rocky. This is not a route for speed tests or a quick circuit at night. This is a weekend run to push yourself and your stamina against the gradients route. It is also challenging in the distances you decide to take on. Though you can't stop on the moors and get a bus if you have had enough, you can plan which public transport to use to travel to Hollingworth and from Huddersfield Road to return from Shineshaw Reservoirs.

In the distance you will see a long strip of evergreen trees climbing up a hill and near here you should follow the path and gates left, which may seem a shame as it takes you away from the breathtaking open land before you here but you are quite high up and quite cold most of the year round as well so may welcome shelter.

Soon you will pass an electricity pylon and see Higher Swineshaw Reservoir before you. The land you are running on becomes paved again and you just follow the beautiful waters downhill. You will deserve the change in gradient on the run to the Brushes area of Stalybridge and Besom Lane. Here you can join Huddersfield Road and get a bus if you are flat-out. This section will improve the overall time because it is downhill and you should warm up body temperature-wise if not muscle-wise heading away from the wild and windy tops.

This is a run to love but it is a 'get covered in mud, push your calf muscles, freeze your face, scream freedom at the pinnacle of the hills' sort of run. It is the sort of route which you need to eat heavily and thaw out from afterwards. This is not a quick mileage-filler before your kids get home or before work.

For a shorter route which is closer to civilisation but still filled with mysticism and beauty, turn left at the top of Cow Lane not right. Thereafter, run straight on along Hobson Moor Road towards Roe Cross and Back Moor – a road not actually a moor, misleading as the name is to newcomers. Here cross over onto Harrop Edge Lane.

Beware of the navigation here though as Harrop Edge Lane can look like Matley Lane on some signs. On misty winter days looking out onto fields here both from Hobson Moor and Harrop Edge is like looking out to sea, being greeted by oceans of white with a sea-spray-like kiss to your cheeks from the mist.

It is a romantic route with old stone walls and it feels like you are floating in heaven in such mists. You may expect to see Jane Austen's Mr Darcy appear out of this weather. The only reminder of where you are is the vague sound of traffic and this is on both Hobson and Harrop. However, keep running down Harrop Edge Lane's public footpath towards the main motorway entrance/exit roundabout near Hattersley where you can get buses back to several towns and the city centre from Underwood Road and Stockport Road.

Apparently for those fitness lovers who rock climb too, Hobson Moor Quarry is now improved (see Useful Websites) after Tameside Council tidied it up and is nearby if you've got the energy! Though this route intersects with the Hobson Moor route it is definitely a steeper run and has a wider range of countryside features such as hills and reservoirs compared to the more singular stunning moorland of the alternative route.

Advantages:

- Stunning scenery.
- For some stretches almost empty country lanes so you don't have to navigate country footpaths or slip and slide over craggy tracks and barely outlined paths but you still get the beauty of the rural nature of the place.

- Stamina testing mountainous hills and inclines.
- The intemperate climate. This will help you if you are training for a specific target or event.

Disadvantages:
- It is not a route to nip around after work; it may be tricky to get to and once running very remote.
- It is dangerous for a lone runner late at night.
- Stalybridge is not always the best place for public transport to all parts of Manchester.
- It is very bumpy past Hobson Moor Road and the hilltop paths can be swampy in places.
- Opening and closing gates can interrupt the run.

Summary:
A stunning, remote route which is an ideal place to get away from it all but surprisingly has a lot more history than its forgotten-looking hills seem to testify.

Mileage:
3.75 miles via Brushes, 2.75 miles via Harrop Edge Lane.

History:
The town of Hollingworth is thought to be named after the Hollyngworthes family. They were landed gentry and it is claimed they were Anglo-Norman and the name derives from houx vert, the French for green holly. The site of Hollingworth Hall was used by William de Peveril after the Norman Conquest for hunting lodges. It was mentioned in literature in 1404 and in 1640 it was rebuilt. The Hollyngworthes had residence at the Hall as far back as the reign of King John. The family motto was said to be: 'Disce ferenda pati' – 'suffer that which must be borne'. It was said to refer to the Battle of 1066 but when your calf muscles are screaming…

In the 17th century the building is thought to have included parts of the earlier, fortified house. The later house had a stone built porch and three storey cross wings, like a vision from a historic tale of battle. The gatehouse was destroyed during the 19th century and the porch rebuilt in 1835, possibly commandeering a coat of arms from the gatehouse. The rest of the house was thought to have been destroyed by Manchester Waterworks in 1944.

There have been suggestions too that the Holisurde mentioned in the Doomsday Book was the town of Hollingworth that we know today and described as 'wasted lands held by the Earl' but it is a pretty and friendly little place, albeit one spoilt somewhat along the main thoroughfare by the traffic levels crossing the Pennines. Yet hopefully, the chance to run this beautiful venue for escape will not be wasted by us runners.

Useful Websites:
www.climbers.net
A rather out of date site for climbers but with stunning photographs at the end of their efforts.
forum.fellrunner.org.uk
Read accounts from other runners.
www.rockfax.com
A site for rock climbing enthusiasts to gather information.

Huddersfield Narrow Canal

Sculpting the soul

You could make this a full loop and run up from Ashton-under-Lyne to the western edge of the Peak District or see the lovely scenes near Uppermill. Then from Uppermill up to Standedge Tunnel and back in a south westerly direction to Ashton's Portland Basin, all along canal towpath but for this one we are starting at Uppermill and running on road to Standedge Tunnel before heading back along the canal towpath.

Beginning in the quaint village of Uppermill run northwards up High Street meeting the Brownhill Countryside Centre and the Saddleworth Railway Viaduct at the junction of Wool Road and Dobcross New Road. Next take the A670 Wool Road and as it becomes Standedge Road edge to the right along Huddersfield Road. Beware, however, there are two Huddersfield Roads around here running parallel to each other and you do not want the A62.

Running up this traffic-heavy stretch with the major A-roads to your left, you are also running parallel to and against the wind of speeding trains to your right but you are drawn forward by all the motion towards Standedge Tunnel.

It is divine to look up the valley with the countryside, the hills, the canal and the timelessness of such a wide open area. The high hills act as a periphery, almost like castle walls keeping the jewel of the valley and its lush, liquid and quiet yet active existence safe. The more you run and see, the more it keeps you moving with the desire to see even more.

Along Huddersfield Road, take the turning for Ward Lane opposite the Hanging Gate public house, cut across the Diggle Fields parkland and get onto the towpath, perhaps meeting one of the Sculpture Trail creatures along the way. The Huddersfield Canal Sculpture Trail is renowned far and wide as artists designed outdoor displays of everything from animals to unusual shapes and those sculptures run alongside the towpath. Sometimes they are easier to spot than others.

A nearby rocky footpath directs you over the top for 3.25 miles to the east side of the Pennines and the Yorkshire opening of the Standedge Tunnel. Crossing the hills completely. A Mancunian heading over to Yorkshire. It could almost prompt a second War of the Roses! Seriously, *OTRAM*'s Huddersfield Narrow Canal route does not take you over the tops covering the Standedge Tunnel itself but if you can't resist have a quick uphill run and look over the eastern horizon following the footpath signs and rockiness, then climb back down and onto the canal towpath after The Diggle Hotel at lock 32W. Next head south west, back in the direction you had run on-road and towards the city.

For tourists or leisure seekers and those with children there are trips through the tunnel on board a glass-topped boat. I think some of us would fear the confinement of such a long trip in a tunnel and as a runner I cannot think of much that would be more saddening than missing the sight of these hills and the valley. However, the opportunity is there for runners coming back on another occasion, or leaving family behind, to sail through the engineering marvel that the tunnel undoubtedly is.

As you jump onto the canal at lock 32 you keep on running on flat towpath and for the most part, certainly at this stage, both sides of the canal are accessible. To your left (heading towards Ashton) the train line brings passengers towards you very rapidly but beyond that you can see the hilltops with monuments such as Pots and Pans Memorial (see other routes). In the basin of the valley itself you pass old mills such as Warth Mill, with its name proudly displayed on ancient signs at its highest point. Later you will also see Dobcross Loom Works.

The heavenly Huddersfield Narrow Canal.

There are many locks in close succession at this early part of the towpath and it seems to be a route more popular with barge owners than some of the other canals in and around Manchester. For us runners, bouncing along the canal path can be repetitive when compared to something like running up a headland but the locks can motivate you to keep going, counting down to your destination, ticking off the numbers of the locks as you pass. For a canal this also feels very open at many points on the rural not urban side of Mossley especially.

Running on, you pass restored sections of the canal and bridges built in the last 10 years. You run past the Transhipment Shed where in times past they moved goods from boats to

89

transport on horses while the tunnel was being constructed. It is now home to the Huddersfield Canal Society.

You then run past a former woollen mill which has been made into housing and at Lime Kiln Lock (23W) you pass under the Saddleworth Railway Viaduct sweetly nicknamed 'Old Sag' locally because it has a noticeable droop. Many of us, especially us older female runners will try not to identify too strongly with that.

Sat on the canal itself close to the point where the towpath is intersected by High Street and Oldham Road is the Saddleworth Museum. This is another well placed visitor attraction, especially for those sailing into town.

Runners who set off from Uppermill will now be back at their starting pointing for this route but keep tapping towpath. The canal takes you to Frenches Marina, just outside Greenfield, which is bordered by the River Tame on the left hand side. There are shops nearby and The Kingfisher pub with a look that suits those with more disposable income than a runner's investment in mud, sweat and tears.

The wharf itself holds up to 20 boats and cost about £1.7 million to build on the site at Knoll Mill. It must be lovely on a summer's evening for hard grafting barge users to have a glass of vino and watch the Peak District countryside all around but most of us runners will note that it is a great use of a once derelict area and decide we can't stay for one and that we will see more locks instead.

Ever onwards but all around things become more urban, more populated and there are often quite a lot of walkers and tourists along the Uppermill, Greenfield and Diggle stretches. The towpath starts to head more westerly for about 0.75 miles, lulling you into a false sense of security that after you have run to Mossley it will be straight back to Ashton when instead you tackle more distance and head south to Stalybridge first.

Run noting the changes along the path with different shaped and sized bridges and different levels of housing alongside the waterway. In Friezland you will encounter Mann's Wharf Bridge and about 0.5 miles later the canal crosses over the River Tame via the restored Royal George Aqueduct and then moves from the district of Oldham into Tameside.

If you were not already running on the right hand towpath you would have to cross bridges here to do so as part of the left hand towpath is fenced off and impassable because of garden landslides and waste. It can be deflating to run a set run and then have to turn and head back along a stretch because a pathway ends so perhaps it is best to switch canal sides on one of the bridges just after the point where Manchester Road crosses over the canal, before Roaches, where the Roaches public house sits aside the towpath and acts as a landmark.

You may notice that around about now in Bottom Mossley you will have reached locks 16W to 14W, and as you started at lock 32W you are about halfway. Well, you can try and tell yourself that as a booster but locks aren't always equally spaced but you are not far off halfway. Run onwards alongside Woodend Mill and see Noon Sun Hill in the distance.

Then at lock 14W the towpath changes sides crossing you over the Winterford Bridge. Here run along the left hand side of the waterway as you head towards urban existence.

Near here the Emmaus Mossley charity shop sells furniture from an old mill but pound on and you will head under Egmont Street and on towards Stalybridge, running through Scout Tunnel near lock 12W, which may be a little unnerving with slim pathways and old wooden beams for support. This area is also very solitary considering it is so close to suburban towns.

Near lock 8W head under the legs of an electricity pylon – that should encourage you to keep moving quickly. This is where the canal had been filled in for a while and the former

Hartshead Power Station stood. The restored canal's route choices seem to have been limited in modern times by other restoration. Further on, the canal reaches Mottram Road in Stalybridge and the towpath widens and becomes paved as the route heads through the town centre.

Along the canal here you can see Armentieres Square and the major role it has in the life of Stalybridge today and the Melbourne Street Bridge, which survived being buried when the canal was filled in and is looking good today. You can see the whale-like hump of Millbrook hill in the distance and sometimes even today still see horse-drawn barges on the canal in and around Stalybridge pulling us back to another time.

The route meets Staley Wharf and the Barge Inn near Peel Street before the towpath becomes very thin with a sharp turn near the site of an old swing bridge. Further onwards the canal crosses the Stakes or Stalybridge Aqueduct over the River Tame; the two waterways seemingly dancing over or around each other for miles. The canal crosses the river again at Clarence Street on what was one of the first iron canal troughs in the country.

The Huddersfield Narrow then runs behind Dukinfield rather than through its centre as it does in Stalybridge. It once served the town well industrially as both Whitelands and Wellington Mills are in close succession next to the canal. Near Texas Street there is also a horse ramp where tired nags who fell in were dragged out and led onto the towpath. We know the feeling! Yet maybe it is time to celebrate because around Whitelands and the nearby Portland Basin in Ashton the Huddersfield Narrow, Peak Forest and Ashton canals all meet. Well, it is time for more liquids because you've finished.

Advantages:
- A lovely view of the valley, countryside, canal, industry and heritage, in one run with no navigation.
- The further into the sticks you go the more you seem to travel back in time with old stone houses and mills from centuries ago.
- You can see many sights such as Standedge Tunnel, Saddleworth Railway Viaduct, Division Bridge, Stalybridge Aqueduct, and the Pots and Pans Memorial on the hilltops.

Disadvantages:
- It will attract tourists, barge users, dog walkers so may be busy and slow you down, particularly in good weather.
- Having to run under bridges and through tunnels will not make this every runner's favourite path, especially on lonely stretches at night.
- Some of the locks can have woodwork that sits near the towpath and can mean accidents, or others slowing you down to use the equipment.
- It is a real shame if you have to interrupt a straight run down one side of the towpath to reverse and cross the canal because of landslides or a short, poorly maintained patch.
- If you first get on to the canal after crossing Sam Road rather than near Ward Lane don't forget to view the Standedge Tunnel entrance nearer Ward Lane. It would be a shame to travel out there and miss it.

Summary:
A countryside, mainly towpath route which gives a taste of the Pennines' historic life and a stunning green valley and then gradually makes you work your way into a more urban era, zone and lifestyle.

Mileage:
8 miles and that is if you don't visit the Yorkshire side of Standedge Tunnel.

History:
Local artists designed pieces for the Sculpture Trail based on ideas given by school children. There is a mural in Dobcross and play areas in Diggle following the themes as well as pieces alongside the canal. Children wrote a poem prompting the 'I Love It Here' sculpture in Water Gate, Uppermill based on stone slabs representing stepping stones. Near Wool Road Bridge a sculpture is a reminder of the mason's marks and tied in with the theme of past construction and 'Through Heathered Hills' wooden sculptures, appropriate to the area which is carpeted in purple in the early autumn, are placed near the Standedge Tunnel entrance.

There are numerous mills along this route with Diggle Mill, Ellis Mill and Warth Mill, which is still used today, near Diggle. You will see more signs of the spinning and weaving heritage when encountering 'The Cathedral' or Dobcross Loom Works that has a clock tower and is a Grade II listed building. Some information states the site was used for making munitions in World War One and Russian submarine parts in World War Two. It was used as a pallet factory for 37 years until 2006 but looks far too beautiful to be a war weapons factory.

Near Mossley a place named Andrew Mill was given water rights in 1765, Scout Mill and Clough Mill got rights in 1820, then Old Roughtown and Carr Hill Mills followed suit. It highlights the intensity of textile heritage in these parts as the canal weaves in and out of these sites. In Stalybridge alone there were eight mills at the time of the Industrial Revolution: Mossley, nearer the source of raw materials such as wool had 20 in 1830.

The summit of the Huddersfield Canal is the highest navigable waterway in Britain standing at 645ft (197m) above sea level between Diggle and Marsden and for some people the celebrations reached similar heights when the canal celebrated its bi-centenary in September 2011.

It is a 20-mile stretch of waterway which was opened in 1811 and re-opened to navigation after £30 million of restoration work in 2001. It had been out of use since 1944. Nearby Sculpture Trail mural plaques inform that it cost £123,804 to build in 1811 and that figure is more than twice what had been originally estimated.

Nevertheless, it was a feat of engineering brought about by the necessity of industry to tunnel through the moorland for industrial and farming purposes. Farming had always been a major occupation in these parts and the Industrial Revolution brought fabric mills to the area. The canal and barges were used to transport wool, finished goods and other industrial products.

Many see the Standedge Tunnel as an engineering marvel as it is the highest, deepest and longest canal tunnel in the land. It is 3.2 miles long and took 17 years for the workers out in the Pennines to construct. Thomas Telford took over the contract in 1807 after Benjamin Outram who had been overseeing it since 1794 gave up in the face of many problems and costs. In June 1809, both ends of the tunnel met and it was opened to sailing traffic in March 1811, with higher tolls backed by parliament to fund the extra costs incurred. There was an opening ceremony on 4 April of that year. Another three tunnels were built through the hills, originally for trains, though only one of the other three is open today taking travellers on Trans Pennine journeys.

Still covered with bricks in some places and rock in others, the hills saw 40 boats a day sail through the mountainous landscape to another county when Standedge opened. Barge users sailed between the towns of Diggle and Marsden, to complete their full canal journey between Ashton and Huddersfield.

No towpath was built inside the tunnel to save costs, so us runners have to climb up over the Peak District hills and leg it to see the other side but we aren't the only ones to have had our calf muscles tested here. Many years ago with no engines and no towpaths for horses to drag boats from, men called 'leggers' lay on top of loads and pushed with their pins against the tunnel sides to coax, goad and propel cargo forwards. Tough work but their calves didn't have the Pennine hills in an upward motion to contend with!

Before lock 17W you will see the old stone humpback Division Bridge which was once the boundary between Lancashire and Yorkshire.

The Diggle Flight of locks was fully restored in 1996. The impressive range of locks set close together take the barges up, up and away through the Diggle Portal and on through Standedge Tunnel.

There is a 'Rail Ale Trail' connected to this route. Trains from Manchester Victoria to Huddersfield calling at stops alongside the canal to allow people a plate, a pint and an absence of police because users avoid drink driving risks. The 'trail' information can be downloaded via Oldham Council's website.

Useful Websites:

www.huddersfieldcanal.com
Visit to get information about the 200-year-old man-made waterway from the people who love it.

www.oldham.gov.uk
Enquire about Huddersfield Narrow Canal and it will list many surrounding activities and sites such as the Brownhill Countryside Centre, the Sculpture Trail and Rail Ale Trail.

www.penninewaterways.co.uk
Great history about the canal and pictures but watch the directions.

www.saddleworth-canal-cruises.co.uk
Find details on the 'Pennine Moonraker' and canal boats trips for when you are not running.

www.saddleworthonline.co.uk
List of activities, information about facility opening times and other nearby attractions.

www.standedge.co.uk
Information on the Visitors' Centre if you do run to the other end of the tunnel and boat trips at the highest, longest and deepest canal tunnel in the UK.

www.visitoldham.co.uk
Information about the exhibitions, facilities and details of which buses to take you there.

Contacts:

Brownhill Countryside Centre
Wool Road
Dobcross
OL3 5PB
Tel: 01457 872598
Email: env.brownhill@oldham.gov.uk

Huddersfield Canal Society
The Transhipment Warehouse
Wool Road
Dobcross
Saddleworth
OL3 5QR
Tel: 01457 871800
Email: hcs@huddersfieldcanal.com

Saddleworth Museum
High Street,
Uppermill
Saddleworth
Oldham
OL3 6HS
Tel: 01457 870336/874093
E-mail: curator@saddleworthmuseum.co.uk
Email: ecs.saddleworthtic@oldham.gov.uk

Standedge Tunnel and Standedge Visitor Centre
Waters Road
Marsden
Huddersfield
HD7 6NQ
Tel: 01484 844298
Email: info@standedge.co.uk

Irwell Valley Way

In pieces or in peace?

The Irwell Valley Way is not a route you are likely to tackle in one day, with over 30 miles of running route it would outstrip a marathon in length but it does give the runner a choice of landscapes. It starts at Salford Quays and heads on to Prestwich and Clifton. It then follows the River Irwell to Bury and then on to Bacup and Rossendale.

Many parts of the trail are well signposted but it can take you around the edges of industrial buildings and quite bleak areas. The stretch near Thirteen Arches Viaduct near Clifton lets you see a Grade II listed structure but the area underneath the structure can be very muddy and the industrial surroundings a little unpleasant. Yet, you are less than 0.5 miles away from the beauty of both Prestwich Forest Park to the east and Clifton Country Park to the west.

A very popular stretch of the overall Irwell Valley Way is from Radcliffe's Asda, via the Outwood Viaduct, over the River Irwell to then meet the waterway heading via Outwood and under Ringley Road West.

Then the trail follows the border of Bolton and Bury between Little Hurst Wood on one side and Nuttall Wood, to name but one, on the other. This woodland area might be tempting to go and explore, particularly if you want to tackle the inclines up the Nuttall Wood side but not advisable if you lose what little footpath there is.

Though BMX bike users like to flip and turn near the Irwell Valley Trail on the edge of places like Fat Hurst Wood, the ground further back is saturated and quite dangerous if you

The Archangel of Clifton, Thirteen Arches Viaduct.

leave the pathways. Though it is wooded, little brooks and very moist ground between the trees mean you could slip, slide or even sink away from a solid route.

If you resist temptation, however, and stay on the Irwell Valley Way you will pass the edge of more wooded areas in the form of Snape Wood before crossing the M60. You will then head east, though inclined to go west, as you don't want to miss Thirteen Arches Viaduct, it being the best structural sight of the route but head east and not only will you see parts of the snaking structure but you can enter Prestwich Forest and Philips Parks, where this section of the route ends.

For another flavour of the Irwell Valley Way you could start at Prestwich Forest Park or Drinkwater Park and run alongside the River Irwell southwards under Agecroft Road, past the cemetery of the same name and into Lower Kersal. This would then put you in Salford proper but running around the tongue or loop that the river makes here can require attention navigationally. You may have to cross the river and find bridges to do so and you will also have to tackle the residential streets in the middle of the tongue-like sort of peninsular.

From here you can run on to Castle Hill Viewpoint or visit The Cliff, the area nearer the water with much sporting history. Shortly afterwards the River Irwell will run towards Salford Crescent Train Station, The University of Salford and you could follow the river in a loop out to the east here, to follow the water completely, but there is not a footpath next to all parts of the waterway. Salford Quays is to the west so you could road run briefly on the Crescent near The University of Salford buildings then turn right down Oldfield Road. Continue as the road becomes Ordsall Lane and takes you to the modernised waters where you can stretch off for the day.

The trail being too long to cover in one day for most runners and walkers it is best to dissect it into pieces. The Salford Trail runs from Salford Quays to Clifton via Kersal Vale. The Outwood Trail, which passes between Radcliffe and Prestwich, was once a railway line but now provides a leisure route through ancient woodland to horse riders and walkers as well as us forgotten runners.

Advantages:
- A lot of choice of where to run when selecting a section out of 33 miles.
- You can get a full flavour of city life, urban sculptures, countryside and leisure.

Disadvantages:
- It is too big to tackle in one go.
- There is too much industry at some points.
- It is not always easy to find accurate mapping of the entire trail.
- Though there is a lot to explore there are many reasons not to stray from the path with this route: industrial sites, boggy ground, navigation nightmares.

Summary:
A long route passing through Quays and staying close to a riverside that visits old mills, modern art and current industry but the entire way is too vast for most people to cover in one run.

Mileage:
Radcliffe/Outwood to Prestwich Forest Park 2.75 miles, Prestwich Forest Park to Salford Quays 4 miles.

History:

The Earl of Chester gave Salford a charter in 1230 making it a free borough. The Irwell Valley Sculpture Trail covers 33 miles and is the longest feature of its type in the UK. There are 70 different artworks, including sculptures like giant tilted vases, from Salford Quays to Bacup which symbolise the trail and the city's heritage.

A Wet Earth Colliery at Clifton Country Park was established in about 1740 and work started there in around 1750. It didn't close until 1928 and was known for engineering firsts, such as steam winding and James Brindley's hydraulic pumping scheme which was used from 1756 until the closure of the colliery.

Thirteen Arches Viaduct or Clifton Viaduct was built in 1848 to carry a railway line from Manchester to Rossendale. It is a Grade II listed structure but the railway line closed in 1966.

The Irwell Valley Sculpture Trail was due to be refreshed by spring 2012 after a £420,000 injection of cash from the Arts Council England, allowing groups to update websites about the route.

The Salford area is seeing land beautified after about a century of neglect in some parts. The Lower Irwell Valley, a square of land between Agecroft Road, the M60, the River Irwell and Bolton Road has a very industrial past, as with several country areas on the fringe of Manchester. But improvements are being made to improve and enhance such landscape areas for recreation and pleasure rather than just being left as abandoned former work sites.

Chatterton Mill was the site in April 1826 of a disturbance when revolting handloom weavers broke machinery and were fired upon by soldiers. Five were killed, as was an onlooker and 69 were arrested. Death sentences were placed on 41 people but they were imprisoned or transported to Australia instead. At the end of the 19th century the mill that had belonged to Thomas Aitken was demolished. The site was made into a Ramsbottom peace memorial in 1923.

Useful Websites:

www.colsal.org.uk
A good website for Salford Trail information.
www.parklover.wordpress.com/2011/04/28/blue-monday-the-irwell-valley-trail/
A website for lovers of the outdoors which covers Irwell Valley Way.

Contacts:

Rawtenstall Tourist Information Centre
Tel: 01706 226590

Rossendale Groundwork Centre
Tel: 01706 211421

Salford Tourist Information Centre
The Lowry
Pier 8
Salford Quays
Tel: 0161 848 8601
Email: tic@salford.gov.uk

Jericho's Woodland

Not quite a city of palms

Bury having a suburb known as Jericho is perhaps unusual to some outsiders, yet when you consider that Moses Gate is also nearby you see the fascination this area has with biblical or Middle Eastern names.

In the baking hot Middle Eastern version Jericho is a city said to be the longest permanently inhabited city on earth. It is also said to be the lowest, situated just a few miles north of the Dead Sea and is known as the 'City of Palms'. Appropriately then, in the Jericho area between Bury and Rochdale we are going to run through the trees. Head out of Bury town centre in an easterly direction, avoiding the big A58 Bury New Road and instead head along Angouleme Way, The Rock, then Bell Lane. Next join Bury and Rochdale Old Road and run past Fairfield Hospital.

There are many buses out this way from the town's public transport interchange but you may enjoy the pounding of streets lined with old stone terraces and the scent of fish and chips everywhere. A very regular flavour in north Manchester. Along the way you will pass an old mill chimney named Melba. Look to your right once beyond the hospital and Melba and you can begin to see the outline of the metropolis of Manchester in the distance but it is to your left we are heading for this route. There are many branches to this route to reach the woodland or peaceful countryside. Next turn left on to Elbut Lane.

From Bury and Rochdale Old Road, about 1 mile further out than the hospital, turn left up Ashworth Road. This road runs through the middle of a V-shape of woodland and alongside areas like Cobb Wood, Gelder Wood and Carr Wood to the east.

After about 0.25 miles a public footpath lets you into Gelder Wood Country Park and alongside Naden Brook to continue heading north. The woodland footpath then takes you to School Lane and on the other side a weir at Ashworth Wood. You then continue heading north. If you follow the Naden Brook up through the eastern most branch of the woodland you will run on past the Three Owls Bird Sanctuary and then see the Millcroft Tea Rooms at Wolstenholme Fold, a Victorian tea rooms and gardens with some history and historical artefacts. Perhaps you will want to stop here for a brew!

To head back to urban land head south again to School Lane via either the same footpath you reached the owl sanctuary on or one heading more south westerly. From here join Ashworth Road again briefly where both north and south of Ashworth Hall Farm there are footpaths onto the west side of the V-shape of woodland in this area. You could meet Kershaw Bridge or further down meet Windy Cliff Bridge to not cross the structures but run left through the Ashworth Valley. Here Cheesden Brook creates weirs and runs through the woodland to later join with Naden Brook. Reintroducing you to Ashworth Road to then turn right and get back onto Bury and Rochdale Old Road.

At Windy Cliff Bridge, however, you could cross the waterway and turn left and head south on public footpaths through Dobb Wood towards Fernises or Wrigley Carr Farms. Here turn right to run along Gristlehurst Lane, past Higher Tack Lee Farm and Lower Tack Lee Farm to then turn left on Birtle Road as it becomes Elbut Lane and re-introduces you to Bury and Rochdale Old Road's busy life.

Beyond Higher Tack Lee Farm you will see wind farm turbines on the horizon and yet this opening up of the countryside is just seconds away from a road filled with public transport and commerce. Up here though you see riding schools and farmland, mounds of country waste next to rustic gateways and field after field of colour and nature.

Tunnel of Hope at Gristlehurst Lane, Top o' th' Wood.

If instead you wanted a more open feel to the run you could leave Bury and Rochdale Old Road near the hospital. Run up Elbut Lane and then Birtle Road before being greeted by a mesh of public footpaths. You need to run for a further 0.75 miles in a largely northerly direction to reach the bottom of Deeply Vale with its Lower Bridge and weir. Here you can select whether to run around these waters sat over the border in Rossendale before jumping back on virtually the same paths to head south again back to Birtle Road and onwards to Elbut Lane and Bury and Rochdale Old Road.

Both Birtle and Ashworth are conservation areas with councils trying to protect the feel of the places.

Whatever loop or path you choose for this route you could if you wished avoid the run out from Bury itself and get a bus to either The Waggon or near to Fairfield General Hospital and Elbut Lane. You could then run upwards with more open countryside to the north and west and increasing amounts of woodland to the east, as you stand on Bury and Rochdale Old Road looking northwards at nature's open plan before you.

Advantages:
- A great choice of diverse types of countryside and woodland scattered on the doorstep of infrastructure.
- A wider range of views, both immediate and longer range, than you may expect.

Disadvantages:
• Sometimes the footpaths take you past or almost through work or building sites.
• The ground can be very mushy and slippy.

Summary:
An unexpectedly pretty and large area of countryside and woodland on the doorstep of residential life. Great for regular, short loops for runners who live nearby or a longer slog for residents who live further afield.

Mileage:
From Bury and Manchester Old Road to Deeply Vale and back 3 miles; to Wolstenholme Fold and back 3–3.25 miles and to Bury and Rochdale Old Road from Bury centre's Metrolink 2–2.75 miles.

History:
Bury's first workhouse was known as the Redvales Workhouse and opened in 1775 to the south of the town. In 1857 a new one was opened in Jericho and this became known as the Jericho Institution in 1929. Later still, it became what we know today as Fairfield Hospital.

Sadly, it seems to be uncertain why Bury, Rochdale, indeed north Manchester in general all love the unusual, exotic and biblical place names it uses. There is Jericho, Moses Gate, Melba even, on the way out along Bury and Rochdale Old Road. Understandably many people assume it is in connection with the strong religious history the area has had at times.

The Industrial Revolution turned life upside down. Once rural areas with people scattered few and far between became a sea of mills and factories instead of green open fields. People were displaced. Many people from the region worked in the mills and even people from as far afield as the south of England or Ireland came to work in the north west of England.

This is where the money was but no doubt it upset people to have to move to grimy industrial places they did not know or to see their own homelands change so drastically and they sought solace and comfort in religion, hence the vast array of different types of faith and worship and the unusual names being on the tips of their tongues in Bury and Rochdale. Jericho is thought to mean his moon, his month, his sweet smell; Moses meant taken out or drawn forth, especially taken out of water or a son, which is appropriate for Moses Gate Country Park (see other routes) with the many waters in and around it.

In Rochdale, just before Christmas on 21 December 1844 a little shop started trading. It marked the beginning of the Co-operative Movement. From £28 starting capital and 28 members it now has over 800 million people in over 100 countries worldwide. The Museum was being renovated at the time of writing but its location, in the little shop where it all began, was set to re-open in 2012. The original Toad Lane store was sold in 1867 but repurchased by the movement in 1931 and it resurrected the original name the Rochdale Equitable Pioneers' Society in 1989, the movement having had many name changes over the years.

Useful Websites:
www.bury.co.uk
You can find information on countryside areas and how to obtain walk and guided walk pamphlets.

www.link4life.org
A Rochdale leisure activities and information website.
www.rochdale.gov.uk
Get information about the borough's sights and leisure activities.
www.spinningtheweb.co.uk
Information about the many places connected with the cotton industry, especially around Manchester and the north west.
www.visitbury.com
For Bury's tourist information.

Contacts:

Bury Tourist Information Centre
The Fusilier Museum
Moss Street
BL9 0DF
Tel: 0161 253 5111
Email: touristinformation@bury.co.uk

Rochdale Pioneers' Museum
31 Toad Lane
Rochdale
OL12 0NU
Tel: 01706 524920
Email: museum@co-op.ac.uk

Rochdale Tourist Information Centre
Touchstones Rochdale
The Esplanade
Rochdale
OL16 1AQ
Tel: 01706 924928

Millcroft Tea Gardens
Roods Lane
Wolstenholme Fold off Hutchinson Road
Rochdale
OL11 5UE
Tel: 01706 642054

Three Owls Bird Sanctuary
Hutchinson Road
Norden
Lancashire
Tel: 01706 642162

Lees, Uppermill and Mossley

From metropolis to mountains

For this stunning Peak District run, which was once said to be the only part of Yorkshire where Lancastrians lived, you can get a 343 bus from either Oldham or Hyde: just one of the ways to take you over the tops and out to Lees, and alight near the village post office.

Once out in this village – which lives an older way of life, advertising 'English' fish and chips and British Legions – warm up in a little garden area just opposite Selwyn's Fish and Chip shop and the village florists. Afterwards run up High Street in the direction away from Oldham until the road itself becomes Oldham Road.

You will see – if your eyes can pass the pain barrier with the inclines – mesmerising rolling green hills and a church on the pinnacle on one of the hills to your right. Keep running along what is quite a busy road, which carries a bus between Saddleworth and Oldham every 10 minutes during the day but is also a beautiful and testing road.

If you look behind you along this stretch you will see Oldham in the distance and Manchester with its metropolitan silhouette on a sunny day too. Back out towards open country you should see the Wharmton Television Mast sat atop the hills as you head out away from Manchester and towards the momentous mountains, which sometimes remain snow covered even on days of brilliant sunshine. You can also see Hartshead Pike, from which you can look over the four counties of Lancashire, Yorkshire, Cheshire and Derbyshire on the road that snakes more up and down than round corners and bends.

You will pass through Grotton and then on your right pass Stockport Road. Shortly after that you should see the beautifully named Lovers Lane on your left before you pound past the Farrars Arms pub and the road overlooks and runs parallel to Greenfield Train Station and the line from Manchester Victoria to Huddersfield. The line also carries the Manchester to Huddersfield hourly service, which doesn't stop at the station but runs very close to the road. It will cause more than a distraction and will certainly outrun you if it passes by as you run the route.

Yet you needn't worry, you can cross the railway line safely over a bridge here and the road will meet Shaw Hall Bank Road and then continue as Oldham Road to the right and Ladcastle Road to the left. If you are running to Uppermill Viaduct take Ladcastle Road to the left but otherwise for this route it is better to continue along the larger A670 Oldham Road. This route takes you to the area of Saddleworth and although it is considered part of Oldham, which is of course in Lancashire, the Saddleworth area historically fell under the West Riding of Yorkshire.

If you wish to have a quick run through the charming village of Uppermill continue along High Street for about 0.25 miles, past the statue of poet Ammon Wrigley, to Willow Bank Pond and then return to the main thoroughfare to pass a mill and run onto Huddersfield Narrow Canal on your left to head back in the direction you just ran out from. However if you want to miss having to negotiate around people and are happy to cut off the quick run through Uppermill, turn off where Oldham Road joins High Street and head south back in the direction towards Oldham along the canal towpath.

Though the towpath is more flat than the hills you have just experienced you need not fear boredom, it will obviously take you on a much more mellow run towards the Mossley area.

The canal just off the High Street at Uppermill will pass the Churchill Playing Fields' track and the waterway, which opened in 1811, will take you past several century-old locks. Many parts of the route have seen new flats built alongside and combined with waterside pubs such as The Kingfisher to try to develop a rather executive feel to the area, very different to the old stone, Yorkshire-esque qualities of the hilly Oldham Road on your run out that way.

The canal will then take you under Chew Valley Road, past more mills and streams to the aqueduct and weirs. Continue along the canal towpath on what is approaching a 5-mile route but you can leave the towpath and run alongside the parallel River Tame in places.

The Waggon Road/Micklehurst Road Bridge crosses both the River Tame and the Huddersfield Narrow Canal and will give you the opportunity to run down the Waggon Road side to Mossley's A635 Manchester Road where you can catch a train or bus back to Oldham, Hyde, Stalybridge or Ashton…or keep on running.

Advantages:
- Stunning scenery.
- Testing inclines and a good distance.
- If you make it to the Brownhill Countryside Centre just above Uppermill you can leave your spouse and children there to be educated on the largely animal exhibitions about the canal's creatures, as you head off to follow your animal instinct and run!

Disadvantages:
- Parts are secluded if you decide to quit early or got injured.
- Watch it in bad weather. There are permanent signs ready to flash to warn motorists the road is closed in winter – but not for those of us who run on our own form of bio-fuel!

Snowy tops above Huddersfield Narrow Canal.

- Check bus and train times prior to the run as they can be unpredictable and you don't want to get stuck out there, especially feeling your sweat freezing without a change of clothes on a winter's evening.

Summary:
A rural stamina testing and incline-filled run through beautiful Peak District mountainous villages with a less taxing return route along gentler canal and riverside paths to clock up mileage and push the muscles.

Mileage:
5 miles.

History:
Perhaps because its surrounding moorland is unspoilt and undeveloped or perhaps because of the wilder nature of the climate here, Saddleworth's archaeological history seems to go back light years. There are connections with the Anglo-Saxons, Romans and it is also believed it has Bronze Age links which would make many people happy on leisure excursions from walkers to metal detector enthusiasts.

Nearby Castleshaw Roman Fort was built around AD79 and artist and poet Ammon Wrigley, who died in 1946, is thought to have worked on excavations there, though nothing is recorded of it. Though the Saddleworth area does have some Roman history it was brought to life mainly though its work as a Yorkshire woollen cloth producer and through its cotton mills during the Industrial Revolution.

A natural chalybeate spring, a mineral spring containing salts of iron, was discovered in Lees in the 18th century and after seeing figures like 60,000 visitors in the month of August 1821 there were plans to make Lees into a spa town but the Industrial Revolution's mills stopped the process. The industrial changes kept the town less populated, with a much quieter 10,000 inhabitants by the 21st century.

The Huddersfield Narrow Canal heads from Huddersfield on to Ashton-under-Lyne. When being built in 1810 the Diggle Moss Reservoir further up the valley burst and flooded Marsden in Yorkshire killing five people. It is said a 15-ton rock was carried 2 miles by the force of the elements: unnerving – but this really is an area that can move mountains.

The lonely, millstone grit land is split between Oldham and Yorkshire's Kirklees borough. The A635 goes over the moor and was named locally as the Isle of Skye road after a pub that once existed there.

Saddleworth's Urban District was given up by Yorkshire and became part of Greater Manchester in 1974. However, some natives still feel a strong connection with Yorkshire, perhaps shown in their love of brass bands and a slightly different sort of lifestyle, as well as the differing types of architecture when compared to many more central parts of Manchester and towns such as Rochdale, with the rows of red terraces.

Useful Websites:
www.britishwaterways.co.uk
To get information on the 2,200 miles of canals, rivers and docks that the organisation runs.
www.visitoldham.com
For information on the Brownhill Countryside Centre.

Contacts:

Brownhill Countryside Centre
Wool Road
Dobcross
Oldham
OL3 5PB
Tel: 01457 872598
Email: ecs.tourist@oldham.gov.uk

Standedge Tunnel And Visitors' Centre
Waters Road
Marsden
Huddersfield
HD7 6NQ
Tel: 01484 844298
Email: info@standedge.co.uk

Longdendale Trail/Bottoms Reservoir

Tunnel vision

On the train journey out to Hadfield (a 30-minute journey which leaves about every 30 minutes from Manchester Piccadilly) the train passes Broadbottom Station and then the land opens up. From then it is no longer the roll of the transport but the rocks that capture your attention.

The hills, perhaps even mountains compared with the flat lands of Cheshire, surround a vast open space that is perfect for runners and which one can see especially well from the grand heights of Dinting Bridge, or Dinting Arches as it is known to natives, looking out over a bowl-like valley.

Hadfield, the end of the line, is signposted as the stop for the Longdendale and TransPennine Trails. These thoroughfares have apparently been used for hundreds of years to cross the Pennine backbone of the nation, with packhorse routes dating back to mediaeval times.

After leaving the station walk across a car park and turn right past a pub called The Palatine, some public toilets and a new housing estate, before turning left into another small car park just before a railway bridge. This area affords space to warm up and cool down before and after the run, or to park there if you drive to the route.

You can then begin your run. The fact that the sandy trail is already set out means you won't get lost or waste time navigating but there is little scope for exploration during the early part of the run, where you are boxed-in by the soil of these old railway embankment-style sides to the path.

Ripples on the water at Longdendale Valley, Hadfield.

Further on, however, the earth disappears, the horizon widens and you are greeted by a chain of blue reservoirs running into the hills on your left. It is a beautiful route as you run along the open pathway and you can look up ahead to see numerous reservoirs: Bottoms, Valehouse, Rhodeswood, Torside and finally Woodhead, which line your route and become a big part of the stunning scenery of the valley.

However, if you decide to run this route on a sunny Sunday you are likely to find that a lot of other people had the same idea with dog walkers, cyclists, walkers, one or two other runners and even the odd horse rider out for the day.

If you prefer solitude the Longdendale Trail is crossed by the TransPennine Trail at several points near the beginning and you can head along that in an easterly or westerly direction. It is not to say others don't use that route, merely that there is more space upon the longer route.

If you do stick with the original trail you can run 3 miles up to Torside, where the route is interrupted briefly by the B6105 and there is an information board about the reservoirs. Up until this point the reservoirs are very visible to your left, offering beauty and encouragement as the trail opens up more and more, becoming quite a windswept guide on occasions.

Despite being in the Peak District this trail is very flat and on quiet weekdays would be an excellent place for outdoor runners to do time trials.

On busy weekends, however, it is a great deal more about building stamina and learning your limitations because this isn't a circuit. If you feel 1.5 miles is the halfway mark after a quick slurp of water it is time to run back the way you came.

Treating the 3-mile mark as halfway seems logical. The interruption of the main road acts as a natural halfway point to the full trail which covers 6.5 miles one way. The trail itself moves away from the reservoirs a little after the B6105, making it good for longer distance runners as the pounding then becomes more about concentration and less about taking in the atmosphere.

Therefore, experienced runners may do a 6-mile route in all, to Torside Reservoir and back but the hardened obsessives will probably then carry on past the end of Torside and on to the end of Woodhead Reservoir.

At Woodhead you will see a closed-off 3-mile long tunnel once used by the transport industry which reached through the Pennine hills to Penistone in South Yorkshire.

Sights such as this and Nine Holes Bridge can be worth the extra effort invested in running on after the trail break at Torside, especially in the right weather and as the trail is less inhabited after the B6105 and you open up to the elements even further. However, this can be a cold, hard run on a bad day despite it being a set trail and you not having to power against three feet of mud with every step and there being few inclines for the Pennine area.

Pathways early on cross the reservoirs and there is a youth hostel at Crowden on the A628 Woodhead Road, near the meeting of Torside and Woodhead Reservoirs but it is on the other side of the reservoirs, if you need a lie down afterwards.

Though you might be tempted to try running back along the other side of the reservoirs to make a circuit it is not really advisable. Woodhead Road is not a road for runners. But there is plenty to see whether you do the 3-mile return (6 miles/10km) or 5 miles then return or even a 6.5-mile run and then return for exercise lovers who just can't stop pounding their feet.

A good thing about this route is the versatility for activities if not for finishing early. You could hire bicycles and come here with family or run on your own, finding complete isolation, probably on a wet weekday!

Advantages:

- It can afford a lot of running without you having to navigate, think about routes or directions.
- It offers a first taste of real, longer distance rural running without the cross-country battle against mud and such underfoot.
- It is refreshing for mind not just body because of the amazing views.

Disadvantages:

- It can be very busy at weekends.
- Though rural and in the Peak District there are no testing inclines and for the runner doing a 10-mile outing this could be a little disappointing or monotonous away from the reservoirs.

Summary:

A relaxed taste of running out in the sticks. Good for the intermediate or advanced runner because of distance not gradients. Stunning scenery but it is best to be canny about when you visit to enjoy the solitude thoroughly.

Mileage:

Dependent on your selection but the main two are 6 miles (Torside and back) or 13 miles (Woodhead and back).

History:

The Woodhead Tunnels were built to take passenger trains from Manchester to Sheffield and the first opened in 1845. Woodhead Two opened in 1853 and Woodhead Three in 1953. It is said passenger services stopped using the route in 1970 and the last ever train passed through the tunnel in 1981.

At the time of its completion by the Sheffield, Ashton-under-Lyne and Manchester Railway, Woodhead 1 was the world's longest railway tunnel at 3 miles and 13 yards (4,840 metres).

They were engineered by Charles Vignoles and Joseph Locke and were known as hell holes by those who worked on them because of their dark, sooty, claustrophobic conditions. When the first was completed it cost £200,000 and 26 lives were lost in its creation. During the building of Woodhead 2 another 28 lives were lost through cholera, worsened by working in the enclosed space. The building had as many as 1,500 men working on it at one point, used 157 tonnes of gunpowder and pumped out eight million tonnes of water – which all would have been very useful to the thirsty or lethargic runner.

The Standedge and Totley Tunnels also cross Pennine routes but the Totley now outstrips the original Woodhead tunnel in length. The National Grid now uses the tunnels at Longdendale to house electrical cables much to the consternation of those who wish to see the lines re-opened for train services.

Construction began on the Longdendale chain of Reservoirs in 1848 and most sources state the work was finished in February 1877. They were formed from the waters of the River Etherow by John Frederick Bateman, to supply water to the city of Manchester. They were thought to be the largest artificial expanse of water in the world at the time they were completed.

As Mr Bateman is quoted as having said: 'Within 10 or 12 miles of Manchester and 6 or 7 miles from the existing reservoirs at Gorton, there is this tract of mountain land abounding with springs of the purest quality. Its physical and geological features offer such peculiar features for the collection, storage and supply of water for the use of the towns in the plains below that I am surprised that they have been overlooked.'

No doubt Mr Bateman would now be satisfied that many people visit the trail to look over and across the glistening valley of man-made lakes he created.

Today 25 per cent of Manchester's water supply comes from here. Anything from about 40ft (12m) to 80ft (24m) deep the reservoirs' waters go on to fill service reservoirs like that in Audenshaw and to quench the city's thirst.

South of Longdendale, on the edge of the Peak District sits Buxton which was a mineral and spa town to the Romans, known as Aquae Arnemetiae. It is still known for its waters today. Another nearby Peak town is Glossop, which until World War One held the headquarters of the largest textile printworks in the world but is now a small market town. There is also Castleton where they mine the now scarce fluorite, known in these parts as Blue John. There are good places to visit in and around the Peak District today adding towns, history and unusual sites to the sights that nature affords the area.

Useful Websites:

www.cycle-route.com
Varied reviews and information about cycle routes.
www.derbyshireuk.net
Information about the history of the area and the place today.
www.peakdistrict.gov.uk
Information about walking routes and the effort and climbs the area entails.
www.peakdistrictview.com
Details on the type of trails, history and which weather suits the route.
www.yha.org.uk
Information on youth hostelling, facilities at Crowden and the chance to book ahead.

Contacts:

Buxton Tourist Information Office
Pavilion Gardens
St John's Road
SK17 6BE
Tel: 01298 25106
Email: tourism@highpeak.gov.uk
The Buxton Tourist Information Office is 15 miles from Longdendale but serves the Glossop area and funding cuts can mean it is better to rely on larger towns in Derbyshire for information offices.

Crowden Youth Hostel
Crowden-in-Longdendale
Derbyshire
SK13 1HZ
Tel: 0845 371 9113
Email: crowden@yha.org.uk

Lyme Park

Stunning but we're prejudiced

From a Mancunian there may be bias but this is one of the most beautiful, spacious and wild parks in and beyond the Cheshire and Manchester area – and many directors seem to have thought so too what with the BBC's *Pride and Prejudice* team using this as the setting for Mr Darcy's 'Pemberley' in 1995 and Colin Firth's paddling in fountains in the park. Apparently, many marriage proposals have been made in the ground since.

For us mere mortals who don't mind being covered in sheep poo and marshy bog before we get our kit off, running kit that is, this is a stimulating and vibrant route to tackle occasionally.

You can drive here and park within the grounds near Lyme Hall but this will cost you quite a bit of money on National Trust-run land (£5, as of 2012 online information). Also you would miss out on the chance to run part of the entry to the park grounds, a substantial measure in a 3 or 4-mile route. Incidentally, when grounds staff were asked if those of us on trainers were charged one worker told me we were charged enough having to walk up the hills here, the effort obviously taxing. So we poor runners putting in twice as much effort as walkers are paying over the odds again!

If you wish to view the surrounding land without parking and payment concerns you can arrive by train, a 25-minute journey to Disley from Manchester Piccadilly. After warming up in the station car park run past the Ram's Head public house, a large establishment, and run to your right up Buxton Old Road and immediately right again to head up Red Lane. This leafy, country lane of large houses passes the edge of St Mary's Church and later passes the holey(!) car park.

On the run again, turn right near the church car park and keep following the road until you see a stile, a gate and a footpath sign on your left and a four-towered building in the distance. You are now viewing the delights of the green and golden grasses swaying in Lyme Park. You won't be running to the mediaeval looking structure immediately and don't be fooled into thinking this tower-flanked building is Lyme Hall. It is an 18th-century hunting tower known as 'The Cage' and part of the original 1,400 acre Legh family estate but it is also a spot to blow the cobwebs away in the strong winds. This is the spot where heaven and earth truly meet.

You could find public footpaths and head left towards The Cage from Red Lane but the last time I ran that area the farmland was heavily fenced off. Though The Gritstone Trail runs from the Hall and beyond the reservoirs to join the distant Mudhurst Lane much of this is beyond The Cage from Red Lane.

From the stile you will also see water in the form of the Horse Coppice Reservoir and further on Bollinhurst Reservoir. It would be nice to head towards these waters and then up to The Cage but unfortunately utility executives have had it fenced off quite severely and it would be difficult to find a route via the side of the reservoirs without having to climb a 6ft spiked fence at present.

For this route, therefore, it is best to run Red Lane in its entirety and finish at the East Entrance to Lyme Park near the little lane where you cannot turn for access to Horse Coppice Reservoir. You will see the large wooden gates and National Trust signs for the park grounds. Just at the gate is a billboard with a map and information about the main landmarks in the park. From here, you should run to The Cage, on to Lyme Hall and beyond to an almost abandoned building called Paddock Cottage but you are spoilt for options on how you tackle the journey and where exactly you taste the wilderness and air along the way.

Hunt the Wind near The Cage, Lyme Park.

Once inside the park you will see many cars quietly appear from nowhere. Runners should turn left, past the wooden toll station for visitors and onwards along a concrete road with no markings. Cars use this roadway too but when it is just runners with the unspoilt land as a backdrop and trees and grounds which look Jurassic in their natural history, it is near perfection.

Soon you will head left, uphill, towards The Cage. The sooner you tackle this the better as the hill gets steeper the longer you leave it to turn off the tarmacked lane. This section is hard work as the grasses are long and in large clumps in many parts so you have to haul your calf muscles higher and higher to overcome them. Some man-made pathways through the grass, almost like green carpet they are so worn, cross your climb but if you left it late to run towards this spectacle this takes more effort.

You can see the parkland with areas filled with cattle, sheep, grasses. It feeds the soul. There are sundials upon the walls and metal grids add to it being a vision of military strength but it is the wilderness of the land which makes this special. The splendour at the end is a prize in itself. On the more urban side you can see distant Manchester for almost 180 degrees.

When you can bear to tear yourself away head onwards parallel to the roadway. Being on the grass here it gives you a taste of wild Peak District acres. View the Grade I listed Lyme Hall ahead of you. Oddly enough you are not approaching the main, imposing entrance. This thoroughfare where visitors have access under a metal arch and character-filled courtyard area, is the back door, so they must have been very friendly aristocrats around here. Seriously, the National Trust owns Lyme Park and the Hall now but as you approach from The Cage you do not see the statues nor the front pediment or colonnade.

The Hall had its once Tudor heritage updated to Italianate splendour in the 18th century. For the romantics among you Lyme Hall would be a good spot to take a comfort break and dream of living here 200 years earlier. Though one hates to break the reverie it will cost you, however, to look around the Hall, Orangery and Gardens…and interrupt vital training time of course. (For prices see later.)

As sophisticated visitors view the inside of the Hall we park pounders may contemplate that perhaps the original owners wanted to display their wealth with their Hall and 'keep up with the Joneses' as it was but perhaps their real love was being up near The Cage, fighting the winds as well as shooting deer, free of the shackles of expectation.

From the Hall, head to your right towards more water and the Timber Yard with drinks and ice-cream facilities, a picnic area and views of the millpond and another possibility for a comfort break. Then, follow the road onwards, like a line southwards from The Cage to the Hall and onwards, past the parked cars and you should head over a cattle grid on your right and a babbling brook on your left. Head up this slight incline – though you may be tempted to detour off towards the woodland.

Further up this hill the path forks in two. Take the right hand route, which is more footpath here than concrete and you should soon see some spectacular views of Cheshire and Manchester again covering about 180 degrees and with vibrant winds. Follow the footpath onwards and you will reach a Lyme Park sign saying you are at John Brown's Corner.

If you can tear yourself away from the views head up the hillside alongside a stone wall which on the right day lets you see the light dancing on the very green grassy ground under the woodland on the other side of the wall.

For extra mileage continue down to the small car park and gate and turn right, up what is said to be called West Drive. This is a lovely stretch to relax, to leap over the brook and sit on the carved wooden bench admiring the woodland from another angle before giving yourself the Sisyphean task of running up the steep hill behind the bench.

From the top here you can see Lyme Hall, The Cage, the Lantern: all buildings on this colourful estate. The surrounding mediaeval deer park and formal gardens of Lyme Park are listed as Grade II in the National Register of Historic Parks and Gardens and you can survey it all from here.

After making it up the hill run back down towards the road and continue on back to the Timber Yard and pond. Within the grounds is also The Knott, a hill popular with cyclists. There are many routes to several landmarks here. Near the little car park not far from John Brown's Corner, just past the gates you can turn left up some steps and then head right towards a now rather battered looking Paddock Cottage. The building is covered in graffiti and semi boarded-up but you are again greeted by the winds from the nearby Peak District moors. You can see the Hall through the trees and The Cage upon a hill to the left.

After heading back to the Timber Yard you can briefly jump on the Gritstone Trail but not all 35 miles of it, and skirt around the millpond and entrance to the children's play area. Next, see the Hall to your right but head left along the roadway and you can follow it to the East Entrance and then run up Red Lane back to Disley. However, you could also climb up to The Cage again, gluttons for punishment must apply and follow existing paths from there to the south side of the reservoirs and beyond. The area sometimes has sketchy footpaths through the farmland, or at least that was the case at the time of my last visit but you may meet a sign offering the Gritstone Trail left and right and a public footpath straight ahead.

From this high point head left to join the end of Red Lane, near St Mary's Church car park, having missed out on the upward slog along Red Lane. Run past a small postbox and towards a grit bin in the corner of the residential end of Red Lane and you should find about 50 steps down towards Disley Train Station. Leap like a gazelle down the steps to then stretch off and get back on the train or get a bus to Stockport nearby or Manchester.

The 199 bus runs between Lyme Park and Stockport. Train services have been hourly for some time but it is best to check with National Rail Enquiries.

Advantages:

- It is a varied route with some amazing views and romance attached.
- You can take the family and dump them by the picnic benches or Hall as you go and challenge the elements. Though you get to see real countryside and views you are very unlikely to get lost on the well set-out roads and footpaths, as long as you avoid the temptation to run via the reservoirs up to The Cage on the way into the park.
- There are times when you can see the inside of The Cage free of charge (from 1pm until 4pm on the second and fourth weekends of every month at the time of writing check the website for offers), and Paddock Cottage at the same times on the first and third weekends each month.
- If you are really beaten after this run you could hire the holiday cottage East Lodge, which sleeps four, and is situated on the edge of Lyme Park!

Disadvantages:

- It can be very busy at weekends.
- Maps give very sketchy levels of detail.
- If you get a soaking in the rain you are a long way from home – even if you live in Disley.
- It could prove costly if you drive here and make a day of it visiting Lyme Hall. (See prices below.)
- A 25-minute trip from Piccadilly before and after the run could make it too time consuming for some who like to just run on their doorsteps – and transport delays aren't unheard of with this route.

Hall to Live For, Lyme Park.

• It may not be the best route in the evenings as some National Trust information states it is open from 8am to 6pm all year round and other information advises checking ahead in winter.

Summary:

A delightful open park with varied routes and terrain for all abilities. Good for mixed ability groups or families to try running together for the first time but even better for someone who wants to test themselves with a taste of vast open land and freedom without fear of getting lost on endless moors.

Mileage:

4.5 miles.

History:

The first Piers Legh and his wife Margaret were given Lyme Park by Richard II in 1398, as a reward for heroic family deeds in battle. Unfortunately, most people's closest reward will be to get in a state, not an estate, for heroism, even if they do battle with the elements for a personal best.

By the 16th century the Leghs had made Lyme their main home and over the next two centuries the estate was developed further with Sir Piers Legh VII instigating rebuilding work. Renovation was continued by successive generations. In the 1720s, the Venetian architect Giacomo Leoni, transformed the Elizabethan hall to resemble an Italianate Palazzo. The piano nobile or main floor is held up by Doric pilasters or columns. The inside of the hall was left unchanged.

During the 19th century the building was restored and altered extensively by Lewis Wyatt who renovated every room in some way and in 1860 the same gardens that can be seen today were set out.

By the 20th century the upkeep and maintenance of Lyme Park had become difficult for the family and so in 1946, just four years after inheriting the estate and just after the end of World War Two the third Lord Newton gave Lyme and the surrounding 1,400 acres of land to the National Trust for us all to share.

Price List:

Gift Aid Admission (Standard Admission prices in brackets).
House and garden: adult £9.50 (£8.50), child £4.75 (£4.15), family £23 (£20.80). Garden only: adult £6 (£5.25), child £3 (£2.70). House only: adult £6.25 (£5.60), child £3.15 (£2.85). Estate entry per vehicle £5. (2012)

Useful Websites:

www.nationaltrust.org.uk/main/w-lymepark
Find out about the historical grounds through the national charity's website.

Contacts:

Lyme Park
Disley
SK12 2NR
Tel: 01663 762023
Email: lymepark@nationaltrust.org.uk

Lymm Dam

Trail past the rich pickings

This may be one of those routes where you are better off getting the bus out to a point and running back rather than running out then getting the bus back. Well, at least old ladies are spared your body odour. Public transport between Lymm and Altrincham, or indeed Lymm and most places, isn't that frequent. If you don't live near Altrincham you will have to get the bus, train or Metrolink out here first as well.

Once the number 5 or 38 bus from Altrincham drops you off in the quaint village of Lymm, run past its white cottages, library and little pond and head from the historic landmark of Lymm Cross, down Eagle Brow, and along the side of the pond area, then past a wooded area called The Dingle.

This will give you time to go and look at Lymm's Middle Dam and perhaps run all the way up to the Upper Dam, the Wishing Bridge and The Bongs. (I didn't invent these unusually named places.) If you do run the loop around here, bear in mind you will have to run back to Lymm Cross before the big run really starts!

However, you can steer to the right of Lymm Cross to see the road bridging over Sow Brook, one of Lymm's many waterways but for another route to see Lymm Dam you can head across the road named The Cross, opposite Danebank and run up Rectory Lane. At Church Green at the top you can see the expanse of water that is built up behind the Dam next to St Mary's Church.

Once you have seen the beauty of the waters and its flora and fauna then run back to Lymm Cross, perhaps using the opposite route this time to create a loop. Then run over the Bridgewater Canal, briefly onto New Road and onto Lymmhay Lane. This should be your

Holy Water at St Mary's, Lymm Dam.

introduction to the Trans Pennine Trail for the day. To head back towards Altrincham and urban civilisation, head right here (though if you had wanted to visit the Pennine Trail Rangers you would have briefly needed to head to the left).

Once on the Trans Pennine heading in an easterly direction the path crosses lots of little lanes and unfortunately you have to run around or past lots of gates or stiles at this point. Nor is it the best stretch of the TPT for signposts. Run past the more residential areas, after Reddish Lane past the shop and the abandoned Railway pub. Not only is it sad because you can't stop for a drink here but it is a shame for the communities nearby that have lost a meeting place and gained a derelict building instead but it is becoming a more common sight everywhere. However, this isn't a theme for the whole trail.

After Heatley it really opens up. This used to be a railway line and the sandy ground and the embankments on either side reveal its past usage but it is beautiful despite its little track of industrial history. Keep pounding although the lovely views tempt you to stop for longer than a quick look and swig of fluids. The trail is fairly straight so it is quite an enticing and romantic sight in the right weather, almost like one long tunnel encouraging you to head for the end.

There are wooden signposts at points here with distance indicators but some of the sites on the horizon might tempt you to run off the trail such as a square church building to the left. As the land is so flat here and much of it open fields, it stretches out forever. On a warm day with a welcome breeze it is a beautiful place to run. You might not welcome that same exposure so much on a torrentially wet day in December though.

Along this stretch is the boundary between Warrington and Trafford MBC. Though you may not be that interested in council boundaries it does help you calculate distances and it means you are back in Manchester proper.

The Trans Pennine Trail and the Bridgewater Canal run in a sort of parallel way for a lot of this route, so you could select where to place your visit to Lymm Dam (at the beginning, middle or end of your run) and select where you get on or off the major paths, although the Bridgewater's path is much smaller heading closer to Dunham.

This is where you will have to decide how far you want to run and which of the many ways to get home you are going to use because you can continue along the Trans Pennine onto Sinderland Road and the Broadheath/Manchester Road area or decide to run back to Altrincham itself, via Dunham.

Altrincham has the better public transport links and you could tailor it to give you a taste of Dunham Massey's grounds but running to Broadheath and getting a bus from Manchester Road to the city centre or running from there up Navigation Road to the Metrolink can give you a longer taste of the Bridgewater Canal.

On the right day the grounds of Dunham Massey are unmissable. Dunham Park itself is a deer park and though you want to stag-ger your running over the week it is worth the extra mileage to see the wildlife, the trees, the little ponds, the colours.

For Dunham Massey jump off the TPT at the junction between Dunham Road and Paddock Lane on the B5160. Turn right and run Paddock Lane, as it becomes Station Road, then it becomes Woodhouse Lane and passes under the Bridgewater Canal. Later, with another name change, this becomes Smithy Lane and after running along Smithy Lane (as long as you don't detour into the park for too long) it then becomes Charcoal Road. Head left at a crossroads with traffic lights at the end onto Dunham Road.

This is where the dream ends. Concrete reality time. You have to run up a hill that seems almost steep after the flat terrain of most of the rest of the route and after passing Dunham

Forest Golf Course on your left, you run through more residential areas. Not long after running under a footbridge you should see Regent Road, Altrincham. Turn right onto this road, then left at the end onto Stamford New Road which should take you to the transport interchange and Metrolink and the chance to get a seat all to yourself…well, after running about 7 miles!

Another alternative or two:
If you wanted to run back out to Lymm around School Lane in Dunham Town, there is a lovely but perhaps risky set of ivy-covered wooden steps down to the trail. Rumour has it among frequent walkers and users that there are kestrels and other birds of prey along this stretch. At this point the ground is wide and sandy and though many people use it, even during weekdays, it doesn't seem to get too clogged or slippy. The land on either side opens up to show Cheshire's wares, with ponds, brooks, and agricultural patterns across the horizon.

Of course, if you live in Altrincham you could run a loop heading to Lymm using the TPT route, then run back this time via the Bridgewater Canal at Dunham Town and Manchester Road. Or run a Bridgewater and TPT loop from Lymm. Yet, unless you are marathon training most people want to cover shorter routes than that, even if it means they have to travel to them in the first place.

The Cross is the area of Lymm that still holds the village stocks today, so don't misbehave or you may find you're on your knees, with your hands in the air and head near the floor for a reason other than physical exhaustion!

Advantages:
- The straight tunnel-effect of the Trans Pennine Trail is excellent for concentration and to focus on just the run ahead of you.
- The straight layout also makes it good for time trials at quiet times.
- The quaint nature of Lymm and natural beauty of the surrounding countryside make it visually worthwhile and prettier than training in a concrete jungle.

Disadvantages:
- Though there is public transport here in the shape of number 5 and 38 buses it is not like being in the city centre for infrastructure.
- On busy days especially at weekends numerous dog walkers and families may hinder you from reaching top speeds.

Summary:
A fantastic route for an intermediate or experienced runner who would like to try something other than a pavement-pounder near home but hates the navigation and map reading of really rural routes. The focus the trail creates makes it a good route for an intermediate who has recently lacked motivation.

Mileage:
To Altrincham via Dunham or the Bridgwater or TPT 6.75 miles, to Navigation Road Metrolink 6.75 miles or to Manchester Road 6.25 miles.

History:
The Altrincham to Thelwall stretch of the Trans Pennine Trail used to be part of the railway line and goes via Lymm.

117

Lymm Cross is a Grade I listed structure. The Cross dates from the early to the middle 17th century and the modern version was created in 1897 to mark Queen Victoria's diamond jubilee. It is constructed of sandstone and it is said to stand on red sandstone steps.

Crosses in mediaeval times were thought to have plain shafts and masonry canopies at the top of a row of steps as Lymm Cross has today and its origins have been traced back to the 14th century but there is speculation an original cross there dated back to Saxon or even Roman times.

One square pillar bares an inscription from 1775 and on the east, south and west sides there are bronze sundials from 1897 and the inscriptions: 'We are shadows', 'save time' and 'think of the last'. Well, the first two inscriptions suit us runners anyway.

The stocks that sit ominously nearby in the 21st century are replicas of the ones from 1775. Though crosses so central to villages were once commonplace it is quite rare to see them now. In Lymm it is where the town crier shouts his proclamations but neither he nor anyone else should say anything too insulting with the stocks being on site.

Lymm Dam was built in 1824 when a turnpike or toll road was created from Warrington to Stockport. The Warrington and Stockport Turnpike Trust, when creating the A56 in the early 19th century, had to build over a then pond and stream below St Mary's Church, building an earth dam to help them do so. The lake this created became known as Lymm Dam. The area was then said to have been part of Lymm Hall Estate and the toll, charging travellers, being situated at the top of a slope near the church, caused some locals to tag the area 'Penny Hill', a label it still has with some today.

The sandstone around the Dam may be as much as 250 million years old, so it even pre-dates the journey time of some of our longest routes. Wild bats live here but as they are nocturnal you would not get to see them during a daylight run.

Useful Websites:

www.lymm.com
Get history and information on famous Lymm residents and landmarks.
www.lymm.net
Get information and news on the village, its festivals and the petty crimes it has suffered.
www.transpenninetrail.org.uk
Find facts about the very long route for runners, walkers, cyclists and all.

Contacts:

Ranger Centre (opposite the Lymm Hotel)
TransPennine Trail, off Statham Avenue
Lymm
Warrington
WA13 9NJ
Tel: 01925 758195
Email: rangers@warrington.gov.uk

Macclesfield Canal

The Macc is back!

You are either a very lucky sports fanatic or you've changed identity, ditched your phone and really are on the run because spots along the Macclesfield Canal are utopia and so is the solitude.

If you took a train out from Manchester Piccadilly to Macclesfield you might have been forgiven for thinking it was too much like hard work navigating your way to the canal – and this is on foot not on a barge.

On a map it looks easy enough to go round a corner from the station and join the canal there. But at the time of writing, a wall was down blocking passageway onto a towpath on one side of the canal and the towpath seemed to stop briefly on the other.

From the station it is best to go along The Silk Road then straight ahead along the A536 Mill Lane and straight on again as it becomes the A523 Cross Street. After ignoring the turnings down wealthy residential streets, turn left onto Byron's Lane and things will start to get a little less suburban.

You should see a pub called the Ye Olde King's Head just before an aqueduct. There will be some steep steps up to the canal but at last, after some running on concrete, you've reached the watery starting line. You can tell this one is a long one, can't you?

Though you might wish to run left towards the city you can't from this point because of that wall and towpath problem so run to your right from here out into the wilderness of Cheshire. There are numerous old stone bridges to run under on this route, the sort where you'd just love

Lithe in the Light of Macclesfield Canal.

to stop and contemplate for about an hour in the summer but in the bleak mid-winter keep your rear moving. Not long past Byron's Lane aqueduct there is an area of woodland with a babbling brook alongside the canal towpath and beyond the gentle water a piece of tree-covered, magical, fairytale forest. The sort of place for a picnic when you've got the time but when you're running 8 miles...

Perhaps about 2 miles into the towpath treading you should see a very tempting public house sat just behind the opposite bank of the canal called the Fool's Nook. If you only wanted a shorter run it might not be that foolish to stop here, cross the bridge, have a drink and then run back again. You would certainly avoid potential public transport problems later. That said, we love distance.

Go through the little white gate, across the tarmac and keep pounding. It's only another 2 miles of towpath until you reach Bosley Locks. On a nice day the brilliant blue sky against the immaculate nearby fields and the well-kept white locks, gates and fences are pretty if a little parochial.

In just under 0.5 miles the Macclesfield Canal ventures over another aqueduct and there are some massive bridges and structures to see in the distance on this route too. If you continue on again, though it may not seem like it initially, you are hitting the edges of Congleton. But the Congletonians have decided to stick their train station quite some distance away from the high street so you've got 3 miles left.

A frustrating 3 miles it is too. It is very easy to miss your exit, particularly when by now your hips are threatening to go on strike and your head may have almost had enough, even if your feet move without you thinking, not unlike a guitar player's fingers: instinctive after years of practise. There seems to be a turn off, bridge and set of steps every few yards that could be the end turn off. However, near the real stop for the station you should see that things get industrial on your left and see a row of shops beyond the bridge, after a road that crosses the bridge.

Well done in covering about 8 miles along the canal and another 1 mile at least up to Byron's Lane aqueduct and steps. There's a bakery which sells some pretty good Cornish pasties if you cross the bridge and knowing train times here you might have a bit of a wait to get back to Piccadilly, even though top speed trains rattle through with frightening regularity. Well, one pasty per mile isn't that extreme when you need carbs, is it?

Advantages:
- It is a stunning waterside route covering a gentle and rather rural stretch of canal.
- Fantastic route for solid distance training.

Disadvantages:
- It is very difficult to leave. Though there are many bridges along the way even if you can find an exit you will be in a position devoid of much public transport and few people to ask for directions.
- The land may be too flat for some runners.
- At around 8 miles this is definitely more an endurance training session than a speed test.
- It is difficult to make your way back to the city centre if you run the Macclesfield to Congleton direction.

Summary:
Testing distance though flat terrain in a very rural location; good for pushing your body, especially your hips to the limit.

Mileage:
8 or 9 miles.

History:
The Macclesfield Canal opened in 1831 after, it is said, the idea to build it was proposed during discussions in the Macclesfield Arms in September 1824. There had been talk of building a railway line along the route but an Act of Parliament in 1826 ensured it was created as a waterway.

Thomas Telford surveyed the route and William Crosley built it at a cost of £320,000. The railways and inland waterways were nationalised in 1947 and commercial carrying stopped on the Macclesfield Canal in the 1960s.

The UK's first narrow canal cruising club, The North Cheshire Cruising Club, reputedly formed on the canal in 1943, during wartime, for those no doubt seeking peace and tranquillity. The people wanted to avoid council fees for boathouses so joined forces but sank when it came to avoiding council rates.

The overall canal is 26 miles long with 13 locks: Bosley Locks sees 12 large stone locks in the space of 1.25 miles. Opening and closing locks will keep barge users fit but they are points of interest to us fit runners journeying along the elevated canal as well.

The canal is part of the Cheshire Ring and joins the Peak Forest Canal at Marple. It travels through areas such as High Lane and Higher Poynton, to Macclesfield, Congleton and then Kidsgrove in Staffordshire before joining the Trent and Mersey Canal to head in a more northerly direction around west Manchester.

Useful Websites:
www.macclesfieldcanal.org.uk
Information about the canal's history and there are maps and pub details to be found.
www.nccc.uk.net
North Cheshire Cruising Club website to join up or buy a boat to get home on.
www.penninewaterways.co.uk/macclesfield/index.htm
Only brief history about the canal but the site offers a virtual cruise too.

Contacts:
North Cheshire Cruising Club
The Wharf
Buxton Road
High Lane
SK6 8AA
Tel: 01663 765581

Ye Olde King's Head
Byron's Lane
Macclesfield
Tel: 01625 423890

Marple

Marple syrup

We don't know how lucky we are here! Marple is a great area for runners as it has parkland, riverside routes and canal paths and the lovely Cheshire elegance but it also has two train stations serving it from more urban areas (Rose Hill and Marple Stations). Though many surrounding villages have the same quaint vibe in many you will find a lot of green spaces are used as golf courses – a good run spoilt, let alone a walk.

If you get off the train at Rose Hill and turn right to run up Stockport Road, onwards as it becomes Station Road, then down Brabyns Brow past Marple Station on your left you will soon join Brabyns Park. This area has recreation land, land for exercising ponies but for this run as long as you don't take on the horses you will get the most from the scenery and mileage by running alongside the river.

Head past the weirs and the Iron Bridge and eventually you should cross the grassland and head up to the Peak Forest Canal. Turn right here and not long afterwards you should be running along one of the skinniest bits of canal you will encounter in the Greater Manchester and Cheshire area. While balancing over the River Goyt on the canal towpath, barges squeeze alongside you, as trains rattle visibly over the viaduct hovering above to the right. This may not be a favourite route for those who don't like heights but either way keep your wits about you for this stretch!

In fact, you could choose to by-pass the riverside element here by turning left at the end of Stockport Road and running straight onto the canal at Marple Locks, a series of engineered barriers for the barges, before continuing on for about 0.75 miles along the canal to the aqueduct. If you choose this route beware of slipping near the locks in wintertime.

Going back to the initial route, about a 0.25 miles after joining the canal from the park you prepare to run into Hydebank Tunnel – and then find it inaccessible alongside the water and find

Country pursuits at Marple Locks.

that you must run up steps or a slope over that stretch of canal. Then after running past Hyde Bank Farm on a lane called Hydebank, you can choose to jump back onto the canal or head up Oakwood Road and through the industrial estate there to join Stockport Road in Romiley and access to the bus and train network.

Sweetly, Hyde Bank Farm has put up homemade signs along the canal towpath offering to sell you tea and snacks, very tempting if all this exercise is giving you an appetite but it may be more of a summer stop-off point for those out walking than a winter warmer for us runners.

Advantages:
- A nice, short run that nevertheless covers two or three villages.
- A run that covers some of the best civil engineering in British canals and makes up an important part of the Cheshire Ring of Canals.

Disadvantages:
- Not one for those who fear dangling off the edge of 100-year-old stonework!
- In darkness it might be easy to have accidents and difficult to appreciate the beauty of the route – a weekend or daylight special perhaps.
- There are frequently many dog walkers (and frisky mutts with muddy paws in the park area particularly).

Summary:
Lovely scenery with interesting sights en route; a quick run that could easily be made into a circuit or extended to be part of a longer route.

Mileage:
Hydebank 2 miles return, including Marple 2.75 miles, Rose Hill 4 miles.

History:
Brabyns Park was once attached to the Brabyns Hall estate and the 90 acres of land opened to the public as a park in 1947. The parkland includes the restored Georgian Iron Bridge. A campaign by Marple Local History Society gathered 2,000 signatures and generated 120 letters of support to restore the bridge and the Heritage Lottery Fund gave £30,000. By 2006, the strengthening work was completed but there is a campaign to find more funds to return the Iron Bridge to its former glory. Brabyns Hall went to rack and ruin, as did nearby Marple Hall and though writer Christopher Isherwood bought the structure it was too late to save it. Rumours abound that the ghost of a headless woman roams the area of the foundations around Marple Hall Drive, near Rose Hill Station.

The Peak Forest Canal's 'Upper' section runs from Ashton-under-Lyne where it meets up with both the Huddersfield Narrow Canal and the Ashton Canal and then heads through Dukinfield. It moves under the M67 in Hyde and on past Haughton Vale and the Haughton Dale Nature Reserve, often running parallel to the River Tame.

The canal then heads through Woodley and Romiley before reaching Marple where it drops 210ft (64m) as it descends the 16 locks at Marple Locks, which celebrated its bi-centenary in 2004. The waterway then becomes the 'Lower' section of the Peak Forest Canal. It crosses 100ft (30m) above the River Goyt by dancing over the three-arched stone aqueduct and it also joins with the Macclesfield Canal in Marple for those wanting to take the Cheshire Ring path. The Railway

Viaduct is about 124ft (38m) high and parallel to the aqueduct. It has 12 arches and took only one year to build in 1865. The Peak Forest Canal next visits Disley and New Mills before heading on to Bugsworth Basin in Whaley Bridge, Derbyshire, where what is thought to be one of the best preserved canal and tram interchanges sits and shows how industry once depended on these waterways.

The canal is around 14 miles long and was constructed between 1794 and 1805. It transported materials such as limestone from the Pennine hills near Dove Stones. Local businessman Samuel Oldknow, who incidentally employed many women in his mills, was a major shareholder in the Peak Forest Canal Company which built the waterway, envisaging more money-making from the venture.

An Act of Parliament was passed to compulsorily purchase land upon which to build the canal. It was given royal assent on the 28 March 1794. The canal was going to rise 500ft (152m) in all with more locks at Bugsworth (or Buxworth as it is also known) but the gradient proved too steep and instead tramways linked up to the quarries leaving the waters to dance the heights most at Marple Locks.

One of the delights about leisure activities in this area is the taste of both urban and rural life and scenery that it provides. Compare running in Eastlands near the Manchester City stadium with the moors near Saddleworth yet they are less than 20 miles apart.

Another running choice is to follow the Cheshire Ring canal system. A misnomer really because the network touches on places in and near Staffordshire, Lancashire and even Derbyshire as well as the county known for its flat lands. The 97-mile network can be run from Marple, along the Macclesfield Canal to Stoke-on-Trent, along the Trent and Mersey Canal to Preston Brook. You can then run along the Bridgewater Canal near Sale to join the Rochdale Canal, the Ashton Canal at Ashton-under-Lyne and the Peak Forest Canal to circuit back to Marple. That may take you more than a few minutes though!

The Cheshire Ring first picked up its name in 1965 in the Inland Waterways Association bulletin in order to prevent the closure or filling in of the section between Manchester and Marple. By the 1960s the use of the canals for transportation of goods had stopped and the waterways were becoming overgrown and neglected. Luckily waterway lovers' perseverance, a trait every runner knows, meant it was re-opened to navigation in April 1974. Today, the network, and its 92 locks are used as a narrowboat holiday route loved by thousands.

Useful Websites:

www.marple-uk.com/ironbridge/discoverytrail
To download a booklet about a trail in Brabyns Park.
www.penninewaterways.co.uk
Get details about the heritage of many canals in the area.

Contacts:

Brabyns Park
Parks, Sport and Cemeteries
Fred Perry House
Edward Street
Stockport
SK1 3UR
Tel: 0161 217 6111
Email: parks@stockport.gov.uk

Medlock Valley Way

Marching through time

At one time the River Medlock was perhaps the most famous natural waterway in Manchester. The Romans, the industrialists, they all used the river for day-to-day life. Yet because of building and expansion in the city centre and because of dangers and the river's strong currents it can be hard to find the river now in the very heart of the city it runs through.

From Piccadilly Station you can run down Piccadilly Approach, turn right onto Ducie Street, seeing but not passing the massive Piccadilly Basin archway on Dale Street as you do. Turn right onto Great Ancoats Street running over Ashton Canal and as you pound along this massive road covered in retail outlets and concrete you will see a green footpath sign to turn left near the junction of Palmerston and Helmet Street. You could of course run directly down Fairfield Street to Palmerston from Piccadilly but you would miss the archway taking that route.

Turn left here and you will finally greet the River Medlock and signs for the Medlock Valley Way. As so much of the waterway has been built upon, running on the Medlock in the city centre can be more like running between points it is known were once along the Medlock. It hides underground for part of the route. From Ancoats, however, follow the riverside path for about 0.25 miles and then you will reach Holt Town at the Mitchell Arms public house. This is the site of the east side Metrolink sitting in the shadow of Manchester City's stadium.

It may well be worth turning off Ashton New Road here, head down Hillkirk Street, then right onto Philips Park Road before joining Ashton Canal on the right of New Viaduct Street. Once on the canal you could run to your right, away from the massive gas holder station and under the shadow of Eastlands, the Running Track, the National Squash Centre and on the left of the canal, Manchester Tennis Centre. Then you could leave the canal, turning left to run up Alan Turing Way instead of running under it. Next turn right into Philips Park.

Running this way will at least give you the opportunity to keep seeing water as in light of all the construction work due to the Metrolink things keep changing and thus hiding or removing existing sights. Manchester City's training ground plans and other sports facilities, maps and plans, signs, even the route of the Medlock Valley Way they all seem to disappear around here.

Instead though, you could make this an interesting urban, concrete stretch. From Holt Town run up Ashton New Road, passing Tony's Stadium Chippy on the right which sits on Grey Mare Lane. It was voted the north west chip shop of the year in 2010. Further on there is a mileage sign on a grass verge telling you it is 2 miles to St Ann's Square. Instead of turning left up the major Alan Turing Way here you can run onwards briefly into Clayton West, which has a true city flavour with signs advertising cosmopolitan dishes such as goat curry. Then turn left up Bank Street, which then becomes Bank Bridge Road and on the left there is a footpath before a railway bridge into Philips Park where you will see both a viaduct and the Manchester Velodrome to your left.

Either route from Holt Town will take you into the park, either on the west side via Ashton Canal and Alan Turing Way or the east side just off Bank Bridge Road. Philips Park leaves a very sweet taste in your mouth whether you stopped for chips and goat curry on the way or not. There is an orchard here where the whole community can go in and pick apples, raspberries and various fruits. Bill Booth, the man that puts much of the effort into this little area, said that as long as the door is open, anyone is free to pop in and eat the fruit so you don't have to interrupt a 5-mile run to gather a kilo of apples first; the parkland and the community give you sustenance for the next stretch.

The sweet urban taste of Philips Park.

Like many runs around Manchester you have countryside, nature and parkland all in the vicinity of busy and bustling urban existence. Where else could you sit and eat home-grown apples while listening to the roar of tens of thousands of football fans? Manchester has the perfect mixture of city and country lifestyles in numerous places and it all suits us runners whether we prefer concrete or grass underfoot.

Once you have explored Philips Park it is probably best to jump on concrete down Bank Bridge Road as the grassy area between Philips Park and Clayton Vale can be a little overgrown and the signs confusing. On your right you will see a viaduct which you should head under to take you from the pleasant community park feel of Philips Park to the urban escapism, tree-lined peace pasture that is Clayton Vale.

I think every runner in Manchester should run this area at least once. The beauty of this area covers almost 0.75 miles to Clayton Mill Bridge and has pathways on both the north and south sides of the River Medlock. You begin to see children camping here and anglers out talking about water quality, the only clue to how close you are to city is often the mumbling of trains around the northern side of the Vale.

There is a Visitors' Centre here and this is a good place to start to wind up if you are not running the whole Medlock Valley Way or visiting Daisy Nook Country Park just outside Ashton-under-Lyne (see other routes) or running to Oldham. This is where you can get buses back to Clayton West or Newton Heath. You could also run right, up Edge Lane and back to the junction of Ashton New Road and Manchester Road for more public transport options.

You do have the option to continue along Medlock Valley Way around the edge of residential land in Droylsden but this is disheartening after the peace of Clayton Vale and tricky as there is a railway line restricting north to south access. You will also encounter other walkways here though, such as Oldham Way and the Tameside Trail.

Though you can't see the river you are running to the south of it. The railway line is south of the river and you cannot cross it near Sunnyside Avenue as the bridge is closed off and has signs saying guard dogs will attack. Run onwards through the tree-shaded pathway behind houses to Cypress Road where you can cross the railway line to your left, head into Weir Clough, immediately over a tiny bridge to your right and then to your right again into Bell Clough, where you are greeted by greenery and Lumm Farm to your right.

Head towards a pond surrounded by Canada Geese and the Brookdale Golf Course in the distance to your left and pound the Hollinwood Branch of the Manchester and Ashton Canal, over the M60 and onwards into Daisy Nook Country Park which sits at the border of Ashton-under-Lyne and Failsworth.

Advantages:
- You get to see some stunning countryside from restored wastelands or industrial lands, just metres away from city attractions and urban life.
- It has a fascinating amount of history covering many eras.
- It breathes life and interest.

Disadvantages:
- Some leisure information on this route can be out of date thanks to changes and planned changes to a vast area, especially around Manchester City's stadium.
- Areas between Philips Park and Clayton Vale and the area near Droylsden can be badly signposted.

Summary:
A vibrant mixture of modernity, community and sheer beauty along the route of a pretty, natural waterway which refuses to be buried in time.

Mileage:
Covering Philips Park and Clayton Vale 3 to 4 miles depending on the route.

History:
The River Medlock Valley runs from Lees, near Oldham, through East Manchester and parks such as Daisy Nook and then onwards to Clayton Vale, Philips Park and finishes where it joins the River Irwell.

From the city centre the 12-mile Medlock Valley Way leisure path runs from Ducie Street in Manchester, passing Eastlands, then heads via Clayton Vale, Daisy Nook and Strines Dale to finish at Bishops Park in Oldham. The first section to Clayton Vale is part of the Number 86 Regional Cycle Route.

The Roman Fort Mamucium was built in around AD78 and sat near the confluence of the Rivers Medlock and Irwell. The settlement of Manchester formed around the fort and the all-important water. It was a timber fort with earthen ramparts built to house about 500 infantry.

It was extended in around AD160 to incorporate granaries, the infantry no doubt getting a taste for butties (or dipping) while in Manchester but the Emperor Severus then came to stop a revolt and rebuilt the fort in stone in about AD200. It was abandoned in about the fourth century but the north gate was reconstructed after archaeological work in 1984. Some of the fort was sliced up with the building of the Rochdale Canal and railway lines but the northern quarter survived.

A vicus or civilian settlement formed on the north and east sides of the fort as the Romans had money, power and supplies so they were the people to congregate around. Military units that visited Manchester included a cohort, part of a legion from Spain known as the Bracaraugustanorium. There were also troops from the Raetia around modern Switzerland, the Tyrol of today's Germany and the Noricom or Austria and part of Slovenia in today's geography.

It is said as well as Mamucium, the Roman Temple behind the White Lion public house on Liverpool Road there was a mansio or hotel opposite the Hilton Hotel on Deansgate.

There seems to be archaeological evidence on the Chester Road side of the River Medlock of a Mithraic Temple, a temple dedicated to the God Mithras, which was popular with soldiers. In 1612 an altar stone was found and dedicated by Lucius Senicianius Martius to Fortune the Preserver. Later, fragments of the temple were discovered by workmen in 1821 near Chester Road.

Today the Roman Gardens have display boards giving an idea of what life may have looked like in the Roman era in Mamucium or Manchester.

It is said in the 1800s bad flooding of the Medlock caused it to burst its banks and it washed away the grounds of a cemetery. Since then the river has been culverted or passed through underground channels from Bank Road to the Philips Park area and Holt Town, Piccadilly and Castlefield areas. Clayton Vale was a countryside area used for leisure in the 1800s.

Bradford, the area around what is now Manchester Velodrome or the National Cycling Centre was once home to a colliery and all the bustle and life that industry and commerce bring. There were print and dye works in the area and even a nunnery. In 1907 Manchester Corporation purchased the land to use it as a municipal tip and it was not until Manchester City Council bought it in 1982 that it began to look like countryside again. There were 250,000 trees of various types planted over 114 acres of land.

The viaduct at Bank Bridge Road, the bridge at Edge Lane and the Bay Horse public house are the only clues that this area of tranquillity was once lively, industrial or bustling, the brick bridge once taking salt over the river and the iron bridge first built in 1900 and rebuilt in keeping with the industrial theme.

There are four ponds within Clayton Vale designated as Sites of Biological Importance because of the rare plant species that grow within them.

Useful Websites:
www.friendsofclaytonvale.org.uk/index
Find out dates for guided walks around the Vale.
www.manchester.gov.uk/info/200102/walking_and_cycling/732/cycling_in_manchester/10
Download Regional Cycle Route 86 maps (hopefully useful for us runners too).
www.medlockvalley.org.uk
For information and history from the organisers of the route.
www.peakdistrictview.com
Information about the Medlock Valley and where to roam in it.
www.philipspark.org.uk/Medlock Valley
Read about the regeneration of this area.

Contacts:
Clayton Vale Visitors' Centre
Edge Lane
Clayton Vale
Tel: 0161 220 1000

Philips Park
Stuart Street
Manchester
M11 4DQ
Tel: 0161 231 3090
Email: leisure@manchester.gov.uk

Philips Park Community Orchard
Tel: 0161 226 3322 or 0161 223 8278 to arrange a visit to the community orchard.

Moses Gate Country Park

A way across the marshy lands

Marshy some of these lands may be but there are 750 acres of them to run across and footpaths heading in several directions. There is a Moses Gate Train Station here and for people just visiting the park this must be in an ideal spot to alight the train. Yet, for us runners who want to cover the park in its entirety the station sort of splits the land in two and would mean if you began there you would have to run something akin to a figure '8' sign sat sideways on.

Therefore, it may be best to start out from Farnworth Station or even Bolton Station to cover this route. Run from Bolton Station to your left and then right onto the B6536 Manchester Road. After about 0.75 miles of retail and residential surroundings the road splits off to weave together the A666 and the A6053 and B roads. You want to briefly follow the houses of the Manchester Road you were already on before the concrete chaos began, then head left through tunnels under the A666 Farnworth and Kearsley By-pass. This all seems to be, if not dangerous, then requiring alertness but almost immediately afterwards you see signs for, and turn along Smith's Road and the surroundings become instantly countrified.

You run along what feels more and more like a country lane and to your left hand side you will see a reservoir with a tall chimney sat in the distance behind it, a pictorial indicator of what life was like here for many years. In numerous parts of Manchester there are masses of areas of water but many of them were built or created, rather than harnessing naturally occurring waters like rivers, to feed the need for power and energy for industry. In the Pennines, Peak District, north Manchester many canals and reservoirs were formed for the Industrial Revolution: to power wheels, transport haulage or water the workers slogging away in the mills and the Bolton area was no different.

Keep running and the road will become Hacken Bridge Road and you will run over the River Croal, passing footpath signs and routes into the park. Head past the Ron Tucker Sports Ground or cricket ground and on your right you will see a public footpath sign which, though takes you into Moses Gate, you should ignore. You will reach a junction with Hag End Brow and Radcliffe Road, opposite the massive Farmer's Arms, where you should turn right. Very shortly afterwards the road will incorporate Smithy Bridge, just before Ormond Street and you should see a footpath or cycle route running underneath where this time you turn right and head into the grassland and trees of Moses Gate Country Park, which you have so far circuited.

A large sign welcomes you to the park and animal sculptures, on this occasion a frog, sits watching life go by. There are pathways to the left to let you run around the numerous ponds that make up the Gravel Pits and this route has numerous footpaths, some named and some merely referred to with coloured arrows, which no doubt make sense if you have seen the key but not everyone everywhere has. The Gravel Pits, the Dragonfly Route, simple arrows on signposts; it is all a little confused. However, the Gravel Pits area is used a lot by children wanting to learn more about creatures and nature and though it is a pretty part of the park it may be a distraction from the main direction for many runners.

Some of the paths can be very muddy. Horse riders are abundant on all pathways here and some paths are set specifically for horse riding or cycling but on others you must be ready to be greeted by horses rearing up, unhappy at your speed of travel.

If you go round the Gravel Pits you will then see Old Hall Farm and head back to the main footpath. If not, stay on the main footpath throughout but both will take you closer to the River Croal and the point where the peaceful parkland is dissected by the very fast A-road

The River Croal crawls round in Moses Gate Country Park.

deceptively named Hall Lane. The footpath has plenty of maps and billboards showing you it is an entrance to the park so luckily you don't just find yourself in the middle of the road because this road has flashing speed signs telling drivers to slow down and there is a lot of traffic here.

Don't run towards Farnworth Bridge over the river but hop over a barrier to run along a riverside path with the River Croal on your right and run through the second section of Moses Gate Country Park towards Red Bridge. If you cross Red Bridge there you will find the Rock Hall Visitors' Centre and beyond it reservoirs at which to sit and contemplate as you eat your ice-cream. Or re-cross Red Bridge and get back on the main pathway towards Nob End.

At present Red Bridge is the only point in the park at which to cross the River Croal other than via a road. However, if you keep pounding the path, running under the shade of trees throughout you will reach more open meadowland and can come off the path, yet there are often many flies down near the river at this point and Wilson's Bridge is boarded off and covered in anti-climb paint so if you want to cross the river from here you would have to run higher, away from the river, back towards the footpath you were already on and then turn right southwards onto it to run over an aqueduct, this time over the River Irwell and along the towpath of a disused branch of the Bolton, Bury and Manchester Canal. The only other option would be to run back to Red Bridge and cross the water, which at that point is still the River Croal.

Continue along the canal which is green in colour through the plants and algae that live in what was once a waterway which objects could sail though. Now it is packed with bulrushes in places and may look like solid ground to some who are unacquainted with it but it is best to tread the towpath.

Pass the bridges along the canal and exit and turn right onto Seddon Lane. Follow Seddon Lane round and then turn left onto Crompton Avenue. Next head right onto Bridge Street and right to where Market Street joins Stoneclough Road and turn right again to run to Kearsley Station and the finish for this route. However, you could run even further along Stoneclough then right onto Bolton Road to cross the M61 motorway. From here run right up Ann Street, left up Lord Street and then right along Church Road. Next turn left onto Gerrard Street or Clammerclough Road to meet Bridge Street. Here you will find Farnworth Station.

Advantages:
- A vast amount of very natural parkland.
- A different route to explore within the park every time you visit what with the Explorer Trail, the Gravel Pits, The Rock Hall Visitors' Centre and the reservoirs.
- A lot of free parking if you drive to the site.

Disadvantages:
- Many horses and horse riders who don't like runners (well, at least our speed).
- Too many choices where pathways are concerned and not enough clear signposting as to the direction they are pointing.
- You can get boxed in on the north side by the lack of bridges over the river.

Summary:
Very natural parkland space which attracts all comers and activities and offers a vast amount of space to explore not far from a large town and industry, yet you can feel miles from day-to-day life. However, it is surprisingly easy to be boxed into and then require step retracing.

Mileage:
Kearsley 3.5 miles, Farnworth 4 miles.

History:
There is nothing biblical about this country park's name. Moses meaning marshy or peaty lands and gate, from Old English gata, meant a way across, therefore the natives usefully named this place a way across the marshy land. Yet like many stunning water-related landscapes around Manchester this beauty spot has industrial connections.

Even though wool was once said to be called cotton, real cotton first started being made in the town in about 1641. The process known as 'fulling' involved the washing, shrinking and thickening of the cloth.

Samuel Crompton of Bolton invented the spinning mule in 1779. The invention produced stronger and finer yarn and gave progress to mechanisation in textiles. He is thought by some to have kick-started the Industrial Revolution but sadly, he died in relative poverty as he didn't have the funds to patent his invention. A statue to remind Boltonians of the fabric of the man stands in Nelson Square today.

John Crompton set up the first paper mill in Lancashire in Farnworth and used the water of the River Croal to aid the industry. Some of the waters within Moses Gate Country Park are called Crompton Lodges today because of the paper mill family's heritage. John's son Thomas Bonsor Crompton patented a method of drying out paper in 1820, which was then a breakthrough for the industry and used waste from cotton production in the paper industry.

131

Rock Hall, now the Visitors' Centre, started to be built by John Crompton and he was granted the lease in 1805 though unfortunately died before the property was completed in 1807. It was granted to John's son Thomas Bonsor Crompton and used by managers of the paper mill. Upon Thomas' death the property passed to his nephew and it was offered up for auction in 1876 upon the nephew's death.

The government officials of Richard I were appointed to mark and measure cloth in AD1100 and Bolton's textile quality was said to be known even widely enough to attract Flemish weavers to come and spin and weave in the 14th century. They brought clog making to the Lancashire town as well but it is tricky for us to get top mileage in wooden shoes.

In 1838 there were 8,621 Bolton people working in the cotton trade. In 1911 that figure had risen to 36,000 working in textiles, 21,000 of them women. There were still 33,000 working in textiles by 1921.

In 1929 there were 247 cotton mills in the area and even in the 1950s Bolton had 103 mills. Sadly, by 1979 only eight remained.

Staggeringly, the Moses Gate site, now filled with wildlife and natural wild flowers was once a chemical waste tip, an industrial site. It is said to receive 350,000 visitors per year and Nob End was declared a Site of Special Scientific Interest in 1988 and a Local Nature Reserve in 2000. The very alkaline soil left as the result of chemical waste before the area was restored means orchids are sometimes said to grow here making it special ground.

Useful Websites:

www.bolton.gov.uk
Look at the council website for a little information about the park and dates for activities there and to email Rock Hall Visitors' Centre via the site.

www.cottontimes.co.uk
A site telling of the Industrial Heritage of Lancashire and its major role in the Industrial Revolution.

Contacts:

Rock Hall Visitors' Centre
Moses Gate Country Park
Hall Lane
Farnworth
Bolton
BL4 7QN
Tel: 01204 334343

Oldham Way/Castleshaw Moor

Are you sure it's over Oldham Way?

The thing about Oldham Way is that despite its size it is harder to find than a confirmed bachelor when those around him want to introduce him to new 'friends'. Every time you think you have caught sight of it, turn a corner and it is gone!

Though the name implies that it starts in and around Oldham and continues in that vein, the reality is far from it. This can be a very vague route which covers some captivating scenery like Castleshaw Moor and Saddleworth Moor but it is largely based on land on the outskirts and to the east of Oldham and really, Oldham Way just finishes on the edge of the town.

It starts at Dove Stone Reservoirs near Greenfield and heads over Saddleworth Moor to Diggle. It then covers the vast cobweb-blowing area of Castleshaw Moor and the Roman Fort and reservoirs there before heading up to Denshaw. You then start to see more urban scenes such as Shaw and Royton before finishing at the Rochdale Canal at Chadderton Hall Park.

The land around Mossley, Greenfield, Uppermill, Delph, and Diggle is such stunning scenery you could run forever here. There are hills, mountains, rivers, canals, reservoirs, war memorials, Roman forts all surrounded by some very testing roads, paths, towpaths, cobblestone routes, slop-laden bogs and moorland.

Because of this and the fact that Oldham Way is so vague instead head along a route of the constituent parts of the set route. Start at the Huddersfield Narrow Canal in Greenfield

Not a blade out of place on Hollingworth and Swineshaw Moors.

(down Shaw Hall Bank Road from the train station and find the waterway at the top of Chew Valley Road). You could start the run even earlier near The Royal George public house where Huddersfield Road meets Manchester Road in Friezland, to have a taste of Tame Valley and to see some signposting for an Oldham Way link but be careful not to disturb the horses training alongside the path. The yellow and green signs for the elusive Oldham Way soon vanish again. Then you run past the vile smell of a sewage works, so, pretty as the area is perhaps it is better to start with the more confined and more firmly structured towpath at Greenfield.

Head along the towpath greeting ducklings and barge owners on very short stays and the path will take you through the edge of Uppermill, past, or rather under, the Uppermill Viaduct which is a giant structure but unfortunately, because of the lie of the land and foliage you cannot see that much of it from here.

After the viaduct head on a slight detour to your right to the Brownhill Countryside Centre which is mentioned everywhere. It is not open on Mondays and Tuesdays and has different hours in winter and summer but basically it has hours of 11am until 4pm, or 5pm on the other five days of the week. It is free to enter and there are toilets open every day it seems. There are also handily posted maps outside to help the runner losing their way or wanting to remind themselves of their goal. The centre has a very well-thought-of Nature Garden too.

Once visited head back towards the viaduct and up a rocky lane rather curiously named 'Delph Donkey' to Delph. It is a walking, cycling and running pathway which was a railway line until 1955. It is said to have got the name from a white horse which pulled the carriage before steam power came along. Well, we hadn't visited then had we? Seriously, if that was the source of the name why donkey and not horse? For alliteration and publicity purposes? Around Oldham they seem to like the link between animal names and geography; the town itself is feathered with owl symbols and signs, a play on the pronunciation of 'owl-dem' used by natives when talking of home.

Nevertheless, aside from the name, the Delph Donkey runs on with notices telling of the history of places like Dobcross along the way but if you wanted moorland freedom for your taste of the Oldham Way you may feel claustrophobic at this point. Do not fear you will see vast open land yet! Here, however, the route becomes a bit industrial with abandoned mills and stones and rocks before reaching what was Delph Station and placing you at Delph New Road.

Prepare yourself for a very concrete section of the run and turn right up Huddersfield Road. Yes, another road with that name. They are abundant in these parts as that is where Pennine travellers would often be heading from north east Manchester's outskirts.

However, up here you do see the land open up beautifully and whereas the Pennine hills near Pots and Pans Memorial and Dove Stones are majestic in their power, rocky obstinacy and wilderness, the hills here have a more refined majesty.

To your left a long chain of hills peep out from the ground in a snake-like spine. You see very well-spaced stone houses scattered across the land but no shops, no commerce; just magically picturesque unspoilt majesty.

Turn off Huddersfield Road onto Waterworks Road and there is a footpath which runs parallel to the lane. Soon you will pass Castleshaw Centre but if you were expecting it to be akin to a tourist information centre it is more of an outdoor pursuits place for schools or youth leaders to hire. Young people can go kayaking, hill-walking or of course Ghyll

Scrambling (wouldn't dream of spending time doing anything else, eh?) which apparently means you walk up or down gorges containing tumbling rivers and pay for the risky privilege. Some of us love outdoor pursuits but might stick to running.

The children lucky enough to be brought here by their schools can then, as we runners are doing, head past Castleshaw Lower Reservoir, up a footpath and visit the land where the Romans once stood while looking down over Castleshaw Upper Reservoir, its arches, the valley and the hills.

Rome itself is a city set on seven hills and it is no wonder the Romans parked here for a while. Hills decorate the horizon in every direction with light dancing over them from the swiftly visiting clouds. It is a shame nothing solid is visible of the fort but there has been much archaeological excavation here over many years. The troughs which kept the enemy at bay by being deep enough to injure their ankles and steep enough not to let them out again once confined are still there in part – so beware!

Thankfully, the Roman Fort is a Scheduled Ancient Monument which means it is protected and cannot be built on. The effect of which means that this wider stunning area cannot be built on either, though with its Peak District National Park setting it is probably quite safe anyway.

After the fort, run on a solid lane past the side of the Upper Reservoir to see a signpost at the end with a sign for Piethorne Reservoir positioned up a rocky and steep-looking set-pathway but tantalisingly, for the first time in a while, an elusive Oldham Way link disc appears as well. There are also signs for the Pennine Bridleway and the Horseshoe Trail. Head left on the flatter pathway but still in the hills towards Delph itself. You can save tackling that calf-stretching rockiness up to Piethorne for a different occasion.

On this route we will make it to the other side! You can see your earlier run up Huddersfield Road, the reservoirs, the fort area and they all seem so distant yet well defined. It gives you a feeling of achievement or satisfaction with your sport to see the basin of a whole valley, most of which you will have covered. If you have run Pots and Pans previously, near Uppermill, you will recognise the memorial on a hilltop to your left and a mast you passed earlier in the run on a hilltop to your right, showing what a vast area you have pounded!

The pathway here back to Delph is set and perhaps you will go past a kind man claiming to be called Ray with a belief (or so he will tell you as he hands you a can of coke) that the former resident of his friend's property bathed outdoors in her 60s. Well, she did until 20 years ago. You do meet some characters in the sticks! Bathing or gassing.

Ray rightly says many people out here need Range Rovers and four-wheel-drives but as you, more bravely, head on foot past the increasing number of properties you will turn right down the Horseshoe Trail. The tomes of rock underfoot here cannot see many horses these days and we runners must be alert on it on slippier days (especially when balancing cans of donated pop in hand).

Head over a quaint little wooden bridge on Grange Lane and potentially past the millpond as it becomes Hull Mill Lane. Then go right onto Palin Wood Road then right again onto Delph Lane or straight on to Delph Lane from Hull Mill Lane and towards the High Street of the most delightful little village of Delph. Here you will find a Co-op and a chip shop. There is also a delightful little humped stone bridge over the River Tame. You can get a bus here from King Street or The Swan but they can confuse because the 350 to Ashton-under-Lyne runs in a loop and seems to stop on both sides of the road within a matter of minutes. But this is where you can get a bus back to Ashton or Oldham and more urban life – if you want to!

Advantages:
- Long. Yes, that is an advantage. You can run up to 40 miles on Oldham Way itself.
- Many types of terrain to pound and numerous sights to view.
- Some of the most stunning scenery you will get to see running around this area. It engraves itself on your heart and soul.

Disadvantages:
- Finding Oldham Way itself, particularly if you get transport to Oldham to start from the town centre – it skirts high to the north and east of the town.
- Being dislocated from civilisation. If you get tired and want to head home you may be miles from the bus route – any bus route!
- There can be numerous other walkers and dog walkers, even on weekdays, near the Greenfield and Uppermill section of the route, which could slow you down.

Summary:
A route with a taste of almost every flavour of Pennine running with hills, canal towpaths, routes down giant old cobblestone paths; sights such as rivers, canals, and reservoirs topped off with a wind to refresh your soul at a Roman Fort and abounding pretty villages.

Mileage:
Greenfield to Castleshaw Centre and back 4 miles plus mileage around reservoirs.

History:
Castleshaw Roman Fort is thought to be Rigodunum, a Brigantine fort but there is no evidence. It was constructed in AD79 but fell out of use in the 90s (AD90s that is) to be replaced by a smaller fortlet in AD105. A small civilian settlement grew around the site which looked down over Castleshaw Valley from its eastern side but that too was abandoned in around AD120.

Archaeologists have been trying to unearth Castleshaw Fort's secrets since the 18th century and now the fort, fortlet and civilian settlement surrounding it are, as stated above, considered a Scheduled Ancient Monument which means they are protected as nationally important archaeological treasures and thus protected from unauthorised change. If you have had the pleasure of running up there you will know why its protection is heart warming.

A road thought to lead Romans from Chester to York across the rocky Pennines via Standedge where the path dipped, took legions – well, quite a few people anyway – through the valley. It was protected in part by the fort which housed up to 500 soldiers meaning substantially more people lived there about 1,900 years ago than do now.

Later, as a fortlet it housed fewer people with under 100 thought to live in the timber and turf monument which had a granary, barracks, hypocaust system (a Roman sort of central heating system) and in the winds up here they would need it. There was also a commander's house and a courtyard.

Sir Thomas Percival discovered it in 1752. Upon finding the fort the antiquarian also remarked that the Roman road east from Manchester to the Pennines was: 'The finest remain of a Roman Road in England that I ever saw,' and though later damaged by ploughing we runners love a straight road out to freedom.

Further excavations are thought to have taken place in the 1950s, 60s, 80s by Greater Manchester Archaeological Unit under the supervision of the University of Manchester and in 1995–96 archaeologists began searching to the south (the side nearer Huddersfield Road) for the vicus or civilian settlement.

However little this run seems to have to do with Oldham, the town itself is somewhere a lot of world traditions began. The site of Lever's Fish And Chip Shop on Albion Street has a blue plaque commemorating the fact that this is the place in 1860 of the birth of the great British institution – the chip! Yes, the potato variety that some of us are no doubt trying to run off. So we can blame Oldham for the chips being down our necks.

It is a town heaving with pubs which certainly seem successful on a Saturday afternoon when many others towns are closing their boozers and that is appropriate because Oldham opened the first ever Yates' Wine Lodge in 1884 giving people the chance to have a drink then get fish and chips on the way home. Some things never change!

The first test-tube baby Louise Brown was born in Oldham in 1978 and a test-tube chandelier in the town's Gallery Oldham commemorates her birth.

Oldham is also filled with fame as numerous celebrities from the world of sport, music and politics started life in the town. On a sporting note semi-retired Manchester United and England midfielder Paul Scholes grew up in Oldham and earlier England, Arsenal and Aston Villa player David Platt. Olympic swimming freestyle triple gold medallist Henry Taylor was born in Hollinwood.

World famous Briton, Sir Winston Churchill, though born at Blenheim Palace, near Oxford, was declared a member of Parliament on the Old Town Hall steps in 1900. Composer William Walton was born in Oldham and his life is illustrated in one of the largest stained-glass roofs in Europe in the Spindles Shopping Centre.

Back in the world of politics and opinion, Suffragette Annie Kenney, who was credited with sparking off suffragette militancy by heckling Winston Churchill was born in Saddleworth. It seems Oldham was the heart of past politics.

Sir Winston is thought to have said: 'I always cherish my memories of Oldham and the warm hearts and bright eyes of its people and I always wish them the good luck I know they deserve.'

Fascinating as Oldham town centre is perhaps these days the good luck should be for those runners covering the whole 40-mile Oldham Way…or maybe even finding it from the town centre in the first place.

Useful Websites:

www.peakdistrictview.com
Look at some of the sights you could see to motivate you or look back on those you have seen to be sure of the names of some of the rocks and ridges.

www.penninewaterways.co.uk
Dip into the waters you may run alongside.

www.saddleworthnews.com
You can't say this place isn't loved. When last checked they had an update of someone trying to steal lead from a window in the previous 17 hours.

www.visitoldham.com
Find some trail maps online (but Oldham Way can be elusive again online).

en.wikipedia.org/wiki/Castleshaw_Roman_fort
For more details about the busy history of the now very solitary land and its inhabitants.

Contacts:

Brownhill Countryside Centre
Wool Road
Dobcross
Oldham
Greater Manchester
OL3 5PB
Tel: 01457 872598
Email: env.brownhill@oldham.gov.uk

Castleshaw Centre
Waterworks Road
Delph,
OL3 5LZ
Tel: 0161 770 8595
Email: castleshaw.centre@oldham.gov.uk

Oldham Tourist Information Centre
Gallery Oldham
Cultural Quarter
Greaves Street
Oldham
OL1 1AL
Tel: 0161 770 3064
E-mail: tourist@oldham.gov.uk

Saddleworth Museum And Art Gallery
High Street
Uppermill
OL3 6HS
Tel: 01457 874093

Peak Forest Canal, Etherow Country Park, Brabyns Park

The Park Side

Get the train from Piccadilly to Disley in Cheshire and once you've alighted and warmed-up at Disley Station turn right and run down Market Street and straight on to Buxton Road. I know it may seem an unorthodox route for a runner considering Lyme Park is a nearby temptation and the train companies even advertise Disley as the station to get off at for the beautiful park. However, this route doesn't include Lyme Park. Yet there is plenty of distance and other parkland to make up for it. First turn left along Redhouse Lane and less than 0.25 miles later you should see and turn left onto the Peak Forest Canal.

You will pass many locks and barge owners along here, especially at weekends. To the right of the canal you can also look down towards the valley and open land near Strines and see the River Goyt, which runs almost parallel to the canal.

Perhaps just short of 2 miles along this beautiful waterway there is a path to your right after a brick bridge. After this, cross Strines Road and find a sign for the Goyt Way, a very well hidden entrance to a path that is covered with foliage overhead. If you take this route you will cross a bridge over the railway line and run down past a gate and over a stone bridge to find yourself next to the woodland of Lakes Road before running on to the Roman Lakes. Take a minute to explore these woods if you like or wait until you have got a bottle of water from the kiosk at Roman Lakes and come back to it because this is very pretty woodland.

If you don't want to hang about, run further down Lakes Road and follow the signs directly to the pond used by canoeists and anglers. On previous visits several families seemed to enjoy feeding the geese to the point where it could look like the entrance to an animal sanctuary. Yet run to the kiosk, avoiding the temptation of the scent of bacon butties, unless of course you must have the sustenance! You might be tempted from here to try and run a circuit of the lake back to the road but unfortunately because barbed wire was placed at certain points you can't. After running to the kiosk, run back towards Lakes Road but this time instead of turning towards the gate you will be turning right along Bottoms Mill Road and then up Low Lea Road.

Don't be lulled into a false sense of security here. There is nothing low about this country road. Think of the north face of the Eiger, then think steeper! Though it is quite a short road it is testing so get your hamstrings stretching. It is a delight. When you reach the top you go back down immediately towards some cottages gathered near a brook on Town Street in Marple Bridge. The little peak is like the epitome of rural freedom on one side and country civility on the other.

Don't get too comfy though. Next run along Lower Fold, which makes Low Lea Road seem horizontal. Perhaps it seems worse because this time it is a concrete road with traffic passing-by too. This is really steep and at the top you can go straight on to Compstall Road or the road forks off to the right to become Glossop Road. I've got bad news. It is the near vertical Glossop Road to the right that you are taking but there is some consolation in that it levels out after about 0.5 miles. Do be careful on this road. Because it is high and lonely but nevertheless an A-road, traffic does speed here and there are sections with no pavement on one side of the road.

You should see on your left about 1 mile after the Glossop Road turning a public footpath leading into Ernocroft Wood, part of the beautiful Etherow Country Park. Well, I did promise more parkland, though it may be difficult to get into the heart of the park at some places and at some times of the year because mud and landslides cause footpaths to be closed off.

The heart and soil of Etherow Country Park.

Once inside you should hit a network of footpaths that let you cross the River Etherow. It is difficult to continue this route if you don't cross the river (though we could always make it a triathlon). Once you've run through the stunning woodland and got across the river turn left and run to the Visitors' Centre. This is a very busy spot on sunny weekends so if you want solitude select a different day to go and perhaps a time of the year when people who don't love running are at home in front of the fire.

By now you might be feeling a bit tired but keep your stamina up and run onto Andrew Street, then Compstall Road and you'll find you've come full circle back to the vertical stretch in Marple Bridge.

Turn right onto the countrified Rollins Lane at the end of which you should cross another river, the River Goyt in Brabyns Park and see a weir nearby. Inside the park there is a pavilion used as a changing area by some. There are football pitches, children's play areas and free parking.

If you run through the middle of the park and past a recreation centre the footpaths become a road. To the right of it, up a slight embankment you will see a footpath used by many runners. Climb onto it and head upwards. At this point you could take the road route back to Marple Station but this route is more charming and though it continually rises it doesn't leave a massive concrete incline at the end as the road route does.

You will again cross the railway line over a stone bridge, head onwards and find yourself at Brabyns Brow where you then turn left back over the railway again to get into Marple Station. Then cross the same line for the third time to catch trains back to Manchester and stretch off. You made it! You've covered two parks, two rivers, a canal and hills that seemed like mountains. It is a stunning route though, isn't it?

Advantages:
- Testing in all ways: terrain, inclines. This route covers just about everything except speed trials and maybe you could work those into some sections.
- It is quite well served by public transport. Disley is close to Stockport and there are buses from Marple to Stockport and trains to Manchester from all those towns.

Disadvantages:
- It is a long run and perhaps it is not best to cover it alone if you are new to the sport.
- On a few occasions the public footpaths could be better signposted which can lead to unwanted detours if you miss pathways but it isn't like getting lost in a city centre network of streets. You know the general direction.

Summary:
One tester of a run with flat canalsides and mountain-like inclines, parkland, concrete and road running. You cover some beautiful parts of the Cheshire countryside in a run that tests every muscle, including your brain for stamina.

Mileage:
6.25 miles.

History:
Brabyns Brow was once paraded with mature beech trees but apparently people complained about droppings from the rookery and they were felled.

Though Brabyns Hall was demolished in 1952 Brabyns Park has a restored, Georgian iron bridge, which still stands today. Dr Henry Brabyn, or Brabin depending on sources, gave the park its name. He incorporated a farmhouse into the original building in 1750.

The last owner Fanny Hudson inherited it in 1906 and she lived there until 1941 when she died during World War Two at the grand old age of 90 years. It was the Hudson family who donated land and money for St Martin's Church to be built in the area and its accompanying vicarage and school.

Brabyns Hall charged people 2d each to visit and look around in order to raise money for Red Cross' funds to help soldiers convalesce there during World War One. In 1949, eight years after Fanny Hudson's death, the 95 acres of parkland was bought by Cheshire County Council on behalf of local councils for the sum of £11,100 but as time was spent by bureaucrats debating how to use the property, floating ideas of having it as an art gallery or public library, the building went to wrack and ruin. It deteriorated and dry rot set in leading to its demolition. It wasn't until the building was knocked down that they realised it had originally been built around a farmhouse 200 years earlier.

Etherow Country Park

The park was established in 1968 and has around 250,000 visitors per year. The park is the halfway point of the 12-mile Goyt Way and covers around 240 acres. Tawny owls often hunt in the Keg Woodland and rare water rails, birds which like wetlands, are found within the woodlands. The Nature Reserve is considered a Site of Special Scientific Interest.

Within the park, Ernocroft Wood houses a coal mine thought to have been mined as far back as the Middle Ages. The estate itself was built by George Andrew in the 1820s, as was Compstall Mill. He created the nearby Compstall village to house his workers.

The River Etherow's source is in Bleaklow and it runs for 19 miles through Longdendale and Etherow Country Park before joining the Goyt in Marple.

Useful Websites:

www.stockport.gov.uk
For background information especially about the parkland.
www.tameside.gov.uk/countryside/etherow
See the Tameside Council website for other Etherow Valley running routes.

Contacts:

Brabyns Park
C/O Parks, Sports and Cemeteries
Fred Perry House
Edward Street
Stockport
SK1 3SU
Tel: 0161 217 6111
Email: parks@stockport.gov.uk

Etherow Country Park
George Street
Compstall
SK6 5JD
Tel: 0161 427 6937
Email: parks@stockport.gov.uk

Pennine Way

The way to see moor

After getting off the train at Hadfield Station you cross a large car park towards the main street, Station Road, lined with stone built houses. Instead of heading down Station Road turn right along Platt Street. Then on your left before the pavement goes through a tunnel, you find the gateway to the beautiful Longdendale Trail (see other routes). If you drive, there is a small car park here.

The first stretch of this trek, which was once a railway line, is sort of hemmed-in on both sides by earth and grass. Lovely though it is to be off concrete, you are in store for a treat once the embankments end and the path opens up to the left to reveal a chain of reservoirs: starting with Bottoms Reservoir then Valehouse, Rhodeswood and then Torside and Woodhead.

The chain of blue and the open landscape really offer you more and more freedom as the start is heavily used by cyclists and dog walkers. To head towards the Pennine Way you can cross the reservoirs between Rhodeswood and Torside on a very safe concrete dam there.

Once over the other side you should turn right onto a sandy path with the glorious blue of the reservoirs to one side and rows of green trees to your left. The beauty of this scenic run is very liberating and though it is tempting to follow an old wooden sign saying Pennine Way, if you do so you will come out on to a lethally fast but lonely-for-the-pedestrian A628 and see only one farm and not find the Pennine Way.

It is better to continue on past that wooden sign, alongside the trees and then left to come out near a lone cottage on the same road with a large gate to the right of it.

Incidentally, if you had carried on to your right along that lane or road you would soon find Crowden Youth Hostel.

The rolling reservoirs and motley mountains of the Longdendale Valley.

This large gate takes you up a stony path, the surroundings widening out and letting you taste some of the most natural, wild air this area has to offer. If you are a runner who loves off-road you will know what taste I mean. You continue upwards and over two stiles and then veer right to find a better defined sandy path running on for quite some distance.

You can see a river in the bottom of the valley to your right as you run along what is now solidly the Pennine Way and to your left there are crags and the ground is mountainous with previous rock slides. If you don't want to miss an amazing sight you can detour from the solid running for a few minutes and scurry up those rocks, though this could be quite dangerous and isn't for everybody. Perhaps you could find a safer point further on but if you do reach the top of that rocky edge it is worth it for the views at the top.

The moors here reach out forever. It is one of those freedom points where perhaps you could scream and not a soul would hear you. The only sound I heard aside from the birds and my breathing on a spring day was the distant sound of shots being fired by hunters enjoying rural sporting life

The ground was lemon and lime with spring grasses and a deep black where the heavy, rich peat showed through near springs. You should be aware of another danger here because of the peat bogs. This can sometimes seem like safe or only slightly damp ground when in reality it is more like quicksand disguised for a British location, dragging your leg three feet under in an instant. Believe me! But you already know you are going to end this run soaked in sweat, filthy, and cold from the saturation of rain, streams, sweat, or a combination of all of them.

This isn't road running but it provokes a fantastic sense of freedom, of being cut off from the outside world and all its hassles. This route does though need careful planning. You don't want to get stuck up on the moors in the dark because no friend will find you if you've left the path. A couple of times I have had to turn off the Pennine Way early and run to Tintwistle's Arnfield Lane via a stream and a heavy-going heather and bracken covered gulley to get back to civilization. It is much better with this one to set off early and do a morning run and if you do leave the path make it a short detour not an unanticipated night on the tops.

Aside from rock climbing detours, carry on up the charming Pennine Way where you can then turn off to your left near Oaken Clough and Laddow Rocks and you will reach Chew Reservoirs. After this, head to your left and down towards a different civilization in the form of Stalybridge's Country Park and public transport back to the city centre.

You may have run about 6 or 8 miles but a large part of you will be sad that it has ended. Unless of course if you did park in Hadfield…

Advantages:
- A taste of freedom and of a high that never dips.
- Part of a route that goes on for an exhausting 268 miles.

Disadvantages:
- It could be quite dangerous as you are some distance from people and transport and have to be prepared with maps, equipment and strength.

Summary:
Some of the most spectacular off road running scenery this region, let alone this area, has to offer but you have to earn the pay off vista with a long, tough run through this unpopulated, raw paradise.

Mileage:
6 to 8 miles.

Top Tips:
Know you will get cold and need a cagoule or another hoodie from your rucksack, especially for when the run ends and you have to wait for transport. Be prepared with maps and other navigational aids.

History:
The Pennine Way covers 268 miles of hill walking, or running, from Edale in Derbyshire to Kirk Yetholm, over the Scottish border. In total 17 per cent of the trail is in the Peak District National Park, which borders Manchester, 20 per cent is in the Yorkshire Dales National Park and 24 per cent in the Northumberland National Park so though you won't visit them being on the run around Manchester you have background to one of the longest UK trails a runner could pace.

The trail visits UK rural highlights such as High Force at Langdon Beck, towards Darlington, the highest waterfall in the UK, Hadrian's Wall and the Lake District.

Edale is about 45 minutes from Manchester by train but it is near to the place where the mass trespass took place in the 1930s, where people were objecting to being denied access to the open country of their homeland.

The Pennine Way route from Edale crosses Kinder Scout but due to erosion deserves care. You could head to the west of it to Jacob's Ladder. Next cross the nearby Snake Pass near Glossop and Bleaklow.

The Way then heads onto Torside Reservoir in Longdendale before heading to Saddleworth and then exiting the outskirts of Manchester to head onwards to haunts in Yorkshire such as Haworth, once home of the literary famous Brontë sisters.

Journalist and rambler Tom Stephenson is said to have been inspired to propose the idea for the Pennine Way based on the American Appalachian Trail. An article written by him in the *Daily Herald* in 1935 and the lobbying of parliament led to it opening in April 1965, making it the country's first set long distance trail.

He was perhaps inspired too by the mass trespass of 1932. As many as 400 people including Benny Rothman, someone who spoke out publicly about the lack of access, set out from Bowden Bridge in Hayfield, to Kinder Scout, where they roamed.

However, violent scuffles began with gamekeepers and a handful of people were arrested, charged and imprisoned not with trespass but offences of violence. Benny Rothman received a four month prison term. He was a young man from Cheetham with Jewish heritage who had spoken about the working class struggles, the need for a right to have access to and spend time on the land, and the need to get relaxation via the area's beauty.

Though the trespassers may have felt they didn't get very far in 1932 their action is still having affects now. A voluntary agreement saw some access granted to Kinder Scout in 1952 and 1958 and Kinder Downfall is now accessible. There are often anniversary celebrations and activities and some see it as part of the reason for the government passing the Countryside and Rights Of Way Act in 2000.

Many people can today walk over 250 miles through the backbone of this land along the Pennines, seeing spectacular views while hoping not to find or cause much erosion to the stunning lands. Around 250,000 users briefly visit the trail each year with 12,000 covering it in its entirety. A Pennine Bridleway is open in places for cyclists and horse riders but for most runners there are spots where public footpaths or roads intersect to let us on and off. This land though is beautifully untamed. Even the famous walking writer Arthur Wainwright got stuck up to his waist in a peat bog here and a warden had to rescue him.

Every year rangers hold events to mark the anniversary of the Mass Trespass.

Useful Websites:

www.nationaltrail.co.uk/pennineway

Get information about the distances, history, and locations the trail encounters.

penninewayassociation.co.uk/

For accommodation particularly in the north Pennines and news about the trail.

radicalmanchester.wordpress.com/2009/11/24/benny-rothman-and-the-1932-kinder-scout-mass-trespass/

Read about the radical Mancunian refusal to be parted from the lands of their spirit.

Contacts:

For Pennine Way information

steve.westwood@naturalengland.org.uk

Philips Park, Clayton Vale and King's Road

Hidden gems

For this long run your number is up – well, you are starting near a bingo hall! If you get the bus or train to Belle Vue then run up Pottery Lane for about 1 mile until it becomes Alan Turing Way. Then run towards Sportcity and Manchester City Football Club's stadium, the National Cycling Centre or Manchester Velodrome, the National Squash Centre, the Regional Athletics Arena and Manchester Tennis Centre. If you are tired just reading all that do not worry, with all this emphasis on sport, wherever you look, even the most tired sports fans can be impressed by some aspects of the homage to fitness and exercise here, something which this city is renowned for.

Yet after all the flash silver and glass structures continue along Alan Turing Way, run over the Ashton Canal and then turn right into Philips Park. Perhaps surprisingly, a monument here tells you it is one of three parks established from public subscription, one of the first municipal parks in the world intended for full and free use by the public and opened in 1846.

That being the case the public should make the most of the area which can sadly look very quiet at times. Admittedly, that said, the last time I ran the route the grass was covered in snow and the 'full and free use' was qualified with makeshift signs warning about ice risks, no doubt from councils fearing legal actions.

Anyway, slip(!) past the rare ice issue and run onwards. Take the earliest turning into the park and run towards the viaduct where all but one of the arches are concreted off, guiding you to the point where you pass into the next area of parkland. If, however, you took a slightly later right turn you would run alongside the River Medlock and meet the viaduct around the open arch.

Shortly after that cross Bank Bridge Road and be greeted by a green metal gate which displays the words Clayton Vale. This gives you the option of running up steps and then turning right towards the Vale or running along the existing path before it leads you back down to the River Medlock and pond-filled and wooded areas that can look fairytale-esque in snow covered surroundings. It gives a sudden feeling of rurality, of clean air and release, considering how close you are to Manchester city centre and its metropolitan madness.

Once enjoying the scenery of Clayton Vale and being spoilt for choice over which pathway to take, on which side of the river, run for about 0.5 miles and you will see a very under utilised looking Visitors' Centre before hitting concrete again at Clayton Mill Bridge. Here, turn right and run up Edge Lane.

This is not a run for either first-timers or short-spin lovers because even though it does not compete with routes like those in the Pennines for testing inclines, the distance is quite long and some concrete roads and lanes require stamina.

However, to cover Edge Lane, turn left to continue along the same named road at the junction with Bristowe Street, then head left along the A622 Manchester Road. This major thoroughfare has seen more digging than an archaeological treasure trove because of the building of the eastern side Metrolink tram system. This has meant that some areas have had diversions and roads and pavements under construction but it should mean that in 2012 there will be stops that can help you shorten this route at Sportcity, Clayton and Edge Lane if you need to. By 2013/2014 you should be able to get the tram all the way out to Ashton-under-

Lyne to start more hilly Pennine climbs afterwards for extra testing. It also means you may have to be flexible about route changes during construction.

For now though, run along Manchester Road until you reach Market Street in Droylsden, once again being back in a busy town centre. Turn right up Market Street, then left along Ashton Hill Lane, then run over Ashton Canal. After that you will join a crossroads of a different Manchester Road (the A635) but carry straight on along Audenshaw Road.

Just before you fear the need to run over a motorway you should see some fairly new houses and a new estate being built to house them at the top of what is called King's Road. There are currently warning signs from the water board that vehicles should not travel down the thoroughfare because of the vast number of potholes but if you are on foot, as long as there is daylight and you are one of the tougher breed of runners, you should be OK. Perhaps it is a warning to heed though in winter weather, however, as in the cold season this is more like an ice skating channel and runs on for over 1 mile to Debdale Park on the A57 Manchester Road. Yes, another Manchester Road. It seems civil engineers were short of imagination for road names when creating this side of town – or gave too many roads the most obvious tags.

All this bad weather skating could make you very tired by the time you reach the A57 and a bus route home but it is worth it for the views of Gorton Upper Reservoir. If you are really struggling once stuck on King's Road where the thoroughfare is an untarmacked, potholed lane rather than a solid road with the odd hole in it, there are no other real thoroughfares off it, however, there are two golf courses to your left and much nearer the A57, Debdale Park, which you can access at some points on your right.

Benchmark restoration in Clayton Vale.

Advantages:
- A real taster of urban Manchester and some of its hidden gems of countryside.
- At roughly 5.5 miles it is good training for 10ks and those events with concrete challenges as you cover public footpaths, concrete and rocky lanes.

Disadvantages:
- Disrupted concrete and potholed lanes mean it is not the best night-time or newcomers route.
- Changes due to building, regeneration and transport projects can mean maps or guide leaflets can quickly be out of date so it is best to check online immediately before your run especially if it is not a regular run.
- Beware not to confuse this Philips Park with one near Prestwich, north Manchester.

Summary:
A run past some of the latest additions to Manchester's leisure life at Sportcity before passing through some of the city's historic connections with leisure in Philips Park then enjoying inner city countryside in Clayton Vale.

Mileage:
5.5 miles.

History:
Sportcity was opened for the 2002 Commonwealth Games and receives around 4.5 million visitors each year. Although it is only about 2 miles from the city centre it is on what was rundown land less than a decade ago. It now has the largest concentration of sporting venues in Europe and a Visitors' Centre which opened there in 2005.

Sale Harriers, Belle Vue Racers and the Manchester Kestrels operate from the arena which houses 6,500 spectators and offers an eight lane running track which is great for housing National Athletics Trials and other events like the Paralympic World Cup.

Clayton Vale was once filled with factories at the time of the Industrial Revolution and there was once a smallpox hospital on the banks of the River Medlock. In 2009 the Medlock Valley Project (which encompasses Clayton Vale) won its first Green Flag and Waterways Renaissance Award from the British Urban Regeneration Association (BURA) for its work to improve 220 acres of public land.

Philips Park has also been awarded a Green Flag. It received it in 2005 from the Civic Trust for the management of the 31 acre public space which is home to many types of wildlife. The park first opened on 22 August 1846 through public funds. It opened on the same day as two others after nearby Queen's Park and Salford's Peel Park, making it the third in the UK. It showed then and still today that where leisure and sporting reasons to enjoy public spaces are concerned, Manchester has always been acres ahead.

Useful Websites:
www.groundwork.org.uk/manchester
A community project to encourage people to get involved in green issues and care more about their local environment.

www.medlockvalley.info
Find information about Clayton Vale and Philips Park and further sections on the major east Manchester route.

www.sportcity-manchester.com
Find opening times, buy tickets and learn more of the history of venues in this area.

www.wildaboutmanchester.info
Learn about tree parties and how to build a pond on this bio-diverse website.

Contacts:

Manchester Leisure (for information on events in places such as Clayton Vale)
Tel: 0161 223 8278
Email: info@friendsofclaytonvale.org.uk

Philips Park Visitors' Centre
Stuart Street
Manchester
Tel: 0161 231 3090 or 234 5000

Sportcity Visitors' Centre
Rowsley Street
Manchester
Tel: 0161 227 3151

Reddish Vale Country Park and the River Tame

Oliver Cromwell's Castle

This route has many urban places where you can set off; opposite Debdale Park in Denton and then run south down Reddish Lane and then near to where it becomes Gorton Road turn left onto Thornley Lane North. Here, bear left at Wilton Street as it becomes Thornley Lane South,

Or for another launch pad, starting your route further away from the city centre run down Hulme Road, situated opposite the entrance to Denton Golf Course and then left along Windsor Road, right onto Windmill Road and past a lot of residential streets and cul-de-sacs with names like Windermere and Kent. There is also a Coniston though we are not running to the Lake District. Head right onto Windmill Lane and keep running until you reach Thornley Lane South, where you meet up with the alternative start.

A tight road junction here means you run right and immediately left from one authority to another; from Denton, Tameside and into Reddish, Stockport in what looks like a cramped residential estate turning, to then continue along Windmill Lane.

More and more signs for Manchester Cycle routes and the Trans Pennine Trail start to appear and on your left you should see a sign for Mill Lane. Head down this road as the area becomes less and less suburban and more rural. Run to the right hand side of the lane and there is a footpath alongside tall trees which separate you from the traffic and houses of the lane. Here you have at last reached a path that is on grass. Finally, you are saved from pounding concrete – unless you love concrete running in which case continue down the tarmacked Mill Lane proper which is alongside.

As this footpath meets the curving road to Hollow Vale Drive at the bottom, head through a tunnel under a railway line and though still on Mill Lane, you are officially greeted by signs for Reddish Vale Nature Reserve.

Head straight on, down the tarmacked but unspoilt country lane avoiding the temptation to turn left immediately after the railway tunnel and you will see the scenery open up. There are beautiful fields of different colours, brambles alongside the track before you are greeted by the sight of a massive railway viaduct in the shape of numerous arches, like a giant snake undulating across the landscape and reflecting in the waters of a large pond or lake area to your left in what is Reddish Vale Nature Reserve yet is on the edge of Reddish Vale Country Park.

Shortly after the lake ends there is a turning to your left but if you carry on a little further you will find the Reddish Vale Visitors' Centre and a car park area. After signing up to do volunteer work in the nature reserve, or to protect wild creatures, head back to the turning at the end of the lake that takes you over the River Tame.

A very interesting sculpture/signpost sits on the other side of the river and if you want to head through Reddish Vale Country Park proper, you should head left here towards the railway viaduct, following the path but not the flow of the river.

If you turn right though, initially you seem to be covering parkland and following the river in the same direction as the water flow. This takes you up a steep series of paths or steps used by rushing cyclists and then past a small paddock of a few horses. Then it largely outskirts the Reddish Vale Golf Course and heads towards Stockport overlooked by the residential tower blocks of Brinnington.

Indiana Jones amidst Reddish Vale Country Park.

For this run though we are going left, against the water flow, north and east in the direction of the beginnings of the river that the Tameside area was named after. However, there can be difficulties navigating the jungle-like pathways in Reddish Vale Country Park. At this point run alongside the River Tame and at some points you will see signs for Arden Hall but some are vague and you cannot follow the river all the way to the Hall.

It is best once you have run some of the more foliage fringed paths in the park and you again find yourself in front of the vision of Brinnington's residential towers, to head beyond Blackberry Lane and up towards the end of Lapwing Lane. Here you can see the Lapwing Centre and Castle Hill High School. Then, over towards the left is a footbridge over the M60.

Once over the other side on Cromwell Road, you could turn left up Far Cromwell Road and onto the footpath to find Arden Hall. Though it has an interesting history (see below) unfortunately it is not open to visitors. Continue up Cromwell Road, then go left onto Ashton Road as it runs over the River Tame and becomes Stockport Road.

On the north side of the river, after about 0.25 miles you should see Hulme's Wood and the Hulme's Lane footpath, a route that will take you on the east side of Stockport Road into Tameside. Turn right and run alongside the river, past Denton Cemetery and head on past Arden Bridge and through Haughton Dale. Then run on towards Gibraltar Bridge and its weir, passing through two strands of Haughton Dale Nature Reserve to reach Mill Lane in Hyde and then head right up to Manchester Road for public transport back to the city.

For completely different routes using train services not buses to reach a starting point you could travel to Reddish South or Brinnington Stations and run north to Reddish Vale Country Park. For some people these would be more accessible but both of these would be shorter routes with a less varied taste of Manchester.

Advantages:
- An interesting urban route as it shows how close vast grassland and countryside is to Denton, Reddish, Hyde and Stockport.
- Lovely scenery at Reddish Vale Country Park and at Haughton Dale Nature Reserve.
- There are carpets of summer hay colours across fields and bluebells in springtime as part of this run is packed with beautiful flora and fauna in the nature reserve, park and woodland areas.
- There is a farm within Reddish Vale Country Park where children can pay to ride the ponies, so a good place to leave a partner with them while you canter off yourself.

Disadvantages:
- Navigation and signs for Arden Hall and the Visitors' Centre around Reddish Vale can be patchy, non-existent or confusing.
- The sewage works near Arden Hall and Stockport Road and the motorway are not the most aesthetically pleasing part of the run.
- It is a popular route with cyclists and horse riders, especially near Reddish Vale which may hinder running times.

Summary:
A sort of city parkland secret only hardened natives tend to know. A taste of the countryside nestled within suburbs with urban living followed by greenery, nature and rural bliss.

Mileage:
4.5 miles.

History:
The original wooden structure of Arden Hall was said by a BBC *Domesday* programme to have been built in 1067. The more recent stone Arden Hall was erected in 1597 and sadly, though not in ruins, is lacking its former majesty and splendour.

For two centuries the Hall was owned by the wealthy Ardernes family who had links with the Arden clan in Warwickshire, whom, it is said, included William Shakespeare's family. The

Hall still has a watchtower at the back looking over the River Tame's valley. There was said to have been a moat around the structure and it was in a good defensive position on Castle Hill.

Arden, also Ardern, Arderne and Harden (apparently) Hall is on the Bredbury or Haughton Green side of Reddish Vale but the Arderne family played a large part in the life of both Reddish and Denton. Their coat of arms was carved on the front wall of the Hall. Originally the site was said to have been owned by the de Bredburys.

The Great Hall within Arden Hall seated 300 people. When John Arderne married in 1522 his family had already been in Bredbury for more than two centuries. Their estates included Arden Hall, Bredbury Hall and Goyt Hall. In 1825 an unfathomable 1,814 acres of their land was sold for £154,773. Oliver Cromwell is rumoured to have stayed at the Hall, known to some as Oliver Cromwell's Castle.

The Forest of Arden in the area once covered: 'the whole face of the country.' Sandford, now in the vicinity of Reddish North Train Station, was once the site where the 'blue bonnets' encamped on their march to Derby as part of the actions prompted by the 1745 Jacobite Rising. Prince Charles Edward, better known now as Bonnie Prince Charlie and his Jacobite forces wanted to restore the crown for the Stuarts but he was beaten in 1746 at Culloden near Inverness and the House of Hanover got to keep the crown. The fields on the Sandford estate became known as the 'blue caps' in light of the highlanders' stay there.

The 400 acre Reddish Vale Country Park was opened in 1985 and the Visitors Centre' now open 365 days a year was once a calico print works fed by the waters of the river. The small tributary of Denton Brook flows into the River Tame and marks the traditional boundary between Denton and Reddish. A Butterfly Conservation Park is situated near the Visitors' Centre and there are romantic names like Sunnyside Woods and Blackberry Slopes here.

Parts of the Country Park link with the Saddleworth, Etherow, Longdendale and Goyt Trails and Ways and also with the much longer Trans Pennine Trail.

Between the River Tame and Haughton Green, coal mining took place for about 200 years disrupting the existence of the ancient woodland. In the 1970s the shafts were capped and trees were replanted to make it one of Tameside's biggest woodland areas. The exposed ruins of the 18th-century Hulme's Pit are the only real evidence of its past industry but it does not stop the Pipistrelle Bats feeding over the ponds there at night, hanging about and trying to reclaim the area as their own.

Useful Websites:

www.reddishvalecountrypark.com
Information about the park with slideshows and message boards.
www.stockport.gov.uk/services/leisureculture/parksandrecreation/countryside/countryparks/reddishvalecountrypark
Background information on the walking routes, wildlife and societies connected with the park.
www.tameside.gov.uk/countryside/tamevalley
Maps and information on places like Haughton Vale Nature Reserve and Hulme's Pit.

Contacts:

Reddish Vale Country Park Visitors' Centre
Mill Lane
Stockport
SK5 7HE
Tel: 0161 477 5637

River Mersey and Chorlton Ees

Gold model

Yep! Something that was a one-time sewage works doesn't sound that pleasant does it? How wrong we can be. This route around the Stretford, Chorlton and Sale areas can seem like paradise on a summer evening. Some reviews claim it is green from dawn until dusk but in the later months of the year Chorlton Ees is a spectrum of gold and browns.

For this route start on the Bridgewater Canal, almost anywhere you like on the vast waterway, however, you are heading to the white building of the Watch House Cruising Club which stands alone at the side of the canal in the Dane Road, not Old Trafford direction from Stretford Metrolink Station. In other words south.

At the white cottage-like building turn off a little path and you will run under a dripping railway bridge along a concrete country lane called Hawthorn Lane. If you follow this along you will pass under a tree-shaded area, past the edge of Stretford Cemetery and see a pond on your right.

Further on you can run up a slope and to a sort of low stile where you can carry straight on, cross and turn left or you can cross and bear right. If you cross and bear right you will be running alongside the River Mersey in the opposite direction to the flow of water and in the evening it is covered in both the setting sun and your fellow runners on a summer's night.

After perhaps 1 mile you will reach Jackson's Bridge which is currently green and yellow and after you cross it you will find Jackson's Boat public house in a lovely spot on Rifle Road for some runners to stop and meet lagging mates or have a well earned Coca Cola!

Your mates may have turned left though after crossing the stile and though they may not have got to enjoy the more open sunlight along the riverside, or seen much of the river at all, they will have seen and heard woodland filled with birdsong and wildlife in Chorlton Ees.

There are several paths marked as 'healthwalks' offering various directions and areas where the trees almost meet to form an archway of foliage. The paths are covered here and in times of wet weather this is probably the better of the two routes. In autumn, this woodland is unmissable.

On the Chorlton Ees route you may find unusual adders' tongue fern foliage and a brick walkway that is evidence of the history of the sewage works past usage of the land here. How much things can change because on a summer's evening this is one of the most beautiful spots in south Manchester.

Bird lovers will also adore this spot reportedly filled with flocks of goldfinch, linnet, greenfinch, redpoll and siskin as they flutter about. There are also herons, reed bunting, whitethroat, blackcap, chiffchaff and gold crest, all known to breed at Chorlton Ees.

Winged creatures aside though, heading towards Sale Water Park, Chorlton Ees routers will end up at Jackson's Bridge (or Jackson's Boat public house). For both routes, after visiting the pub, run up Rifle Road, again filled with amateur footballers, cyclists and horse riders on a summer's evening. You then join concrete civilization again – well, paradise doesn't last forever. After running (with care) across quite dangerous roads at the roundabout at Junction 6 of the M60 you will reach Old Hall Road.

Keep running past the Dane Road turning on your right and onwards for less than 0.25 miles to Broad Road where you do this time turn right. Run along Broad Road for about 0.75 miles and you can finish at Sale Metrolink Station. Instead you can run back down the paved

Have Mersey on me as the River Mersey looks towards Chorlton Ees.

area, past the library and council buildings of Sale Waterside and get back on the Bridgewater Canal if you want a second go – maybe covering Chorlton Ees this time if you covered the River Mersey last time and vice versa...Or, you could just stretch off and congratulate yourself for finishing training!

Advantages:
- The beauty of Chorlton Ees and the River Mersey.
- It is a nice adaptable size for a regular circuit.
- It is a stress-busting route if you run to help gain relaxation.

Disadvantages:
- On some summer nights there can be too many other runners if you like a little solitude.
- Some of the Chorlton Ees pathways and healthwalks offer too many footpath choices. Head west if you lose the route.
- The very concrete finish after such a beautiful, natural run.

Summary:
A mellow, but largely flat area to use as a regular training route to clock up mileage, which offers the chance to switch off because you are surrounded by beauty and nature but also a place where the Ees really comes into its own in the autumn.

Mileage:
2.75 miles.

History:
The beautiful Chorlton Ees was once Withington sewage works but it was closed in 1972 and the land restored under a project called 'Operation Eyesore'. Many footpaths now lace the area and are easier to run on than the brick thoroughfares sewage workers once used.

In more recent years it has adopted the name Chorlton Ees and Ivy Green Nature Reserve and is rated as a Site of Biological Importance. The Mersey Valley Countryside Warden Service which manages the area, started in 1978. The Ees can be accessed from a cobbled road off Brookburn Road in Chorlton as well as via footpaths and walking routes near the River Mersey and the Bridgewater Canal around Stretford.

It is thought the River Mersey's name stems from an Anglo-Saxon word meaning boundary but the water itself was prone to straying from its sides and flooding the area.

In 1841 a stone weir was built by William Cubbitt and John Tompkinson, upstream of the Barfoot Bridge near the cruising club, to stop the structure being flooded. The weir was a second attempt to try and harness the water after a flood on the 17 August 1840 washed away the engineering. It was last used in 1915 and thus has been out of action for almost a century.

Throughout the Middle Ages the town of Sale was known for farming but it had a thriving cottage industry making garthweb, a woven product used for making horses' saddle girth. The building of the Bridgewater Canal in 1765 and then the railway lines though the area in 1849 meant Sale changed from a farming community to a commuter town. Chorlton seemed slightly isolated at one time and used the market and transport at Stretford to go about daily life.

Useful Websites:

www.jacksonsboat.co.uk
Information about the public house with a nearby liquid landscape.

www.merseyvalley.org.uk
Information about the Mersey Valley, walks, conservation and things to see.

www.trafford.gov.uk
Search the council website for information about parks in the area and wider routes such as the Bollin or Mersey Valleys.

Contacts:

Chorlton Ees
Brookburn Road
Chorlton
M21 8EH
Tel: 0161 881 5639
Email: s.marshall@manchester.gov.uk

Jackson's Boat
Rifle Road
Sale
M33 2LX
Tel: 0161 905 2647
Email: paul@jacksonsboat.co.uk

Mersey Valley Visitors' Centre
Rifle Road
Sale Water Park
Sale
Cheshire
M33 2LX
Tel: 0161 905 1100
Email: info@merseyvalley.org.uk

Roman Lakes, Marple

Strine on my legs

With its quiet sophistication and its olde worlde feel Marple is not exactly the kind of place where you should anticipate danger. Yet every time I have run here it has resulted in some problem or other with a bad fall at Marple Locks once and drivers like something out of a Sicilian plot wanting to boost my speed with a motorised push on another occasion.

Ordinarily once you leave Rose Hill Train Station in Marple and head along Stockport Road until it becomes Oldknow Road and then cross Arkwright Road to head down Faywood Drive, you reach very mellow countryside the road then becomes Lakes Road.

From here you sort of veer right, turn right down Lakes Road, a very steep, pothole decorated lane, beautifully surrounded by woodlands and the River Goyt. Lovely as the effervescent greens and the water-filled sights are around this steep downhill roadway it is one to watch, especially in winter, thanks to potholes the size of moon craters and the gradient of the stretch. The thoroughfare can also be busy with other leisure users, walkers and traffic taking canoes and water sports equipment down to the lakes.

Once at the bottom of the lane you are positioned between the areas of Marple and Mellor. Run to your right past the side of North Lake and then on past Main Lake, set with dainty bridges and life frozen in time, with young boys fishing, a sight you rarely see now and families out walking together. You can get a booklet for £1 from the café here entitled *Rambles Around Roman Lakes Leisure Park*.

Once past the Main Lake head alongside the River Goyt overlapping and crossing some parts of the Goyt Way route, past the weir and then under the giant arched viaduct which carries the Marple railway line. Afterwards you pass an octagonal shaped building and run onwards. After seeing very rustic wooden signposting advertising the Goyt Way and other routes turn right and cross the Packhorse Bridge, a lovely little stone humpback bridge which seems to have crossed time. After traversing it jump down with care onto the very slippery stone slabs that were probably a forerunner to paving stones (or a cheap alternative).

Look back towards the almost fairytale bridge and enjoy the sight and the ambience, especially if the sun is sitting on the top of its curve, a perfect setting for a prince to kiss a princess. Imagine long flowing hair dangling towards the river as the couple meet from either side of the bridge, from other worlds. Back in the real world you are about to greet hell!

Run up the vast banking before you and head up some very narrow steps, some of which have wood at the rim to stop them sliding away into oblivion but it does mean they are easy to trip over and require more effort to jump onto. Keep jumping up the winding, steep, numerous steps like the wicked, suffering character in the fairytale and your calf muscles will be pushed at the first real uphill challenge of the day. Hopefully, the runner in you will not hate the challenge though as you could instead continue after the Packhorse Bridge along a path to a lighter incline that would take you on to Plucksbridge Road but which runner chickens out?

After jumping more steps, you will hear more and more traffic after the semi-peaceful lake area. Soon you will reach the busy Strines Road. The B6101 road is edged with middle class residential houses and flying four-wheel drives. Step over the last steps, made of stone, with care, and onto the thoroughfare.

You can turn right and head straight up this road until you reach Marple near Rose Hill and Stockport Road if you want a concrete finish. However, for more time with nature and water the Peak Forest Canal runs behind the houses, if you can get there! A public footpath sign across the road from where you joined Strines Road invites you to head up what looks like someone's drive. If you take on this challenge beware as this access route is little used and survival experts that live off their own body parts on TV would no doubt fail to enjoy tramping through the jungles of 4ft high nettles here.

If you yourself do not wish to risk the nettles you could run up Strines Road a little further towards Marple and then turn left up other canal access paths, pounding the towpath past bridges and cyclists with towpath rage eager to ring their bell at you if you dare to block their route. There are also barges with friendlier owners.

After jumping on the towpath near Strines Road turn right, the towpath and bridges naturally take you across the canal. Run around 0.5 miles further on and you will reach the marina/mooring area at Top Lock, Marple Locks. This is where many barge owners come to train to dip their way through the close succession of 16 locks that make up Marple Locks and where the Peak Forest Canal meets Macclesfield Canal. You will see to the left a sign for Stoke-on-Trent, 33 miles away, and Middlewich some 40 miles away (if you are ambitious or energetic enough!)

Again you have a choice about routes here because from Top Lock you can run along the left hand side of the Macclesfield Canal instead of the Peak Forest Canal and after a short distance turn off the towpath to your right and onto Church Lane. At the end of this lane, turn left onto Stockport Road and run for about 0.25 miles to Rose Hill Station. Yet more enticingly you can take the route whereby you run alongside the numerous locks from Top Lock and see the splendour of civil engineering from way back and run under and through stone tunnelling viewing the surrounding lands as you go.

Instead of heading back from Rose Hill some people will find train access better from Marple Station on Brabyns Brow. If so, when you have seen enough of Marple Locks run north or south to the point where Station Road crosses over the Peak Forest Canal and jump on to concrete and head down Brabyns Brow to Marple Station.

Advantages:
- Stunning countryside and scenery.
- Good access for two train stations that serve Manchester and many stops along the way.

Disadvantages:
- You can be slowed by other leisure users, especially at weekends, such as cyclists, canoeists, dog walkers, ramblers!
- Though Marple Locks are interesting they can be slippery in bad weather and tricky to run on.

Summary:
A see-the-sights run rather than a stamina or speed test but you are surrounded by beautiful, mellow countryside, civil engineering and a wealth of hidden history in this very polite, quiet place for peace.

Mileage:
3 to 3.25 miles.

The fairytale humpback Packhorse Bridge at Strines.

History:

5,000 of Marple's 7,000 acres of land are in the green belt but that was not always the case. The area was once a bustling place for workers and deliveries to mills that peppered the canal and river basin. Marple was handily placed for having natural water to power mill wheels and to obtain raw products such as limestone from the nearby moorland, which came from the Peak District to Buxworth by tramway and was then ferried along the area's canal network to places with industry including Marple. (See Marple route.)

Where Lakes Road crosses the River Goyt buildings used to stand that were once connected to mill owner Samuel Oldknow, hence one of the nearby road names. His Mellor Lodge and his mill manager's Marple Lodge sat on different sides of the river (had to keep class barriers, you know) but Oldknow's house became a girl's school in the 1930s before being abandoned and sadly demolished in 1949.

Once you cross the bridge near the bottom of Lakes Road and bear right you reach the scene where the mill once sat. Oldknow had owned the 400ft (122m) long Mellor Mill or Bottom's Mill as it was known (hence the name Bottom's Mill Road). The mill was powered by three water wheels, one 22ft (6.7m) in diameter but no doubt not reminiscent of those at fairgrounds to the many children who worked at the mill. Though the pauper children, said to be from Clerkenwell in London, were treated well – by orphans and paupers standards – they worked for 4s or 20p a week, grinding for 13 hours a day (almost like the effort required for these running routes). It was said to be the biggest cotton mill of its kind in the North West in its heyday and employed 550 people.

In the 1780s, about 70 per cent of the increased 3,000 person population of Mellor worked in the textile industry. Industrialization came in about the 1760s and Mellor Mill was built between 1790 and 1792. The mill was ravaged by fire in 1892 but the nearby Corn Mill survived until the 1930s. Now, no sign of either survives.

The Roman Lakes, misleadingly named, have a history dating back to 1086, not quite to Julius Caesar. In the Victorian and Edwardian times hundreds of tourists visited the Roman Lakes for leisure pursuits, taking trains out to the country to drink in the tearooms and float around the dance hall. Indeed, it is said one-armed bandits still sat on the site ready to arm-wrestle visitors out of their shillings in the 1960s.

Between the Roman Lakes and the weir is Mill Lade, the name for a watercourse or re-directed water channel that was used to power mills in times past. Samuel Oldknow created this lade to keep his mill running and his fabric stretching and rolling.

The 'Roman' tag which prompted the name Roman Lakes was said by the Marple Local History Society to have been dreamt up in the Victorian era to add romanticism and was often applied to the Packhorse Bridge or humpback bridge that leads up the hillside to Strines Road. The bridge itself is built of stone and dates back to the 17th century. It seems to have stone posts positioned there, perhaps once holding a gateway or toll to charge those crossing the River Goyt.

Thanks to Oldknow's entrepreneurial spirit (and his large mill) a network of roads, railway lines and canals came to this quiet country area which may otherwise have been a little cut-off. There are hopes that the vast history of Marple and many historical artefacts can one day be housed at a museum in the town. Indeed one Mellor couple's discovery of crop marks in their garden in 1995, which went on to unearth an Iron Age Hilltop Settlement and 10,000 years of archaeological evidence is a fascinating find.

Useful Websites:

www.marple-uk.co.uk
A website detailing walks around Marple, heritage and photography and links with Marple Locks Heritage Society.

www.mellorheritageproject.org.uk
Look into the magnificent discoveries of 10,000 years of history from Mesolithic to Bronze Age to Roman and Mediaeval archaeological finds in the area.

www.romanlakes.co.uk
Learn of the area's nature trail, history trail and other activities.

Contacts:

Roman Lakes
Lakes Road
Marple
SK6 7HB
Tel: 0161 427 2039
Email: info@romanlakes.co.uk

Top Lock Marine
5A Lime Kiln Lane
Marple
SK6 6BX
Tel: 0161 427 5712
Email: Info@toplocktraining.co.uk

Running Hill Head

Moor tops please

Ever think you have gone over the top with your running? Not until you have tried this route. This 4-miler starts amidst quaint Peak District villages. After alighting the 350 bus from Oldham or Ashton-under-Lyne at Uppermill warm up near the canal there and then run up High Street, turn right onto Church Road and pass an equally rustic little village pond where the ladies save their coffee morning biscuits for the birds.

One difficulty in Uppermill is that the signposts are tiny to ensure they are in keeping with the rest of the village designs. This makes them whimsical but does not make them easy to see for pragmatic purposes, for drivers, runners and so on. Still we are not running that fast and we only need to make a couple of turnings in the pretty village. After running up Church Road the residential estates and wheelie bin numbers begin to reduce and the number of dog walkers lessens as the incline increases.

Keep on the same road as it curves round and overlooks a lovely church next to a field sometimes filled with ponies. Continue on past a burial ground, feeling half dead yourself with the incline already but enjoying the increasingly widening scenery and Church Road then becomes Running Hill Gate.

Carry straight on up the near vertical country lane surrounded by green fields and old stone walls and gradually the country lane becomes a track, a ridge between two fields, which is where ground begins to get rockier underfoot and when you have to begin to take real care about where you are stepping.

This is not a route I would recommend for everyone. You have to spend a lot of time looking down to see where your next footstep should be and that in itself can be exhausting over a long distance but without set footpaths damaged ankles upon the moor tops, especially if you are running alone, would not be a good thing. (Jane Austen's Willoughby does not visit here much.) Choose patches of gorse rather than the edges of clumps of grass and the running is more like leaping from spot to spot with some speed behind it.

Next climb over a very bucolic stile alongside a country gate. Then step alongside, or carefully over, a cattle grid. Then to your left Running Hill Gate meets Running Hill Lane. You could turn right here and head along Baker's Lane but for the route covered here the gradient continues!

Run straight on for over 0.25 miles more and not long into this stretch you step onto Peak District National Park land. To your right on a little area of private land you may see water dripping off giant rocks carved out of the landscape. Not that you are encouraged to encroach on private land but you are likely to hear the dripping of the waters in this very solitary and even eerie place from what footpath there is at this point, ground out of the grass.

On a day filled with brilliant sunshine the wind and the dripping sound are all you can hear in this spot, which allows brilliant views to the north and over moorland to the east and also a hazy look at central Manchester on some days, to the west.

Continue past the dripping water rocks and after reaching the disused Running Hill Pits area turn to your right but look behind you for a spot on the horizon to keep checking back to, that way you will know if you run off course, especially to your left, as that is the worst option here. You want to head over the top of the hills to Holmfirth Road and have a stunning view of Yeoman Hey and Dove Stone Reservoirs.

Basically you want to head south to meet Holmfirth Road but you might choose to run over this land via Broadstone Moss and Broadstone Hill or via the less respectably named Dick Hill but whichever route you embark upon here you are guaranteed no footpath.

This area once housed quarries and there are the remnants of little buildings used by the workmen and worn areas of ground where carts must have been dragged along the earth but this route is not for the faint-hearted. It really is not a route for those new to running or professional sports people for that matter whose ankles are worth a fortune and do not want to risk injury. This route is a tester. It would be good for someone training for a long distance race or marathon. A stamina builder.

When running this route the soggy peat areas are like quicksand and if you get sucked up when running up here alone you could be stranded for quite some time. Leap from gorse and heather covered areas to flat, stable looking rocks but you should take great care with the rocks on wet days, avoiding the cutting megaliths and slurping peat bogs.

Having briefly landed one foot in the peat to then have it steal my trainer and see steam coming from my footwear (from solid hard running energy, not bad aromas, I think) I had to wrestle nature to get my trainer back or face a one-legged race for the final 2 to 2.5 miles. This is taxing.

If you cannot stomach so 'routeless' an existence you could leave Running Hill Gate for Pobgreen Lane and follow footpaths across Primrose Hill and past the old quarries but if you did so you would miss the wilderness, height and testing inclines of the full Running Hill Gate and surrounds.

After seeing a lonely, wind-battered tree on top of the moors and feeling like the only soul on earth, free of all earthly concerns and on top of the world, you look out on the other side soon after to see Dove Stone Reservoir. It is set in a valley surrounded by plantations spoilt only by the fact that a stonking great A-road crosses horizontally in front of you with cars travelling on to Yorkshire at break-neck speeds.

After hurdling over barbed wire the good thing about reaching the road is that for most of it there is a footpath and thus solid ground again. The views are again spectacular but largely less wild towards Yeoman Hey Reservoir, Irontongue Hill, Dove Stone Reservoir and the weir and less wild still throughout the valley towards Greenfield.

You will start to be greeted by airless cyclists forcing themselves uphill as you look smugly at the downhill journey to your right. Run down Holmfirth Road for about 1.5 miles and into the valley. Once Holmfirth Road becomes less rural and houses start appearing the road changes to Manchester Road, Greenfield and you can get a bus back to Ashton-under-Lyne or Oldham here. Instead you can continue to run up Manchester Road and on footpaths alongside the road and the River Tame to quieten the runner's spirit for another day – and crank up your mileage returning from Mossley.

Advantages:
- Stunning scenery. You are visiting the top of the world!
- A taste of moorland solitude without being too far (well) from transport.

Disadvantages:
- No real set paths so it can be dangerous to ankles if you don't take care.
- A route that needs planning the first few visits, maybe even a day off work. This is more fell running than jogging around the estate to get trim.

Draw me in to Running Hill Head.

- Not a travel-light route. You really need maps and water for this one.
- It may be good to take a fellow established runner in case of accidents but this would destroy the solitude of the run.

Summary:
One of the most breathtaking routes imaginable but one which could easily afford injury. It requires planning, daylight and a real desire to run on free land. Perhaps a once or twice a year treat for the established city centre based runner but not a beginner's route.

Mileage:
4.75 miles.

History:
As Running Hill Head is such an isolated location, a place of fields and farmland, its history, at least that known by anyone other than long term locals, is short or fairly unknown.

Running Hill Head Pits look out over Diggle and are a favourite with rock climbers. Nearby Ravenstone Rocks are thought to have got their name after the Roman occupation around AD5 of the area to the west of what is now West Yorkshire was called Rheged. It is said it covered modern day Cumbria and Lancashire, sub-dividing into North and South Rheged, hence some people connecting the sound of the Roman name with that of place names such as Ravenstone.

Many gatherings of rocks in this high area – excellent for looking out across the horizon – are once thought to have been sentry posts or boundaries upon the hills that are the long-standing natural boundary between the east and west of northern England.

Useful Websites:
www.fellrunner.org.uk
Get details on results, up and coming race meetings and even details of race cancellations.
www.peakdistrict.gov.uk
Information for visitors, teachers, walkers and of course runners on where to visit and what to see.
radicalmanchester.wordpress.com/2009/11/24/benny-rothman-and-the-1932-kinder-scout-mass-trespass
Read about the battle to try and free the lands for the people.

Contacts:
Peak District National Park Authority
Aldern House
Baslow Road
Bakewell
DE45 1AE
Tel: 01629 816310
Email: customer.service@peakdistrict.gov.uk

Stamford Park & Canal Course

Layer it up baby!

After trekking across the city centre in an attempt to get a train and then going back to Piccadilly Gardens for a bus out to Ashton-under-Lyne I was glad to finally see the east Manchester town which seems to be getting more superstores and more super-sized with every year.

After trying to warm up between the bus station and train station juggling an A–Z and backpack the size of Kilimanjaro and watched by helpful onlookers with pints and cigarettes in their hands, I was glad to get concrete crunching. Who knows what's round the next corner?

On this route though you should turn right from the bus station, head up Wellington Road, continue up Penny Meadow and where it reaches a complicated triangle with Crickets Lane and Mossley Road the simplest route is to then run along Beaufort Road which is on your right. It is also easiest as far as your feet and lungs go as there is a slight decline after you pass Tameside College.

Go straight to the end of Beaufort Road then at the end turn left down Stamford Square and you should then see on your left the gates to one entrance of Stamford Park. Just inside there is a map of the municipal masterpiece (not to be confused with Stamford Park in Altrincham, Trafford). For this route it is best if you go up the right hand or Astley Road side in the direction of the Rose Gardens, up to the boating lake just over Darnton Road and back down the originally left side, the Mellor Road side. That way you are probably going up the steepest side but it is better on wet days and may be better for getting your bearings at times.

On the day I ran it, however, delighted as I was to reach grassland for my shins sake, it then started raining in June…then thundering and lightning and then throwing down hailstones the size of blueberries – five a day I could definitely have lived without. I will run through most conditions but I had to join four park workers, a drenched new Mum and sleeping baby and another couple of park visitors gathered in a shelter pretending not to be scared by one of the worst storms I've ever seen in England.

After about 30 minutes with toes uncurled just enough to run I went up to the boating lake, via temporary swampland thanks to the downpour and back down through small but beautiful woodland on the other side. Down the Mellor Road side you will see woodland, cascading waterfalls which are particularly visible on rainy days and gargoyles in some walls and bridges from the days when the land belonged to the elite and was part of a deer farm. Extreme as the conditions were, it has to be said there can be rivers of water on the established footpaths forcing you onto swampy turf, so maybe it is not the best parkland to run through in extremely bad weather.

After reaching the starting gates of the park again cross Stamford Street, turn right and very swiftly left, to run down Clarence Street (further away from Stamford Square) and head along the road which crosses over the Huddersfield Narrow Canal.

Don't be tempted to detour thinking that is the best way to reach the towpath when you see some steps off the main footpath, as that is railway land. After about 0.25 miles you will see a mill and a big chimney, which indicates the canal but you must get onto the towpath on the right hand side of Clarence Street, on the side of the canal furthest from Stamford Park. You would run towards the mill for Stalybridge but this *OTRAM* route takes you in the other direction so go left away from the mill…and if you are unfortunate, towards some hissing geese protecting their young.

Though you won't see much of the town itself you are soon running behind Dukinfield. Your route will show you lovely old locks and canal bridges but nice as they are to view, the towpath narrows. Some of the bridges and other parts are cobbled so it can make a slippery path at times, or one risky for ankles if not tackled with care. But we runners have trod on tougher turf than this.

After about 0.75 miles some steps distract you from the main towpath and towards a massive railway viaduct under which you will hear the River Tame running. You can't see the river clearly in many places here and along the earlier canal but don't be too annoyed because you have to get off the towpath here anyway; so even if the view was open you would have to leave it as the towpath ends temporarily at the next bridge. Cross the Asda car park, seeing another vast mill and chimney to your left and head down the side of some industrial buildings across the road. Signs will show you the Huddersfield Narrow Canal which you just ran, to your right and the Ashton Canal to your left. Now it is time to head left onto the Ashton Canal.

Soon after this on the Ashton Canal you will pass a Sea Cadets branch, despite us being inland and some aptly named barges may be around. Then you can see some beautiful humped, cobbled bridges and charming crossings and at one point, the Portland Basin. The Ashton Canal which you are pounding along crosses over the Peak Forest Canal, which crosses over the River Tame. It is more like a watercourse than a dry run but an interesting sight.

On wet days here, as with many other towpaths, it isn't necessarily a mudbath everywhere but you tend to end up running forwards, do a semi-circle up the banking round a puddle, forwards again, up the bank round a puddle again in a repetitive motion like an inebriated snake! This aspect of rustic towpath running can feel like an exercise class on some days...unless you are prepared to get your feet thoroughly soaked. Yet this canal affords some stretches of real pleasure with green foliage and dancing light, especially in the right weather and it has more charm than tarmacked towpaths.

Keep pounding and you will begin to see railway sidings on your left which means you are close to Guide Bridge Station, your finish line. You will pass under or go past a dainty looking bridge which leads to your right, onto Pottinger Street. Don't take that route but it is a good indicator of where you are up to, less than 0.25 miles from the station itself.

At this stage there is the towpath and a sort of secondary towpath higher up the same side, nearer the railway sidings. Soon you will see a brown, wooden railway bridge to your left. If you want to get back to Manchester city centre run over this and across the car park to the station.

After the endless sidings and commercial train parking areas the passenger station seems a little lost but very welcome at the end of a run probably only 3 to 3.5 miles in length but taxing in bad weather with cold, wet feet you haven't felt for some time! The car park does offer a good space to stretch off. You will need the opposite platform for trains on the Marple or Hadfield lines but you are nearly home.

Instead of using the railway bridge you could keep pounding the towpath briefly until the canal reaches the junction of Audenshaw Road, Stockport Road and Guide Lane. You will again see Guide Bridge Train Station and St Stephen's Church here to help you get your bearings.

Advantages:
- A full range of terrain: concrete, parkland, canal towpaths, cobbled bridges.
- The paths are surrounded by interesting things to see such as Portland Basin, old red mills, historical bridges, the River Tame, a viaduct and barges.

- There are numerous chances and choices. You can adapt the route, cut pieces of the route out, change waterways. You could run to Ducie Street in central Manchester or the route has cycleways and towpaths that guide you. On another occasion you could run the Huddersfield Narrow Canal out to Stalybridge and beyond.

Disadvantages:
- Perhaps not the best route on dark, wet nights – you could easily fall into the water and the canal section would not be good for the vulnerable running alone at night.
- Watch out for closing time changes at Stamford Park, especially in winter.
- Getting to Ashton-under-Lyne in the first place is sometimes more time-consuming than you may expect.
- It is a shame that though you see so many mills and thus history along the way there is little information about the buildings that the town's industry was founded upon.
- There are numbers but no names and little information about the numerous bridges en route.
- Once on the towpath it is hard to jump off especially between Ashton Canal's Portland Basin and Guide Bridge.

Summary:
A route with very varied terrain and a chance to cover the hidden habitats behind urban existence. You can adapt the length once you know it better but towpaths are hard to get off at some points, especially when you are many feet above a river.

Mileage:
3.25 miles.

History:
Prince Charles reopened the Huddersfield Narrow Canal after 50 years in 2001. It stretches 20 miles from Huddersfield to Ashton-under-Lyne and has 74 locks. It has the longest canal tunnel in Britain, Standedge Tunnel and its summit is the highest navigable waterway in Britain. (See other routes.)

The Ashton Canal once had spurs to Stockport and Hollinwood and is part of the Cheshire Ring today. It links the Bridgewater and Rochdale Canals with the Huddersfield Narrow Canal and Peak Forest Canal.

Stamford Park's origins got tired workers out of a rut. Cotton mill workers, slogging six days a week wanted somewhere to relax on their day off. Living in very poor conditions during the Industrial Revolution a public space was much needed and in a report in 1844 it was said the area lacked 'convenient space for exercise'. It was felt there would be moral and physical benefit from such a space and it was urged that Lord Stamford grant land for the purpose.

By 1856, when there was still no park the cotton workers decided to raise the money for one themselves. Yet once the campaign began many different layers of society chipped in and mill owner Samuel Oldknow (see other routes) died donating £7,000 for a park and the maintenance of an infirmary in his will. By 1872 the committee instructed their solicitor Henry Darnton to buy Highfield House. This makes you wonder why we do not call the land Oldknow Park rather than Stamford Park today but the Stamford family did help.

Other information states the Stamford Park land was originally owned by Robert Lees of Hazlehurst in 1668 as a deer park named Highfields. It later became the property of mill owner

Abel Harrison. He donated Highfield House and land when he died and the Earl of Stamford gave further land on the border of Ashton and Stalybridge which was combined to make what is now the park. It finally opened in 1873 to give cotton mill workers a leisure area and there was even a ladies gymnasium – though why it was so different to a mens gymnasium is probably down to the culture of the time.

In 1891, Chadwick Dams, the former mill reservoir, was made into what is today called the boating lake and for many the park has a tradition of marking the border between Ashton-under-Lyne and Stalybridge and thus Lancashire and Cheshire.

Between 60,000 and 80,000 people were said to have turned up for the opening of the park for which £15,000 was paid on 12 July 1873. The Joseph Raynor Stephens Memorial was opened in 1888 for his work to promote a fair wage and the rock work was done by George Briggs, whose father Francis Briggs had been a landscape gardener to Joseph Paxton who designed the gardens at the Derbyshire stately home, Chatsworth House.

An aviary from the 1950s has been demolished but a replacement, thanks to changes to the park through lottery funding, is due to open in 2012.

Useful Websites:
www.ashton-under-lyne.com/places/stamfordpark
See pictures of the park and read about its history and present day activities.
www.tameside.gov.uk
Find out about opening times, friends' groups and the Stamford Park's history, but you can also look up Portland Basin here or send messages about the facilities.

Contacts:
British Waterways North West
Waterways Office
Waterside House
Waterside Drive
Wigan
WN3 5AZ
Tel: 01942 405700 (for all canals)
Email: enquiries.northwest@britishwaterways.co.uk

Portland Basin
Portland Place
Ashton-under-Lyne
OL7 0QA
Tel: 0161 343 2878

Stamford Park Friends' Group
(Meet at) Stalybridge Civic Hall
Tel: 0161 342 3348

Stockport's Vernon and Woodbank Memorial Parks

There's competition!

There is much parkland around the Manchester area, some wild, some cultivated and perhaps when compared with places on the scale of Lyme Park or Tatton Park the parks in this route don't have anywhere near the same impact. They are closer to urban life though so can prove very regular mileage-clockers and very welcome tastes of nature.

From Stockport Train Station run down the north eastern leg of Station Road, cross Wellington Road South and run up and along Wellington Street, Churchgate and Spring Gardens until you cross St Mary's Way and reach Turncroft Lane on your left. Tackling the busy streets head left again past some industrial buildings along New Zealand Road until you reach the vertical plant-covered tunnel steps of Vernon Park, which, if tackled uphill, tests your stamina and arm muscles with the sheer concrete climb.

Run past the bowling greens to your right, on past Vernon House and you should soon see the gates that mark the entrance to Woodbank Memorial Park.

Once in the park you can take the right or left hand paths and run in a loop, skirting past the Woodbabk Park Athletics Track and Woodbank House. The park's pathways offer you the chance to run on concrete or just to the edge on the grass for different terrain but you can still find your way or cut straight across sports grounds and grasslands.

Manchester as a whole is a sporting city. On a warm August evening in the school holidays but there can be runners out in threes, numerous individual runners, 20 or 30 people playing cricket, bowls, cyclists; Woodbank Memorial Park is the home of Stockport Harriers Athletics Club and, of course, a ferret walker called Andrea with 'Ben the ferret' on a lead, apparently!

In short, it is busy. Especially during summer evenings and if you like to breathe rural air and freedom when you run you can do so in nearby countryside and at neighbouring parks; but Vernon Park and Woodbank Memorial Park to generate a very communal feeling to the grassland. Some people will love the challenge of out-running others or talking to other runners. Some will just be content that the sport is so well loved.

The eastern side of the park lets you run alongside the River Goyt and is a tree-shaded pathway with a lovely taste of nature. You may run into the skateboarding area with mounds of soil and then return or head back though Woodbank over grassland but for either you should run a loop back towards Vernon Park and the north roads back into Stockport town centre.

After you run back through Vernon Park to New Bridge Lane turn left away from the River Goyt and then veer right to take a very concrete run along Carrington Road and then on to Great Portwood Street.

Great Portwood Street is where things get tricky because the centre of Stockport is like a maze. You can run the concrete and longer route – but perhaps easier route – along Knightsbridge and Great Egerton Street, then go left along Wellington Road South to turn right for Station Road. However, you could go straight on from Great Portwood Street onto Warren Street, along Merseyway, and to Chestergate and the bus station. There are signs from the bus station for a footpath to Stockport's Grand Central Train Station and Chestergate is underneath the useful Wellington Road South, which leads to Station Road and a platform home. However, it is best to stick to the A-Road of Knightsbridge then Great Egerton Street and go left up Wellington Road South to Station Road. Stockport Station can be strangely difficult to reach if you stray too far from the Wellington Road South access. Even though you can see trains high up when crossing the viaduct, you can't get to them. Stockport Train Station has rather a small entrance for quite a big terminal.

Advantages:
- The sporting feel to the parkland, especially to Woodbank Memorial Park in the summertime.
- A good regular loop; a mileage-clocker for those living in the neighbourhood.

Disadvantages:
- The parkland might feel too full of other sports and athletes.
- Central Stockport can be like navigating a mirrored maze for a newcomer.
- The parks don't give much directional information and it is easy to confuse Vernon Park with neighbouring Woodbank Memorial Park.

Summary:
Perhaps a mileage-clocker for those who live nearby but especially beautiful when laden with bluebells in springtime. You can combine sights like routes by the River Goyt with runs near the athletics tracks and seven football fields but probably more for social sport than personal bests.

Mileage:
Very dependent upon how far you run within the parks, but 3.5 to 5 miles.

History:
In Woodbank Memorial Park, Peter Marsland built the house between 1812 and 1814 with the help of architect Thomas Harrison of Chester. In 1921 the former mayor Sir Thomas Rowbotham gave Woodbank Hall and 89 acres to the town as a memorial to those who died in World War One. He then gave a further £2,000 towards the refurbishment of the house, which reopened as a museum in 1931 but closed in 1948. In 1953, glasshouses were built to replace those lost in neighbouring Vernon Park.

Vernon Park was opened in September 1858 but one of the reasons for it being so welcomed by mill workers was because of their involvement in making and building things within the grounds, which include splendours from fountains and ponds to bandstands and cannons.

The Vernon Park area was re-opened in September 2000 after a £1.6 million Heritage Lottery Fund grant and other monies amounting to over £2 million in total. The park has a museum and café. A marker on a bench was placed to commemorate the 150th anniversary of Vernon Park becoming the 'People's Park' or 'Pinch Belly Park' as it was known, on 20 September 2008.

Useful Websites:
www.dashathletics.co.uk
A family friendly club giving young people the chance to excel in athletics.

www.stockport.gov.uk
Look up the heritage of trails, ways and riverside routes as well as parkland in the council borough.

www.stockportharriers.com
Visit the website about the club which has over 400 members and does off-track training as well as running on the athletics track for more sprint orientated ambitions.

Contacts:

Dash Athletics
Email: dashathletics@yahoo.co.uk
Tel: 07863 299863 (Mike Frost, Club Secretary)
Tel: 07974 743639 (Joe Frost, Head of Coaching)
From six years to senior age groups. Train at Woodbank Memorial, Vernon Park or Hazel Grove High School.

Parks, Sport and Cemeteries
Fred Perry House
Edward Street
Stockport
SK1 3SU
Tel: 0161 217 6111
Email: parks@stockport.gov.uk

Stockport Harriers And Athletics Club
Woodbank Memorial Park
Tel: 0161 494 1604
Email: jerzygeorgesh@btinternet.com
Jerzy Matuszewski – Membership Secretary
Public Training Times:
Monday, Tuesday, Thursday: 6.30pm until 8.30pm
Sunday: 10.30am until 12.30pm

Vernon Park Museum
Turncroft Lane
Offerton
Stockport
SK1 4AR
Tel: 0161 474 4460
Email: parks@stockport.gov.uk
Largely used as a business or conference venue but still a part of the park's heritage.

Falling through light in Stockport's Vernon Park.

Styal Country Park

Wellies and wax oils

Wealthy as this area appears, with the main roads filled with darting four-wheel drives and sports cars, Styal Country Park could also be described as a rose between several thorns. Parts of the park are less than 0.5 miles away from Manchester Airport on one side and about the same distance from Wilmslow on the other, meaning that if you start your run from Wilmslow Station you may have to avoid a humming sea of oversized commuting vehicles which could almost challenge America for planet rotting emissions.

Aside from gases, parts of Wilmslow are very charming as you run either right along Station Road, down Swan Street, right onto Church Street past the church along Chancel Lane. Then continue along Cliff Road before turning left down Styal Road towards the park. That is a route with more character. Yet you could go from Station Road (after going right at the station), right again along Manchester Road, over a roundabout and continue along Manchester Road until you turn left, again onto Styal Road.

Either route will take you to the southern edge of one of the most underrated spaces in Manchester. Although many visitors travel to Styal Country Park to see Quarry Bank Mill and the museum, which can mean, depending on timing, you are running around crowds of schoolchildren on trips, aside from dog walkers few people seem to come to appreciate the nature itself and its beauty. At Wilmslow Station signs often advertise the beauty of Tatton Park's manicured plant-life when Styal's nearby stunning nature seems to be almost ignored. In the autumn, however, the park is breathtaking in colour and vivacity and you don't tend to notice how low the planes ready to land nearby are because of the height of the trees and the sound of raining conkers.

Some runners may be tempted to get public transport to the airport and head out to the park from there. Though when tested it could be thought a bit risky because if you take the Ringway Road West route, the four-wheel drive owners haven't bothered to furnish us leg-users with luxuries such as pavements. It seems few people head out this way on foot.

If you decide to leave the airport in the other direction and do a massive loop of Thornley Lane, Runger Lane, Wilmslow Road and Altrincham Road, it is a gargantuan route and very lonely with some stretches through motorist tunnels and the need to run along a service type road like those near motorways. You can also lose your way more easily in the airport's concrete jungle on the sections closest to the airport bus station.

Therefore, you can either get a train to Wilmslow Station, Styal Station, or Heald Green if you want a longer concrete run into the park (down Styal Road and Hollin Lane). Or you can get a bus to Styal. If you wish to bring your own vehicle here there are plenty of parking spaces within the park though it is perhaps a little more of a squeeze on sunny weekends when the estate vehicles filled with six dogs at a time unload…and unload…and unload.

From Styal Road one route into the park is near Twinnies Bridge. Once off the road which crosses the river at this point, there is a footpath that runs directly through the park towards Quarry Bank Mill. It is nice but this path runs straight through fields alone. If you head slightly to your left you can follow the line of the river towards the mill seeing some absolutely stunning natural colours skirting the water, with bronze and red plants edging the riverbanks. The waters are so beautiful they are reminiscent of a Japanese lake.

This is a National Trust park and so much better maintained than some areas around Manchester which are heaped with litter and there are also many bridges across the River

Bollin. Some of the structures are fenced off on the south side of Quarry Bank Mill, so when running your route ensure you can cross the river (or have the extra energy to find another bridge).

After running a winding path alongside the waters, sometimes in tunnels created by various trees' branches meeting overhead, then passing a weir, you will be greeted by Quarry Bank Mill itself and its gentle gardens. Areas here have cobbles underfoot but also explosions in footfall after your relative peace. This would be a good place to leave relatives while you went running on a weekend but can be a burden because of the number of tourists to navigate around at times.

Keep running up the steep path behind the mill area. At one point along the river there is a giant tree trunk that has fallen, which crosses the width of the river. It hasn't been put there by staff, it isn't park 'furniture' but for those that have seen the film *Dirty Dancing* and who are desperate to see the woodland on the other side of the river…Get someone to talk you out of your temptation to test your balance on it! Freezing and sliding off when perched high above a river, especially on a rainy day, can be a daunting experience.

Stay on the right hand side of the river as you head north. This leads away from the tourists at the mill to some winding footpaths and heavy tree coverage, making it extra dark at night but majestic with seasonal colour. After the footpath dips again you head down to the River Bollin where you can see a second weir through the trees, gushing out frothing waters.

After this the pathways skirt Styal village, yet if you turn left through a stile or kissing gate you can continue down into a narrow valley made by the River Bollin. It is even more dense in its woodland and even more like something from a fairytale than earlier riverside spots with its wooden humpback and stone bridges, some drowning in foliage. You will pass or run across

Bridging the seasons in Styal Country Park.

Chapel Bridge, Heron's Pool Bridge, Kingfisher Bridge and Oxbow Bridge along this section of the run. This area is much quieter than the tourist magnet mill area. It is also more testing for the runner with steps and steeper pathways than the flatter area at the Wilmslow end of the park.

About 0.25 to 0.5 miles later you should see the private Norcliffe Hall to your right. Although that land is private, a roadway behind it should lead onto Altrincham Road and past Styal Cricket Ground pavilion. Turn right at the end to run through Styal village and return to Manchester via Styal Train Station or run the Hollin Lane, Styal Road route back to Wilmslow. If you do head back to Wilmslow again be aware of the steep dipping road with no pavements at times. It may be good for testing calf muscles but motorists seem to want to test their vehicles out on it too.

If you continue along the river for too long, tempting as the sight may be it just opens out into very lonely land and you shouldn't follow too far after Norcliffe Hall or Bollin Giant's Castle Rocks. Heading north will leave you with the aforementioned Heald Green public transport options or services from the airport.

Continuing south however, head past the former orphanage which was made into a women's prison in 1962. You can't help considering it is a strange place to put offenders really when Styal and Wilmslow are so wealthy and picturesque, yet the prison had one of the highest suicide rates in England and Wales in 2003. How the other half live. Yet it should remind those of us who are running that we have the freedom to keep pounding…well, you are only 1 mile or so from Wilmslow.

You can cut back onto the parkland or stay on Styal Road for the last stretch of the loop back, heading back up Cliff Road or you can cross the river within the park and find a steep footpath which takes you past Wilmslow Rugby Club's ground and onto the more residential King's Road.

At the end turn left onto another Altrincham Road (the A538) and run towards Lindow Common. Considering this area is famous for the almost 2,000-year-old man found buried there, very little is actually stated about him on the signs or plaques which detail flowers and animals. Still the area is beautiful. Again, a rose between thorns as it is surrounded by a residential loop and heavily subscribed roads; but it has Black Lake within it, which can look stunning on a sunny day and the Common has numerous pathways for runners to cover. This extra coverage of King's Road, Altrincham Road, around Lindow Common and onto Altrincham Road again until it leads to Water Lane, Alderley Road and Station Road could add as much as another 2 miles to your run. It could perhaps be part of a one off longer run but may be better suited to runners living nearby who want a regular route, rather than it being a finish for tired feet that have already covered Styal Country Park and surrounds.

Advantages:
- Stunning scenery.
- Somewhere to park-up safely.
- Miles of woodland pathways, open fields and concrete roads to cover.

Disadvantages:
- You are restricted to crossing the river at certain points.
- Wilmslow's traffic is horrendous but the station there is much better served than Styal and easier to reach than Manchester airport.

- Visiting the mill and gardens can prove costly. (See the website.)
- The country area itself can make for a short run if you don't include Wilmslow or Styal village.

Summary:
A stunning country retreat, well-kept paths, with charming weirs and bridges but like a hard sweet, less likable on the exterior but lovely in the centre. The surroundings can provide the runner with distance but are less attractive and in parts dangerous because of traffic levels.

Mileage:
Wilmslow to Styal return 4 miles, Airport Ringway route to Styal 2.25 miles, Airport Runger route to Styal 3.25 miles.

History:
Quarry Bank Mill is a Georgian reminder of the Industrial Revolution with displays of how cotton was made into cloth and with Europe's most powerful working waterwheel to inspire you to keep moving!

Lindow Common has Black Lake at its centre, in Welsh Ilyn ddu, which is where the name Lindow came from. Lindow Man was a body from the first century AD, well preserved because of the nature of the peat bog. He was found at the nearby Lindow Moss. The body was found in 1984 and is now kept at the British Museum.

Lindow Man was about 25 years old, about 10.25 stone (65kg) in weight and may have been the victim of a sacrifice. He was struck at the back of the head with an axe, suffered a knee to his back which broke a rib, was strangled and had his throat slit after death. It seems that someone disliked him! It is said that all he got as a last meal was charred bread. Good for carb levels, at least.

The peat bog of the area preserved his body to give scientists evidence and they used radiocarbon dating to tell when he was around. Other human parts have been found there but Lindow II, as he is officially tagged, is the most famous find.

The heathland area of the common was used as vital grazing land in centuries past so your feet are running over historic land for many reasons on this route.

Useful Websites:
www.britishmuseum.org/explore/highlights/highlight_objects/pe_prb/l/lindow_man.aspx
Find out about visiting Lindow Man at The British Museum in London.
www.nationaltrust.org.uk/main/w-quarrybankmillandstyalestate
National Trust information on Quarry Bank Mill, Styal Country Park opening times and contact details as well as information on other parks and estates.

Contacts:
Styal Country Park
Tel: 01625 445896
Email: quarrybankmill@nationaltrust.org.uk

Swineshaw Reservoirs and Moor

Reaching the top of the world

The forthcoming section of running is spectacular but first you must do the dull bit and get a bus straight to Brushes or Besom Lane off Huddersfield Road, Millbrook, from Hyde, Stalybridge, Ashton or Oldham, although some services are only hourly.

On Huddersfield Road you should see entrances to Stalybridge Country Park near Brushes Road and a little way up Besom Road. Both of these roads border Walkerwood, Brushes and Lower and Higher Swineshaw Reservoirs. This is confusing because about 1.5 miles further north, up Huddersfield Road there is another Stalybridge Country Park entrance – and they don't seem connected landwise. The pieces of land are considered part of the same park officially but they are separate areas of land one at Carrbrook and the other at Millbrook. The park areas are only connected via access footpaths and not one big stretch of continuous green parkland.

Back near the major area of parkland at Brushes you can enter the land just off Besom Lane, near what is now the closed Commercial public house or near the Brushes Road area between the Commercial and the equally closed Prince of Hearts. One of the problems with this route is that you are spoilt for choice with pathways near Brushes, some of which are poorly signposted.

It is best to enter off Besom Lane and begin to head towards Walkerwood Reservoir's left hand side. It seems that this area was once frequented by more visitors and it was home for more farmers but now it is almost resident free. There is a chain of reservoirs in this section of the park and it is this and the surrounding scenery your run is really here to encapsulate.

With the love of the open countryside and freedom it embodies, you may want to run up the more natural, greener right hand side of the reservoirs as you look at them from the bottom of the first one, Walkerwood. However, it is best to run up the established tarmac lane on the left hand side rather than trying to find separate footpaths on the right as there is no set pathway to serve alongside the waters at reservoir height.

Yet like a continental driver on English roads if you love the exploring element of running and hate to see all that open countryside, grass and moorland without your feet visiting it, you cannot help but edge to the right, running across little bridges and up banks between the reservoirs, which in themselves are like a speed test up Mount Everest.

No matter how you veer and how many ruined old stiles and signs of earlier footfall you see, you cannot run up the right hand side of these reservoirs on one long path. The only way to try to see them from the right would be to run on the moorland tops near Mottram-in-Longdendale and Hobson Moor (see other routes) and that is too detached from this run and much higher than the height of the waters you visit to run this route.

So, perhaps reluctantly at first, plod up the tarmac lane which hems the left of the reservoirs to enjoy good views of the surrounding Pennine hills. There are strips of trees or woodland between the lane and man-made lakes. Along this path you may see hungry horses wanting you to stop and feed and pet them and one or two stone houses quietly placed away from city life. There is a large gate before the stone houses, providing you with the temptation to go right again but that would leave you needing to return frustrated to the original path. As you climb the tarmacked lane, which one runner said is 'hard work' it inclines noticeably after the second reservoir, Brushes Reservoir, and it 'brushes' away more than fatigue.

You reach a block of knobbly concrete on your left and over the stone wall on your right you can look back over Brushes and Walkerwood Reservoirs to see Manchester's city centre landmarks. You could also see them upon reaching Walkerwood, peeping through the v-shape made by the hills on both sides of the valley, yet seeming amazingly close considering how rural the vantage point feels.

It is captivating up here, especially on a sunny day. The earlier part of the lane was dotted with blackberry bushes but now it veers around to the left looking much more open, lonely and wild. The hills that you've watched since Besom Lane or Brushes Road are shrinking, or rather you have climbed them, a good sign for any runner's sense of achievement.

The path gets more gravel-like or stony as you climb a little further and veers to the left as you reach the end of the run alongside Lower Swineshaw Reservoir. This is likely to be the last time you'll see any other people, on a wet weekday certainly, yet in summer I met around eight to 10 people near this stretch; cyclists and dog walkers looking at us 'runner creatures' puzzlingly.

You do not get to see much of Lower Swineshaw Reservoir because of trees but you are probably drinking in the colours and patterns of the land. In summer the hills on the right hand side of the chain of reservoirs with Hobson and Hollingworthall Moors atop are bleached yellow from sunlight. Beyond Higher Swineshaw you will see Irontongue Hill. Yet your left hand, more shaded side, is covered in purple heather. This side is Harridge Pike, exploding with colour in early autumn and with views of Buckton Quarry.

At the end of this testing lane there is a signpost and a bench welcoming you to the final reservoir in the chain, Higher Swineshaw Reservoir. Here you can breathe in well-earned fresh air from Pennine hills and Peak District Moors. You can see the colours on the hills and moors around you: bleached yellow grasses, rolling carpets of purple heather, or the green of England depending on the season and the side of Brushes Valley you view.

If you run to the right you can look back down the chain of giant ponds and see the city dazzling in the distance, while being dazzled by the natural beauty of your surroundings. You can look up to the stone walls and moorland tracks of places such as Hobson Moor on the right of the reservoirs as you approached.

However, you can also head towards the sign for Tintwistle, right from Higher Swineshaw as you approached, then left and head past a gate, onto a bridleway and then over a stile to reach the fantastically named Irontongue Hill. The land here can be very uneven but the scenery towards Chew Valley and Longdendale unmissable. The grazing sheep are unlikely to be happy to see you but you will be happy with further, even higher views, this time of Chew Reservoir, Tintwistle, Mottram Church, further north, east and south. Then look and head back with care towards the sight of the chain of reservoirs you have just conquered and Manchester itself.

Up here there are many places to see, which at times offer 360 degrees of pure, stunning, stimulating, wild, beautiful Peak District land, spoilt only by electricity pylons sitting like unwanted guests at a picnic.

Near Higher Swineshaw Reservoirs I met a skinny pensioner, well, a man soon to reach his 65th birthday, named Steve Clegg who has been running in the area since his youth, first as a cross-country runner at school and then he used to run for East Cheshire Harriers. He had a better knowledge of every track and dustway on the tops than Ordnance Survey.

Steve told me nostalgically that there used to be a farm up near Higher Swineshaw, serving tea in the 1950s and a boy scout outdoor pursuits centre towards Lower Swineshaw. I don't know if his local history was as strong as his geography but Steve said he had to rest up more with his running these days. The pensioner now only covers 8 miles three times a week!

185

Kissed on the winds around Harridge and Irontongue Hill.

Looking on with nodding understanding and not mentioning mere 10-mile weekly targets, I let Steve run off so he could 'eat what he wanted and enjoy a pint' because of his training.

When it is time to leave this, if not secret garden, then semi-forgotten wilderness, you can head back down the tarmacked lane you ran up, alongside the reservoirs but this time downhill. Disappointingly after all that effort the signpost informs you that it is only 1.5 miles to Brushes Valley but the upwards leg of that stretch felt like a marathon

For variety and to cover as much of this raw Eden as you can, as it would rarely be a weekly run for most people. It is very tempting to go to the left of this last Higher Swineshaw Reservoir (as you approached on your run) towards Buckton Quarry and round Harridge Pike. If you do for another magical vantage point, you must stick to the footpath here as you approach the looming hill after Higher Swineshaw before you bear right and follow the sweeping signposted, sandy footpath round.

The path you are heading for is not directly left of the path as you were approaching Higher Swineshaw but sort of 10 o'clock on a watch dial from there. To turn left and then bear left would take you on a footpath-less route to try to continue to run back over the tops and is frustrating because of the lack of footpath, unless you wanted to view more than run, as with Irontongue Hill.

On the set footpath, once over the main incline of this craggy, rocky, sandy and even at some points possibly dangerous stretch heading north, you can see Buckton Vale Quarry across a divide and the suburbs of Carrbrook and Millbrook and all their residential life. You can see the city often in a haze and you can see Hartshead Pike across the valley, the landmark near Ashton-under-Lyne and the wind-power generators on the tops beyond them.

You climb a last stile next to a gate and urban existence begins to re-appear. Shortly after the footpath veers right you then have to decide whether to go left or right. Turn left to reach Huddersfield Road via Besom Lane at Millbrook, where you began. Or you can run right towards the signs for the Tame Path and the Pennine Bridleway (PBW) and run towards Carrbrook.

Either way the stresses you escaped and the tingling sensation of freedom on the moors seem to begin to swap positions as you hear blasting music and sirens. Dog walkers and more and more homes appear; the speeding cars and kids with toys all increase in numbers. However, as the gradient and downhill motion take you off the tops with amazing pace, especially when trying to catch a once an hour bus, you miss the land already but it leaves you with a staggering sense of well-being.

If you know Manchester's landmarks these viewpoints amaze you. If you don't know Manchester's landmarks they amaze you. This is a breathtaking route by any standards. The height is staggering and apart from the odd creature that looks like a wallaby, for many parts there is more solitude here than Wuthering Heights could muster.

Sorry to break the reverie but you could, of course, at this point cross Stamford Golf Course and join the Tame path; run down to Spring Bank Lane / Grove Road instead and join the Huddersfield Narrow Canal towpath back to Stalybridge centre. Or, after all that moorland air, just get the bus from here back to Stalybridge or Manchester centre.

Advantages:
- You cover almost every type of terrain.
- Stunning scenery to the point where your mind, body and soul are stimulated by the views.
- It allows you to climb to the tops along safe, not uneven, tarmac with less dancing over moorland clumps of grass and heather.
- It is not far distance-wise from the Brushes – but it is not exactly effortless!
- It allows you laps of hill repeats that aren't really that long – one of the best ways to strengthen legs when running.

Disadvantages:
- Getting lost if you stray from the path and maps are scarce as many fringe rather than cover this area.
- Too vast a choice of pathways and potential other routes in the early stages (via Brushes) and then no open access alongside the reservoirs, just the left hand side path.
- You could injure yourself on the moorland terrain and unevenness. Buckton Quarry area is quite rocky and dangerous and you may need trail running shoes if you become a regular.
- There is no stopping for an energy drink here so you may need to take supplies.

Summary:
A short run offering a vast mixture of reservoirs, rural parkland and moorland peat bogs and tarmacked lanes to give a circuit or a return journey run which is easy to extend but the terrain and need to stick to paths must be respected on the tops.

Mileage:
Either Besom or Brushes return route or Harridge Pike circuit 3 miles.

History:
Buckton Castle was built on the site of a pre-historic fort. It was a 12th-century Bailey Castle and Norman Motte or mediaeval ringwork. It has been protected as a Scheduled Ancient Monument since 1924. It sits on top of a sand ridge 1099ft (335m) above sea level near Carrbrook.

This, the oldest surviving building in Tameside, would have been built from wood and stone, local materials, as a defence building. Such structures were not created after the reign of Henry II (1154–89) so it may have been one of the last of its kind to be erected.

Building began on the chain of reservoirs: Walkerwood, Brushes, Lower Swineshaw and Higher Swineshaw in about 1864 in order to serve the fluid needs of the population towards Manchester. Indeed, in other parts of Tameside the supply of water was so important to the culture of the time that well-dressings, ceremonies almost revering the source of water supplies took place, adorning the structures and surrounding them with flowers. Such ceremonies still take place annually in areas like Gee Cross.

Stalybridge Country Park was created in the early 1990s and saw off plans to put a tipping site in the Brushes area of the town. It had a Countryside Visitors' Centre but park volunteers said it closed in 2009 because of local government cuts. The Pennine Bridleway passes through the park.

Useful Websites:
www.carrbrookvillage.users.btopenworld.com/warden
Let wardens show you the rural routes they know well to then run it yourself.
www.countrysideaccess.gov.uk
Check out the right paths to take so you don't face dead ends.
www.tameside.gov.uk
Information about the countryside, activities and the Countryside Rangers Service. Also some history of the area.

Contacts:
Countryside Ranger Service
Tel: 0161 330 9613

Tatton Park, Knutsford Entrance

Don't get in a rut – with the deer!

You are spoilt for plains and ironically planes, on the train out to Knutsford. Once the journey passes the designer refinement of Hale it picks up the stretching plains that reach as far as the eye can see before Ashley. There you start to see thatched cottages and a floral 'English country garden' theme not as obviously apparent in and among nearby Derbyshire's alternative strong and strenuous terrain.

One word to describe Cheshire's countryside – apart from the blatantly obvious flat – is courtly. The 13-minute train ride from Altrincham is a delightful passage or you can get the train from Piccadilly and out to Knutsford, which takes 42 minutes.

Once you disembark at Knutsford, turn right but don't be misled by the brown sign which panics you into thinking Tatton Park is 4 miles away. The Rostherne Main Entrance reached by car might be but the Knutsford Entrance, the one for us runners is only about 0.5 miles away (unless of course you're on a real burn out!)

After you've turned right at the station you can run along Toft Road and then Princess Street until it becomes Tatton Street, or run further back along the parallel King Edward Road until

It's hall landscapes at Tatton Park.

190

it joins Tatton Street. Both streets are the commercial thoroughfares of an olde worlde town but King Edward Road, with its 'Museum in the Street' heritage signs is probably more atmospheric and thus good to see but also more likely to be too busy to run along at any real speed.

If you take the Tatton Street route to Tatton Park Gates you go past the Lord Eldon, which has won the acclaim of being Camra's pub of the season in previous years. As long as you don't stop for a bevy, Tatton Park's Knutsford Entrance is at the end of Tatton Street.

The park opens at 8am for pedestrians and 11am otherwise (9am for pedestrians in the winter but is closed on winter Mondays). With all these changes it is probably best to ring or check online before you visit the park, especially if you are travelling a long distance to it. Regular users may be well-versed it its opening hours but for the rest of us there are contact details below.

One of the great things about running over parkland such as this is that there are many areas to warm-up and cool down when training, which more urban routes don't always afford. At the Knutsford Entrance there are toilets, granted cold mobile type toilets but they are very handy before you set out and a blessing if they stop you getting caught behind a pine tree!

Now warmed-up, you can head alongside the main thoroughfare, which is a concrete and shorter but busier route of around 3.5 miles, or take the golf course route to the mansion, to the left of the main thoroughfare, returning via the main stretch for a more scenic and longer return trip of 4.5 miles. Those undertaking heavier training could cover the perimeter of the park for around 8 miles or even run to the Rostherne entrance to begin with, mentioned earlier.

Running on the main thoroughfare or even along the enormous Tatton Mere to the right or up the side of the golf course offers so many positive distractions. There are many spots to stop and admire the views as you get your breath back. The park has around 500 deer in it and they can often wander along to say hello. The colours in the park are magnificent in autumn time and it looks so unspoilt in the snow-covered winter season too.

The golf course route begins with a very slight incline but offers a delightful chance to be on the grass. Some people like concrete running for its directional guidance and as there is less chance of getting a twisted ankle in potholes and so on. Personally, I've always thought it better for the soul and the physique to run on the natural ground which has more give but with this run the choice is yours.

After a while you reach the kissing gates that give you access to fields jammed with rutting deer, fallen tree stumps and the flora and fauna of country living, including mushrooms the size and shape of sponge tennis balls. Then you enter woodland shaded with serenity and solitude where you are instructed to keep to the path. This is probably the loneliest point of the whole run so make the most of the chance to roam alone, sit and think or have a water break.

This park sees thousands of cars enter at the weekends so knowing you have a little plot to yourself, even for just a minute or two, is divine, especially if you visit during the autumn in time to hear it raining conkers and pine cones.

After this you reach open land and a brisker wind before greeting civilisation again as you head towards the mansion and surrounding stable-yard, farm, gardens and adventure playground.

Next you pass the Rostherne Entrance to the 2,000 acre park; 1,000 acres of which are open to the public. You then head along Knutsford Drive again towards the town, past the enchanting Melchett Mere on your right, then the massive Tatton Mere – complete with speedboats on sunny days, to your left.

Both meres are beautiful but it may be best to run alongside the very straight Roman Road to the end, rather than on the tarmac itself, dodging cars as you go. It's likely you will then have more opportunity to be safely distracted by the beauty that surrounds you and there will be more solid concentrated running for the athlete training for a specific event and of course the need to escape the scent of sheep poo might speed you up!

It is free for pedestrians and cyclists. Vehicles are charged £5.00. The park closes at its earliest in winter at 5pm and last entries are at 4pm. It is open longer during summer months but it is best to check the website for details on prices and times.

Advantages:
- It offers a multitude of routes and variations for all abilities.
- Different abilities can go together, run different routes and meet at the farmyard at the end – feeling like flogged horses!
- Everyone is there for leisure; you shouldn't be harassed by rattled commuters blocking your route.
- There is somewhere to park.
- It is a beautiful park and you will love the calm it provides even if you only visit once in a while.
- You won't spend half the route navigating like you may on moorland or open countryside routes.

Disadvantages:
- The low flying planes may be interesting to some people, an irritation to others.
- There is only one train to Knutsford every hour for a lot of the week meaning if you miss getting back to the station in time on the return leg…
- It is easy to get carried away and just want to do a 2-mile run and end up covering 6 or so (that may be an advantage though!)
- Events held throughout the year may occasionally disrupt your running so it is wise to check beforehand. Weddings held there may mean you might not be the only one wanting to run!
- Beware the park closing times. Time changes with the seasons can disrupt your plans.
- Though it's free to enter on foot it will cost at least £4.50 in a car.

Summary:
A deer park country estate with stunning views of nature which is good for those who don't like navigation but want some grass underfoot and who want to leave their car – or their family somewhere – as they pound the patch.

Mileage:
Mansion 3.5 miles return, via golf course perimeter 4.5 miles. The park perimiter is adaptable but 8 miles return.

History:
Tatton Park has a history dating back to Bronze Age farming and has been home to herds of deer since the 13th century. In the late Tudor period Tatton was acquired by the Egerton family who owned the estate until the last Lord Egerton died without heirs in 1958. Maurice Egerton bequeathed the estate to the National Trust and council funding meant it was managed by

Cheshire County Council from 1960 to 2009 when Cheshire East Council took over. Each year over 750,000 people visit the 1,000 acres of deer park, mansion, gardens, Old Hall, Rare Breeds Farm and to see the events.

Useful Websites:
www.tattonpark.org.uk
For prices and opening times and the history of the park.

Contacts:
Tatton Park
Tel: 01625 374400
Infoline: 01625 374435
Email: tatton@cheshireeast.gov.uk

Trans Pennine Taster – Hyde to Broadbottom

Apples and Armageddon

In and around Manchester there are many points at which you can jump on and off the Trans Pennine Trail, some sections of which are very well signposted and directed, sometimes even too much so, others barely hint at the existence with stickers on conveniently placed posts and fences.

This run might of course only be a small part of your overall plan to run the entire Trans Pennine Trail but for this route we will start in Hyde again and run first from Mill Lane, through the ever-faithful Haughton Dale Nature Reserve.

Follow the path alongside the River Tame and admire the delightful sea of bluebells on the hill-faces to your right in springtime. Soon you will cross planks of wood forming a bridge across a small crevice, which from a distance reminds the onlooker of an Indiana Jones set without the ropes (or the really severe drops, of course).

Head onwards and the path takes you, with screeching calf muscles, up 35 steps – I know, I've counted every single one of them! At the top it is a narrow path and there is quite a steep drop down the hillside to the river and though it is not fenced off you are not up there for long because within a few feet you drop down 35 steps and turn left onto Gibraltar Bridge.

See ridges along Mottram Old Road from Werneth Low.

After crossing the bridge you are spoilt for choice. You can head up moss and foliage laden pathways surrounded by stone walls which scream with historic ambience. Instead you can turn left and then almost immediately right to follow the wooden sign up to the Peak Forest Canal. However, for this route you should turn left and keep on a short distance instead of heading up to the canal. Run on the path past giant Sycamore trees and then it will take you through a long tunnel under the canal and again under the railway line to take you towards the Trans Pennine Trail.

There develops here an element of secrecy near the trees and canal tunnel but soon things change. Head to your right, up Apethorn Lane where there are houses, though small in number. Just before you reach the junction of busy A-roads a wooden sign for the Trans Pennine Trail offers you an option to turn left for a 6-mile run to Stockport or right for a 5-mile run to Broadbottom, though it does not feel that far when you have covered it.

Turn right and the trail then curves round to the left offering a tarmacked path for walkers (and us runners one supposes) and a muddy lane aside for horses. This sadly is where the route fails slightly because although it is part of the massively well-known walkway it is like something out of a sci-fi movie. This was once the Godley to Apethorn Railway and because of that the path is placed between embankments. It is jammed between muddy slopes and on top of the embankments streets set at a higher level look down over the route.

I love the character of Hyde but have to admit that for the runner below, the tarmac and the signs about horses not galloping go on, and on, and…You are very exposed to the residential streets and there are rarely chances to turn off the Apethorn to Godley stretch of the Trans Pennine Trail. Imagine a movie where a nuclear problem had virtually ended mankind but the infrastructure and foundations of life remain unused and you are the only human left; on bleak days that sums up this stretch of the run with the endless monotony ahead of you and seemingly lifeless streets above you.

Thankfully, as the land opens up, you see a bridge at Brookfold Lane, Godley. If you try to continue you are fenced off by private woodland and boundaries and you must then climb or step precariously down the ledge at the side of the bridge to then run under it – not towards Mottram Road but right towards the more countrified Green Lane.

You then run onwards and see a muddy path which offers the chance to head up through a gate for Green Lane; a more defined pathway but less open. However, you can head on, sort of leftwards through Brookfold Farmyard over very muddy, even fen-like ground, before stepping over streams and through Brookfold Wood.

Here the path is non-existent and it is, as Shakespeare put it in *The Taming Of The Shrew*, a case of jogging until your feet turn green. You can see Werneth Low high on the hill to your right: its poignant war memorial and the pylons of Windy Harbour. As you step through horse manure and over fields without a set path it takes you towards Greenside Cattery and both ways take you to Mottram Old Road (the A560) as horses and cows look quizzically at you.

From Green Lane turn left and after you reach Greenside cross the road, which some people use as a car-racing track and almost immediately you join the right hand branch of the sweetly named Apple Street. As the incline rises you are tempted to turn left into Lowend Farmyard to see over a ridge and head into open space. Instead carry on past the farm and shortly afterwards to your left the stickers point you to Broadbottom or Botham's Hall Farm. If you headed to your right here you would reach Idle Hill and a place with a name such as that can't be desired by exercise junkies!

Head down Cown Edge Way along the side of the farmland, initially on a path into which a tractor has ground its identity and have the opportunity to stare over the vast, green countryside to contemplate the amazing difference when compared to that Armageddon feeling on the Trans Pennine near Apethorn.

Next, head left, downhill and along the narrow but defined pathway, through Back Wood with its swerving, dipping route, delicate little stiles and bridges and a floral welcome in springtime. This route heads slightly further south than the neighbouring area of a similar vibe, Broadbottom's Great Wood.

As you near the end of Back Wood, run past a vast number of small steps on the opposing embankment which would take you onto the Etherow/Goyt Valley Way and though curiosity here may make you itch to see more, continue through the outskirts of Botham's Hall Farm, avoiding more curiosity-inducing signs for an area bucolically named Woodseats.

Head onwards, or left if you ponder the footpath sign, up Leylands Lane and towards Hodge Lane or Moss Lane, either country road will take you up to Broadbottom Train Station and to transport to the city centre. The Hodge Lane route, however, has you clinging to a steep hillside, jumping over brambles and gives you a last taste of country rurality and freedom through nature. Next step over a little bridge and almost without warning onto the train station platform, amazing the fed-up, on-looking, delayed commuters with your exhausted, sweat-covered arrival.

If you have a long wait for a train or an urge to continue running, head out of the station onto Mottram Road (yes, another Mottram Road) then onto Market Street, Lower Market Street and then right onto Lymefield Terrace and here you will find the Lymefield Visitors' Centre. The building has displays and information about local heritage and wildlife. It also has a maze but is unfortunately only open at weekends. Another attraction here is Broad Mills Heritage Site.

Advantages:
- Varied locations and surfaces.
- The chance to run part of a major distance trail.
- If you head left at Broadbottom Station, up Mottram Road then Broadbottom Road you can join another trail on the Chain Bar Way.

Disadvantages:
- The Trans Pennine tarmac stretch from Apethorn to Godley is restrictive and draining.
- The route carries so much fascinating history but hides it in the mud.
- There are many sections where you cannot pull off or choose to quit, where you are boxed in and have to follow only the Trans Pennine route.

Summary:
A metamorphosis of scenes, visions and feelings that takes the runner on a long tour without feeling over-challenged and gives a slice of the differing vibes of the suburbs of Manchester and the western edge of the Peak District.

Mileage:
4 miles.

History:

The Hodge Lane Dye Vats are 18th-century stone vats which were used by the Hodge Print Works and are said to be part of the earliest textile site in Tameside. Grey cloths would have been bleached with lime in the giant, connected vats and then laid out in the fields to dry – like us post-training semi-anaemic runners! The site, minus flattened runners, was excavated by the Greater Manchester Archaeological Unit in 1986. (See Trans Pennine Trail at Sale for more background information.)

Useful Websites:

www.ldwa.org.uk
Long Distance Walkers' Association
www.tameside.gov.uk/countryside/etherow
Lymefield Visitors' Centre

Contacts:

Lymefield Visitors' Centre
Lymefield
Broadbottom
Tel: 01457 765780

Trans Pennine Trail at Sale

Take many steps but leave no trail

The Trans Pennine Trail in its entirety is over 200 miles long but for a taster of it around south west Manchester and Cheshire start this route by running from Washway Road, up Harboro Way and straight on to Harboro Road in Sale. As you are pounding the concrete thinking this tree-lined residential area is nice but wondering when things open up, the road becomes Carrington Lane and about 0.5 miles, maybe a bit more after that, there is a sort of stile entrance over a gravel bridleway on your left with signs stating this is Route 62 on the Trans Pennine Trail. It also suggests the path is good for walkers and cyclists; well, it is very good for runners too!

Turn right up the path and you will be amazed at the speed with which the concrete jungle and residential motor sports become pathways arched with nature, leaves and trees. It opens up to become rural very quickly and you can see acres of crop land and grasses in front of you, for you to pound past.

Soon you will encounter the forestry of Dainewell Woods that could easily be the setting for children to find fairies in the forest. The dancing light and delicate shapes of the plants makes it a great place for a good imagination. But the woods become more and more dense as you run on and less suitable for exploring yet the beaten track of the Trans Pennine Trail (or TPT) is more than adequate.

Continue on and you will see signs for both Dunham Massey and Stretford. Take the route towards Dunham Massey out towards Altrincham and further out of the city. Even though the forest is dense on this stretch don't worry because the pathways are very clear and easy to run along. On a weekday you will rarely encounter anyone along most of this route, once you've legged it through suburbia.

A later sign offers you directions rather than destinations and you should choose west here but really this is where the navigation ends because after running on past farmland with a fenced off pond you will reach Woodcote Road and see fields filled with palominos and donkeys and signs telling you not to feed them or you'll lose your fingers or clothes!

Keep on running (without a donkey's assistance) past a water treatment works and down the rest of Woodcote Road which then becomes almost cobbled and you'll see a few houses and stables with chickens pecking wild outside. At the end turn left onto Sinderland Road but be careful, this is where motorists let rip after leaving behind the congestion of Broadheath and there are no footpaths. Though you will be on this road for about 1 mile, footpaths do not appear until 0.25 miles later so it won't feel risky for long but some of the scenery here, especially in summer, can capture all your attention with golden fields filled with cereal crops. It is perhaps not the best route on a winter's night without high visibility clothing.

You could run all the way down Sinderland Road turn left and back onto Manchester Road to clip short the end or continue running up Washway Road or even find public transport from here if you've had enough. But which runner is a quitter? You would miss some more wonderful sights if you did take the shorter more suburban route. Crossing the road with care you can follow the TPT (yes, you are still on it) towards Dairyhouse Lane with rolling farmland towards Dunham and Altrincham. Some of the scenes here are stunning and make you glad you live or run in and around the edges of Manchester and in this case, Cheshire.

Unless you are going for a really long run don't be tempted to jump over the steps on your right and continue along the Trans Pennine Trail. On Dairyhouse Lane continue along the concrete and past a pub called the Bay Malton on Seamons Road to join the Bridgewater Canal at Seamons Moss Bridge. You're back on the old faithful Bridgewater again.

Turn left along the canal path and run past the bucolic bench, past the marina, view the odd shark-fin shaped apartment blocks and duck under the bridge that is Manchester Road. Then continue along the towpath past Timperley Metrolink station and get off the towpath at the next Metrolink stop which is Brooklands.

Here, after running up the path back onto concrete, head north west past the cemetery and run down Marsland Road at the end of which you will find the Washway Road, Harboro Way junction and the finish line to a circuit…or if you're mad enough you can start the whole thing again.

Advantages:
- A beautiful way to get away from things. Straight from a residential area onto the Trans Pennine Trail and the route then becomes more and more countrified.
- Some amazing scenery in summer.
- The TPT paths are well maintained so you won't feel like Indiana Jones on a swamp crossing.

Disadvantages:
- It could prove difficult navigationally on a dark winter's evening. You could easily fail to see the signposts for the trail at some points like Sinderland Road or the turning for Dunham Massey.
- On Sinderland Road there are no footpaths so without high visibility clothing the end stretch could be dangerous when it is dark or the weather is bad.
- Sometimes the signs offer too many options. If you are new to the area you may not know for instance that Dunham is more rural than Stretford and therefore better running ground, or which town is west or east.

Summary:
An intermediate route that might be good practice for a 10k if you've used it regularly enough and have got to know the route. This section alone is too rural and long for beginners but easy to tailor for those who want an even longer run, like continuing along the TPT at Dairyhouse Lane.

Mileage:
5.75 miles.

History:
The Trans Pennine Trail cuts through Manchester from Hadfield via Stockport, Sale and Altrincham but the entire trail links the North and Irish Seas (or east and west coasts of northern England if you prefer). It runs coast to coast, Hornsea to Southport, or vice versa, at 215 miles long (or 346km). The website claims the route is mainly level which is somewhat difficult to imagine at parts of the route near, say, Hadfield, considering the gradient of the Pennine land but the stretch near Sale and Altrincham is certainly quite flat.

The trail's highest point is on Woodhead Pass in the Peak District. It travels through the Pennine area with its rugged and dramatic scenery, through Longdendale Valley, before reaching Stockport and following the River Mersey onwards to Sale and then on towards Southport.

An inaugural walk and cycle ride in May 1989 prompted the beginnings of the TPT but funding had to be secured and areas prepared with signposting and groundwork. The trail was officially opened on 13 September 2001. In July 1996 the TPT was designated as the British section of the E8 European Long Distance Walk Route but we can run that another time.

Werneth Low – Via Hyde

Chuffin' cheek!

If you have already tried Werneth Low from the Romiley side you will know it is not one for the quitter. Nevertheless, it is not one to be missed either as it is one of the best viewpoints around Greater Manchester.

If you start in Hyde town centre at the bus station or Hyde Central train station run up Market Street, past the timeless market vendors braving all weathers and singing to Frank Sinatra or somebody, as they do so.

Run on up past the numerous side roads then past the junction with Union Street and onwards until boxer Ricky Hatton's gymnasium greets you on the left and the road becomes Stockport Road if you continue on or Dowson Road if you fork right here.

If you can resist the signs for body massages, or tattoos, then whichever road you take is up to you as they will both lead to roads up to Werneth Low. However, for this route we will run via Dowson Road.

Once past the junction you run over an old stone bridge which spans a route for another day, the Trans Pennine Trail (see other routes). This route is specifically for cyclists and runners. It has a look of a former railway line route converted for leisure that skirts the city and many such paths make up the TPT as it is known.

Continue until you reach a point where Dowson Road becomes Stockport Road to the left and ahead and turn left. This part of Hyde is known as Gee Cross and it takes you to Joel Lane (the extra steep way up to Werneth Low) or Higham Lane where there is a milder incline and it offers a Visitors' Centre too before you reach the pinnacle.

In the memory always, Werneth Low, Hyde.

Joel Lane will have you panting and spluttering on a summer's day but when you reach the top there is the temptation to stop for an energy drink at the Hare and Hounds, where it must be the 800ft (243m) above sea level altitude and the view of five counties which makes you feel light-headed, not the beer!

Whichever lane you take (Joel or Higham) turn left onto Werneth Low Road and head towards two sort of television masts or communications towers at Windy Harbour beyond the Werneth Low War Memorial. This will cut through Werneth Low Golf Course so watch some people's aim but it is nevertheless a tarmacked road not a footpath.

Near the mast there is a very disused looking car park type area and an abandoned Portacabin which is a crying shame when you drink in the visions of landmarks around Manchester from there: Mottram Church, the site of the old Roman Fort of Melandra in Gamesley, Hartshead Pike, the moors behind Oldham, Rochdale, Bankswood Park in Hadfield, Shire Hill in Glossop and the Longdendale Valley. Alternatively on the other side of the mast there are scenes of more gentle countryside towards Broadbottom and Compstall. Luckily for the uninitiated there is a metal plaque which shows you the direction, name and distance of the various landmarks.

From there you can also see and run to, the nearby war memorial. You run across grassland to reach this point and there are benches and a bracing wind at the spot most of the year round as you see more sights. Afterwards head along the set footpaths back through the grassland to Higham Lane Visitors' Centre and back down to Stockport Road.

As you are returning via Higham it is probably most varied and definitely more testing to go up the steep Joel Lane and then do a loop by going back down Higham Lane. This route, however, means you will miss seeing the Visitors' Centre before the viewpoint so perhaps it is best for newcomers to go up via Higham Lane.

Once back at residential level on Stockport Road head back to Market Street and enjoy Hyde's compassion with a cup of tea – and get stick about what you look like or where you have been running.

Advantages:
- A beautiful viewpoint of Manchester which covers virtually 360 degrees and has plaques informing you which landmarks you can see in the distance.
- It is motivational. A visit to this site and its views will re-invigorate your love of running and inspire you to cover new places.
- Disabled people can get access via Higham Lane and everyone can eat a hearty meal at the Hare and Hounds at the top.

Disadvantages:
- It is very steep, especially if you take the Joel Lane route.
- A lot of the run is standard residential streets and roads so stunning as the Low's views are those en route don't match it.
- A little school at the bottom of Higham Lane can make things busy at home time.

Summary:
A high climb on the Joel Lane way up but a more gentle descent from one of the most fantastic viewpoints of all of this great city. You could even re-route things slightly to finish at the pub and eat there – if you didn't put other diners off their dinner!

Mileage:
4 miles.

History:
In 1920, over £14,000 was raised to buy Lower Higham Farm and its land and in 1921 a war memorial was placed on the site at Hackingknife as a monument to the 710 local men who died in World War One. During the 1970s, Greater Manchester Council, Tameside Metropolitan Borough Council and Hyde War Memorial Trust established Werneth Low Country Park and it was opened by the Duke of Gloucester in 1980.

Close to the pub there is said to be a World War Two bunker which housed telephone lines to Whitehall and a telescope for runners and ramblers to see the views. There is also an ancient burial site nearby.

A dedication made at Werneth Low in 1921, stated romantically that it was bought to be kept forever as an open space for the health and well-being of the community. The views are still ethereal on a sunny, spring day, or even on a snow coated blue skied winter's day, indeed almost any day of the year. However, it is a shame the mast is not so heavenly nor the abandoned looking state of things near Windy Harbour.

Useful Websites:
www.tameside.gov.uk
Find a map of Werneth Low and view its history and information about its location.

Contacts:
Countryside Ranger Service:
Tel: 0161 330 9613

The Hare And Hounds Public House
Werneth Low Road
Hyde
SK14 3AA
Tel: 0161 366 5526

Werneth Low Country Park
Lower Higham Visitors' Centre
Hyde
SK14 5LR
Tel: 0161 368 6667

Werneth Low – via Romiley

How can you go low?

God knows why they have such a penchant for deceptive names around the area but this stunning viewpoint of south Manchester is anything but low!

After alighting at Romiley Station turn left up Compstall Road run past all the shops and then turn left up Sandy Lane. Yet if you want to avoid the shoppers turn immediate left out of the station, up Guywood Lane then right along Marsden Road to join Sandy Lane.

Either way, once you join the residential climb that is Sandy Lane keep going straight on as the road becomes simply 'Greave'. Yes, strange name but your hamstrings might agree – you'll grieve. Just after Aysgarth Avenue, as you see Greave Primary School on your left you should see Werneth Low Road on your right and suddenly out of a world of lollipop men and school runs you are running up a stony lane which is an almost vertical climb.

You may see a donkey on your left here who I think is symbolic because you will need a stubborn 'ass' to keep moving here.

The rocky lane has the tarmacked country lane element and to the side footpaths and bridleways. Testing as this 13 per cent gradient is, enjoy it because after the quaintly named Top-o'-th'-Low cottage, 0.5 miles after starting the climb, you reach a triangle made by Cowlishaw Road and suddenly, road-wise, this country lane atmosphere develops almost A-road tendencies. In fact, if you felt beaten you could take the right turn down Cowlishaw and back to Compstall Road and Romiley Station.

Don't fear just because the traffic becomes more urban the views don't just become those of city life. You can see Manchester's Beetham Tower from here and try to decipher which

Hillslides on the Romiley side of Werneth Low.

landmarks you are looking at over the green ocean of countryside in between. You can smell real fresh air: it is that stuff peppered with the fresh feeling of freedom and you can feel the wind cooling you down.

For most of us who wanted more of the same and didn't quit at Cowlishaw keep running past the Hare and Hounds public house, handily placed if you need another water bottle.

Soon after you will meet turn offs such as Joel Lane and the stone-cottage clustered junction with Higham Lane and Mount Road but if you are in it for the full slog keep going along Werneth Low Road and you will see many pathways to the gloriously placed war memorial.

You can see this from many points in the area during day-to-day life and it may make you smile to remember running to it later. After running to the memorial you can continue along Werneth Low Road, past the golf course, before you reach a place known as Windy Harbour. This gives more views out to the east and sights of Longdendale Valley, Mottram Church, and the Peak District. Both here and at the war memorial there are silver metal plaques which show the direction of all the landmarks you can see from up here and the distance to them.

This is a fantastic viewpoint but it is very poorly signposted and a sort of hut looks abandoned and damaged. Beyond the urban links a bench on the precipice here looks like it is perched on the edge of the world. There is a stunning panorama from up here and it is well worth a pause for reflection. After this things get increasingly concrete again, so enjoy!

When refreshed, continue east along Werneth Low Road. You've earned a lot of the downhill that is around you now. Go down Cock Brow near Windy Harbour avoiding the cattle farms' inhabitants thanks to cattle grids. Run down one of the most beautifully named thoroughfares in Greater Manchester named Apple Street and you could take a left here across fields to cut out the very end where it joins Mottram Old Road. Either way turn left at the end and run past elements of Werneth Low Country Park and see the memorial you ran to earlier crouched on the top of the sun-scorched hill.

Keep going past Green Lane and the football ground and into Gee Cross. Pass Higham Lane on your left (where you could have taken a short cut earlier to get down from the Low but would have missed some of the best bits) and go past The Old Tannery public house. As the road becomes Stockport Road carry on past Joel Lane (another lighter route exit, when heading downhill anyway!)

At the crossroads turn left to continue along Stockport Road and then left along Pennine Road. There are still some inclines to come but you will soon see the road become Greave again and no doubt your body is really grieving now. Keep running along Sandy Lane and then right to the station and after just over 5 miles running have a very well earned slurp on a drink, or two!

Advantages:
- Fantastic for stamina testing. If you are training for something big it doesn't get much more challenging than parts of this!
- Amazing views of the countryside, of Manchester city centre and surrounding towns.

Disadvantages:
- Very few – though your quads may disagree for the next few days!
- The concrete return part of the loop may spoil the solitude for some people.
- Not good for quick-run people or concrete lovers who like the flat.

Summary:

A towering tester with 13 per cent gradient yet minutes away from a 14-minute train ride to the city centre. Ideal for wilderness runners who are stuck with city centre lives.

Mileage:
5.25 miles.

History:
Werneth Low Country Park is a 200 acre green space set about 9.5 miles from Manchester city centre. You can see the Pennine hills in detail and it is said even the silhouette of the Welsh mountains on a clear day.

After a public appeal in 1920 the War Memorial Committee of Hyde Borough Council purchased Lower Higham Farm to place a memorial there to the 710 men who died in the Great War (1914–1918) from the area.

On the altitudinous site known as Hackingknife a £2,000 memorial was placed which is the memorial that still stands fighting the elements today. No doubt Hackingknife got its name from the slicing winds there on some days.

The Hare & Hounds public house sits in the park and is said to overlook five counties and stand at 800ft (243m) above sea level. No losing your sea legs at this bar then – or more importantly your land legs!

Useful Websites:
www.tameside.gov.uk
Gain information about the history of the area, parking and mapping.

Contacts:
Countryside Ranger Service
Tel: 0161 330 9613

The Hare and Hounds Public House
Werneth Low Road
Hyde
SK14
Tel: 0161 366 5526

Werneth Low Country Park
Lower Higham Visitors' Centre
Higham Lane
Hyde
SK14 5LR
Tel: 0161 368 6667

Woodlands Road to Heaton Park via The Cliff

Cliffhanger

This route starts by offering you some concrete terrain with culture. After getting off the Bury Metrolink line at Woodlands Road and having just enough space to warm-up on a grass verge, head north west up the incline of Woodlands Road towards a residential area, heavily populated by varying religions.

Running straight along Heath Street, Tetlow Lane and Broom Lane can be a roller-coaster incline-wise and it means crossing many busy roads but you get to see a multi-cultural part of Manchester and run through an area with a high Jewish population.

At the end of Broom Lane turn left to the pelican crossing and on the other side of Bury New Road you should see a gateway and path which takes you back on yourself into the actual woodland and means you avoid the steep bank you would have to run down if you had crossed straight over from Broom Lane (unless you want to run that steep bank route, of course).

Whichever route you take to get there it is well worth the effort when you see some of the nature down by the riverbank on The Cliff; an area made famous by the fact that the Manchester United team used to train here apparently until 1999. Today, as the river flows near Great Cheetham Street West and Cromwell Road near Lower Broughton Road there is a training academy for Manchester United FC and the club still holds academy matches there today.

The foliage and clearings are beautiful at any time of year but when you run even further away from Bury New Road you can see Castle Hill Viewpoint to the north, then you find steps and a wooden path which run alongside the River Irwell.

The river itself is quite wide here and as things open up it is tempting to race off and do some sprinting along the wooden path. However, it is easy to miss the fact that some of the route is stepped and not being vigilant could result in injuries.

Following the river you will pass an arching footbridge which you should run on past. Lovely as it is on the opposite side with wide open football pitches and fungi filled glades, the path soon runs out and leaves you jungle trekking before being fenced off from any attempt to cross the later bridges.

Captivating as this riverside stretch is it can be irritating during hot weather because of the number of flies and midges. However, as long as you aren't blinded by them you can use it as a reason to run even faster!

If you specifically want to see more sights along here it is good to run past the arched footbridge, under Littleton stone bridge and on to the weir. You will then reach Jubilee Bridge where you are again fenced off from reaching the infrastructure but it gives you the chance to look over to Manchester United's former training ground and see the turf that was run on by sporting legends. Yet in your reverie don't forget this route will see you locked out and you will have to run back the way you came.

It is also tempting to think you can get up to Littleton Road via the Racecourse Hotel or its beer garden but they are fond of fencing around here not just football. So just after passing the first footbridge keep running along the path then veer off slightly to your right onto tarmac and Kingsley Avenue and then left onto South Radford Street or instead, from the path, head onto Rushley Avenue and straight on to Northallerton Road. Either way, if United fans can tear themselves away turn right, up Littleton Road and towards the Cussons' factory.

Whether via Littleton Road or osmosis you should head north-west past sports fields and alongside some points of the river until the road becomes Kersal Vale Road. Then at the roundabout after seeing more riverside bridges, scenery and access to the Irwell Valley Way, turn right up the seemingly endless hill that is Rainsough Brow.

After the bucolic waterside running and the ghostly empty streets near Woodlands Road and Kersal you begin to notice a more settled sense of community here – were it not for the hill taking all your focus.

This is one of those endless, intense stretches on a route where you get so involved in wanting to reach the finish you almost forget where you are. The road eventually flattens and becomes Hilton Lane and then Scholes Lane after a crossroads and as the traffic gets heavier so do your legs.

Yet like the well-earned victories United player Scholesy has given the Reds success is nearly upon us. About 0.5 miles down Scholes Lane turn left onto Bury Old Road and skirt past the edges of Heaton Park's greenery on the right to head to the Metrolink to the city centre, stretching off in the car park or on the platform on a quiet day!

(See Heaton Park for a separate route onto the parkland.)

Advantages:
- Very mixed terrain; concrete, grass, wooden slats, sand. You name it. There are also hills and flat stretches. Good for training for a mixed terrain event.
- Some of the hills are real stamina builders and some are close to the end of the route forcing you to push yourself when you are already tired or tested.
- This route is already testing but it is easy to lengthen it as well by running on the Irwell Valley Way at Rainsough Brow or round Heaton Park when less hardy individuals have already quit.

Disadvantages:
- Some of the fenced off roads and bridges can mean access difficulties and you having to run back the way you came if you're not careful, which can be maddening.
- It may not be the best route in summer if you are too distracted by the flies.
- Not a beginners' route because of the intensity, or one for women who feel vulnerable running alone at night. Though most people are friendly you might feel uncomfortable in some of the quieter semi-abandoned residential areas near Woodlands Road and Cheetham Hill and Littleton Road in Kersal.

Summary:
A route for intermediate to advanced runners that builds stamina, calls for adaptability and demands a strong focus on the hills and inclines.

Mileage:
4.75 miles.

History:
The Manchester United FC chairman began renting 'The Cliff' in June 1938 for use by the Manchester United Junior Athletic Club but Manchester United bought the ground for training in 1951.

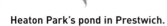

Heaton Park's pond in Prestwich.

In the early 1950s United stars were training on the hallowed turf of the pitch at Old Trafford but to avoid needless damage all training was moved over to the Broughton site.

Floodlights were installed to help players training at night, youth teams and for the public youth matches. An international rugby match was held there in 1952 as well. Unfortunately for the team it seemed some people could see a little too much there as the press and opposition spies were gathering training tactics from United because of the openness of the site and so United moved to the Trafford Training Centre at Carrington.

First team, reserve and academy training now takes place at Carrington but the youngest players still use The Cliff, as have the England team prior to matches at Old Trafford.

The Cliff will not just see you excel in your running. In 1952–53 in the first year of the FA Youth Challenge Cup United pasted Nantwich Town's Youth Team 23–0 with players such as eternally renowned Duncan Edwards and other Busby Babes scoring as many as five goals each. United's youths lifted the trophy that first year winning 9–3 against Wolverhampton Wanderers on aggregate, so The Cliff knows the pinnacles of sporting talent.

Useful Websites:
www.heatonpark.org.uk
To see what is on and find your way around the interactive map.

Contacts:
Heaton Park
The Farm Centre
Manchester City Council
Manchester
M25 2SW
Tel: 0161 773 1085
Email: heatonpark@manchester.gov.uk

Salford Sports Village
Littleton Road
Salford
M7 3NQ
Tel: 0161 604 7600
Email: salfordsportsvillage@scu.co.uk

Wythenshawe Park

Cannon past the opposition

Most people in training would say they are either concrete runners or that they like their cross-country with all the flora and fauna it entails. Swathes of people now seem to be out pounding pavements in suburbia – avoiding the cost of being a gym member and not having to put up with the grunting of that neighbouring sweater on a gymnasium-based treadmill. Either way lots of long traffic-filled thoroughfares in Manchester might start a runners congestion charge if some zealous bureaucrats start counting runners' footfall.

Brooklands Road, near the Brooklands Metrolink Station is just such a tree-lined residential route. You can run from the Metrolink station for about 1 mile in total along the straight road which can be mentally taxing because it goes on forever with no corners or twists.

Finally, at the end, you will reach a roundabout and should turn left here on to Altrincham Road. Watch the pace of change here because there are constant development works putting up new supermarkets and tarmacing new roads in retail parks or industrial estates. The pavement here is also part footpath and part cycleway so it is easy to stray, only to find you have someone trying to pull a wheelie up your spine or being boneshakers of a different kind.

After passing the retail parks, the ubiquitous McDonalds and the overshadowing urban reminders of the 1960s and 1970s in the form of residential tower blocks you should see Wythenshawe Park on your left.

Though nowhere near as majestic as Manchester parks like Heaton Park or Cheshire's Tatton Park, at weekends Wythenshawe Park is packed with families; youngsters and players

Black and white Wythenshawe Hall.

out seeking their moment of glory on the football pitches that won't quite challenge the World Cup but do give a similar endorphin buzz. In summertime fields of light-coloured grasses look similar to wheat fields and give a golden edge to the park as your desperation to get out of urban life and onto the parkland rises.

Eventually, after about 1.25 miles as you see and hear motorway traffic in the distance to your right and you almost reach the pedestrian subway under the M56 on the other side of the road, before that you should see a sign for Spinney Road on the right hand side of the road. Opposite Spinney Road turn left and you will see a tempting country-lane-style path to your left but you need to head straight on, up a more narrow path by the side of a sort of gate and you have reached Gib Lane and Gib Lane Wood.

It is one of the things to love about Manchester, a secret that outsiders and maybe even some natives who don't do exercise don't know but one minute you can be in a city of concrete and the next you are in country heaven. The woodland here is very pretty with large trees which have outlived generations and there are the scents and smells of rural locations. For those who prefer running surfaces with more give the grass, bark, leaves and mud start about here. Follow the path along the edge of the park rather than heading straight onto the wide fields.

If you keep following this path you then reach open grassland and it feels like running on carpet or even a trampoline with the rubbery spring in your step that the parkland gives. You can run this path to the end until it meets Wythenshawe Road or turn left slightly earlier and see benches with 6ft high wooden carvings towering as back rests. Run onwards over the grassland filled with dog walkers. I passed a lady in a wheelchair out with her dog who visits every day. She said she had to. Maybe that was for the dog's sake but perhaps it was the draw of the park.

Head on past a statue of Oliver Cromwell, stood with a proud, adversarial pose, looking at the front of Wythenshawe Hall with its Tudoresque style, black and white timbers and the smell of burning logs during some seasons. Behind the Hall there are gardens with information boards teaching you about different sorts of trees. There is a Courtyard, Tea Rooms, a Visitors' Centre, a Park Warden's Office and toilets.

A lot of people gather in this area, which is such a contrast to the silence and solitude of the Wythenshawe Hall Park Gardens just behind the Hall. There, the shading of the giant trees is a delight on a hot day and a little brook and fountain stone, although the monument is not often filled with water, are an escape from civilization. You can see the back of the Hall from here in a less imposing brickwork design but beware if you come in the evening as this area is locked. It is best to check for opening hours.

Just beyond the Courtyard there are tennis courts and a tarmacked road which maintenance vehicles use. Head right and then left towards the Athletics Track which is a meeting place for the Sale Harriers Athletics Club.

From here it may be tempting to run back towards Altrincham Road south of the park or Moor Road to the west. However, alongside the northern edge there is a lovely wooded area which almost reintroduces one to their youth. It is filled with bark covered footpaths, wildlife and wooden sculptures. Behind it Wythenshawe Road continues and if you rejoin the residential world here it may save you the longer distance and repetitive nature of re-running Altrincham Road and the south end of Brooklands Road which you ran earlier.

Instead run left along Wythenshawe Road and then, no doubt feeling hot by now, right up Warmley Road, right again up Wendover Road and continue along it as it becomes Cranleigh

Drive. The change from housing association properties to large, manicured-gardened middle-class wealth increases with each stride here. At the end of Cranleigh Drive turn right onto Brooklands Road.

You will reach the straight road just after St John the Divine Church and run up past the Belmore Hotel and you can finish the run and cool down at Brooklands Gardens – just across from the Metrolink Station. Here there are neighbouring shops and garages and the Brooklands pub at which to buy well-earned drinks (or takeaways, a pint of lager and a pie to quell your post-run carb cravings!)

Advantages:
- For those who don't like concrete running the monotony is broken by the park.
- For those who don't like cross-country style running and having to navigate but want some grass training this route is ideal.
- It is handy for a start at the Metrolink and there are plenty of bus routes along the way if you can't get home on foot.

Disadvantages:
- You won't find much solitude on this route if that's what you are looking for.
- There is a lot of traffic alongside the road stretches.

Summary:
This is a 5-mile route for intermediate runners. It offers a taste of urban running in Manchester's bustle but also the delights of nature and a feel for heritage and culture in the city.

Mileage:
5 miles.

History:
The park is set in 270 acres and contains three Grade II listed structures in the form of the North Lodge, the statue of Oliver Cromwell and Wythenshawe Hall. The park was given the Green Flag Award in 2010 for reaching the national standard for parks and green spaces and you can enjoy a cup of tea at the Courtyard tearooms which opened in 2008.

Since the 1300s the Hall has been the home of the Tatton family and in 1643–44 the site was besieged by the Cromwellian Parliamentarian soldiers during the Civil War. Robert Tatton was a Royalist and would not concede (until two cannons were brought in from Manchester in the February of 1644, little choice then really). It does leave you asking why a statue of Cromwell stands in its grounds though. A change of direction perhaps, after being beaten?

By 1830 the fields around the Hall had become parkland. In 1926 Lord and Lady Simon bought the Hall and parkland when the city council was hoping to make Wythenshawe a 'Garden City', moving people out from the city centre to slightly more countrified surroundings.

Like several other Manchester parks it was given to the city to be kept forever as an open space for the people of Manchester and glad we are too.

Useful Websites:

www.manchester.gov.uk/info/200073/parks_and_open_spaces/2242/wythenshawe_park/1
It lists diverse events such as stargazing with the park warden and many other activities.

Contacts:

Manchester Triathlon Club
PO Box 450
Sale
M33 0AS
Tel: 07583 742652
Email: mtc@man-tri-club.org.uk

Wythenshawe Park
Manchester
M23 0AB
Tel: Park Office on 0161 998 2117

Wythenshawe Wheelers (for adapted cycling)
Tel: Sue Blaylock on 07753 428937

Ambitious Feet

If you love the routes in this book but see them as weekly training for a big event or want to cover a big run there are several ways you could perform a life changing battle with your breathing and fight with your feet, from being organised with hundreds of others to the solitudinous slog for charity, or ever onwards to meet a life's ambition while being more free than disorganised:

The Trans Pennine Trail

Starting at Southport, then Liverpool (I know, many true Mancunians will feel a shudder) you head through Lancashire countryside and towns like St Helen's before reaching the Mersey, Trafford, Stockport, Tameside and heading off into the Peak District National Park. The trail heads for Yorkshire and on to Hull then Hornsea at the east coast. A mere 215-mile (346 km) test of your training achievements!

Coast to Coast

Initiated by walker Alfred Wainwright this tester covers three national parks; the Lake District, Yorkshire Dales and North York Moors. It starts at St Bees in the Lake District and ends at Robin Hood's Bay on the North Sea coast 190 miles (360km) away. Obviously, if you try this one you might be allowed to stop once or twice en route!

The Pennine Way

You are crazy aren't you? But doing this would incite envy from some. This 268-mile (431km) run up the backbone of England will enchant you with sights that you will remember for a lifetime. Not one where you should lose your wits though as you run from the Peak District, through the Yorkshire Dales to Hadrian's Wall and on to the Cheviots. You will need a mountain of motivation to reach your peak!

Manchester 10K

Pound the paths with about 38,000 other people in springtime – most running for charity – and enjoy the city-sized equivalent of patriotism. Run with friends or challenge workmates and pass world famous sporting sites like the central metropolis' major football grounds. Enjoy the beat of the music and the atmosphere or run it simply because you love Manchester and love running and you feel it your duty to pound it at least once in this lifetime!

Royton Trail Multi-Terrain Event

A 5.5-mile multi-terrain run around Tandle Hill Country Park.

The White Peak Marathon and Half Marathon

Said to have been initiated in 1977 by Dave Mitchell, the Peak District based route goes from Thorpe to Cromford Meadows following the Tissington Trail. Then it goes on to Parsley Hay and the High Peak Trail and Cromford are taken on. The Half Marathon follows the High Peak Trail from Friden to Cromford.

October time is generally a good month for North West Marathons to test you with autumn elements not just mileage.

Special Races

There are so many races, nationally organised ones, club ones, 10k, 5k, half marathons it would be impossible to include them all. Ask Google for the ones closest to your part of Manchester. Further afield, five of the top 10 scenic runs in the UK according to www.runnersworld.co.uk website were in the North West, in fact Cumbria. However, here is a selection of some of the terrain on which you can train:

Bowdon 5k June

It has been held since 1999 so is a fairly new race but has produced times of 14.33 and 16.32 for men and women respectively, the flat terrain of the area no doubt aiding speed. www.altrincham-athletics.co.uk for application forms.

Cloud Nine Hill Race March

Usually held in March time with a £5 entry fee, free soup and it comes highly recommended, though challenging in reviews. See www.congleton-harriers.co.uk for information.

Congleton Lions' Run Day October

See www.congleton-harriers.co.uk
A half marathon which started in 1983.

Dunham 5k May and June (2009 series)

First held in 2002 Dunham Massey is a beautiful Georgian mansion with deer and a pond in the parkland. According to the www.altrincham-athletics.co.uk website the race is favoured by women because of the safe parkland running environment.

Manchester 10k

A very popular and enjoyable race but get in quick because it can prove difficult to get an entry place.

Passing Clouds Fell Race

A 9-mile run for over 18s where you climb 1,800ft. It is organised by www.congleton-harriers.co.uk.

Tegg's Nose Fell Race

Tegg's Nose 7.5-mile fell race is run by Macclesfield Harriers and competitors ascend a joyous height of between 1,100ft and 1,600ft at Bullocks Lane, Sutton near Macclesfield, usually in August time. It is an economy run at only £2 for the 2011 run which should suit everyone's pocket but you were charged again to get into the Sheepdog Trial fields.

Trafford 10k

First held in 1990, largely on flat terrain, Carrington and Partington are some of the areas it covers. Look at www.altrincham-athletics.co.uk for more details.

The Herod Farm Race

A Glossop area 3-mile run, which was first held in 1989. You may be running some time with this one as the website has stated a landmark public house has closed then later states that it is the finishing point. Register on the night but for pre-run information see www.glossopdale.org.uk.

The Shelf Moor Race Usually September

A 6-mile race that includes three aircraft wrecks. You can climb the steep James' Thorn on an 1,800ft contour to see one or go to the top of the Peak District to see two more at 2,038ft! Stunning views on the right day. See Glossopdale Harriers website for details www.glossopdale.org.uk.

Wilmslow Half Marathon Usually Late March

Perhaps you only go running about 5 or 10 miles a week to keep fit, chatting with your mate as you go. In that case be prepared to be shamed by geriatrics and people that run the distance between Manchester and Leeds and back every week then do another 20 miles for fun. They don't hang about at Wilmslow Half Marathon and in 2009 Michelle Ross-Cope broke the course record covering the mere 13 miles in 1hr 12min and of course we must not forget the 35 seconds. Michelle who trains 100 miles a week has been running since she was 12 years old and runs for Great Britain.

Remember these Top Tips to be Tip Top

- Stretch and warm up properly at the beginning and end of every run. It can seem tedious but if you don't want the flexibility of lead the next day.

- When running a one-way route start furthest away from home and run back to avoid the temptation to quit early. This way you can also get the boring transport/logistics out of the way first.

- There is more motivation when heading for home. You can have a supersize energy drink waiting for you on arrival – and a pizza menu!

- Run with a friend. It gives you someone to compete against, someone who will ensure you don't get lost on wild routes, someone to gee you up when you'd rather watch a soap opera for the eighth time that week.

- Run alone. Yes, I know it contradicts the earlier advice but so do people and their different ways. If you run to get away from other people and stress, run alone and find solitude.

- It's time for the feet to hit the beat. A lot of runners are obsessed with taking their ipods, Walkman's, tambourines, maracas, whatever musical device you care to mention. It is good to have a beat to run to.

- Run straight after work. Don't get comfy on the sofa and then expect to have the motivation to go out in winter temperatures and run 5 miles. Relaxation time is precious and you don't want to waste half of it feeling guilty, thinking you should be out running, so do the running first.

- Have varied length, regular routes close to home. You might want to wriggle out of crossing Manchester when public transport is down but if you have a 2 or 3-mile regular route near home you've no excuse. Often it is easier to run than feel guilty about not having done so.

- Use insoles. Weighted insoles make your feet heavier to up the intensity. Earth negative heel positions or the heel being lower than the ball of the foot, makes it like walking uphill or adding more incline on the treadmill. It also straightens up your posture.

- Run towards traffic not on the left when you have to take to the country roads. If pavements are non-existent or clogged up with snow and you are forced to run on tarmac at least let the driver stand a chance of seeing you. Well, at your speeds!

- Don't run straight after a heavy meal. If you expect to do your best on mega challenges such as the hills around Marple after six doner kebabs or a Sunday dinner you've underestimated Marple!

- Stay in touch. You may not need, or want, your mobile on a 3-mile run on your doorstep but for moorland which is new to you, in winter, take it just in case.

- Take your anger, upset, frustration, negative thoughts out on the running. Not only does it help you move faster but like the endorphins it makes you feel better afterwards.

- Have a goal or target. Whether it is to run 10 miles a week or to train for a marathon next summer targets help you get moving.

- Have a notebook or training log to note best times and distances for motivation purposes but also so you can write down the runs that you enjoyed or the ones you hope to tackle in future.

- Visit council and park websites for information on days out and guided walks which you can involve your family with or find areas that may become new favourites.

Useful Websites:
www.transpenninetrail.org.uk
Get information on events, places, maps and history along the route.

Contacts:
Trans Pennine Trail Office
Tel: 01226 772574
Email: info@transpenninetrail.org.uk

Athletics Clubs and Organisations

One of the good things about the Manchester area for the runner is the versatility of surfaces. You can go running through parkland, set trails, inner city concrete running or even running alongside waterways, on moorland and fell-running on the outskirts. If you are new to the area or want the best tips from seasoned runners, or maybe want someone to motivate you with your training it might be best to join a club, of which Manchester has a selection, including:

Altrincham Athletics Club

www.altrincham-athletics.co.uk

Founded in 1961 and based in Timperley this is an all terrain club with over 200 members. First membership fee is £35 for men or women.

Congleton Harriers

www.congleton-harriers.co.uk

Over 100 members of all ages and abilities at the club which has, literally, been running for 25 years. All terrain – road, fell, cross-country, trail – and the club members meet several times a week. Some members even enter marathons and races on the Continent, as well as the London Marathon. The annual membership fee is £15 at present but there is a £21 sign-up fee as well. You get membership to UK Athletics for race insurance though.

East Cheshire Harriers

www.eastcheshireharriers.co.uk/clubhistory

The club is based in Ashton-under-Lyne but over the years has become an amalgamation of more and more Tameside clubs like the Dukinfield Harriers and the Tintwistle Harriers. The subscription is more expensive than some though at £80 per year but see the website for discount categories.

Glossopdale Harriers

www.glossopdale.org.uk/races

Fell running for adults in steep hilly countryside, sometimes with very bleak conditions but there is some running for road runners. There is a £10 membership fee and you can download an application from the above website.

Macclesfield Harriers & Athletics Club

www.macclesfield-harriers.co.uk

Adult membership is £20 for the year for those competing and there is often a waiting list for junior members due to the popularity of the club. See the website for contact numbers. The club formed in 1897 but reformed fully in 1945. It has a long history in cross-country but in recent years has excelled in marathon running and has an 8-lane track, field facilities and a clubhouse thanks to lottery funding granted in the 1990s.

Manchester Harriers

www.manchesterharriers.co.uk

Based in Gatley near Stockport the Manchester Harriers have over 200 members but are always looking for new members. The club was founded in Fallowfield in 1886 and in the 1970s established a British indoor record in the 3,000 metres through member Ricky Wilde. Adult membership is £35 per year.

Sale Harriers

www.saleharriersmanchester.com

According to information from the well-known athletics club they have approximately 800 members. They cater for all standards, from new runners up to international level runners. The cost of joining is £40 for seniors, £20 for associate members, children, students and the unwaged. See website for details.

Salford Harriers

www.salfordharriers.co.uk

It meets in Moston, north Manchester, though track is held at Sports City. The club was founded in 1884 and has weekly road and track sessions but gets involved in some worldwide running events as it did with the World Mountain Running Trial in Blackburn in 2011. Membership is £25 per year.

Stockport Harriers and Athletics Club

www.stockportharriers.com

The club has over 400 members who train at Woodbank Park Athletics Stadium, Woodbank Park, Stockport. Membership is £28 per year but the club caters more for track and field runners than distance runners.

Trafford Athletic Club

www.traffordac.co.uk

The club meets at a £1 million facility in Longford Park in Chorlton-cum-hardy and originally formed in 1964. It was previously known as Stretford Athletic Club. Over 100 members have competed at international levels, including the Olympics, in less than 50 years of history. Membership was £35 in 2010.

Useful Websites

Though most runners would rather be pounding grass or concrete than reading about it there is more and more useful information available now to let you take your sport further. In *On The Run Around Manchester* each route has given you handy hints for websites for each particular run but this page gives you more general websites to surf before you stride off into the sunset.

www.climbers.net
www.cycleroute.com
www.nationalparks.gov.uk
www.nationaltrust.org.uk
www.ordnancesurvey.co.uk

Find out about mountain rescues and learn more of the dangers of hill running.
www.kmrt.org.uk

Get your maps and grid references here.
www.fellrunner.org.uk
www.go4awalk.com
www.ldwa.org.uk
www.peakdistrictinformation.com
www.peakdistrictview.com
www.walkingbritain.co.uk

See pictures of the places you want to run to or clarify exact names or details of those you have already seen.
www.geograph.co.uk
www.rockfax.com
www.saleharriersmanchester.com

Find out about the fixtures and successes of the 2011 British League Champions. The site includes information about an intra club for fell runners.
www.saleharriersmanchester.com

The website covers track and field, cross country and road events and you can download a membership form.
www.stockportharriers.com

Get information about how to warm-up and stretch to your limits or how to handle injuries.
www.sportsinjuryclinic.net
www.thestretchinghandbook.com

Last Word

Manchester is a city with a vast history of adaptability and variety. During the Industrial Revolution this was the place of innovation and wealth, of production and a change of life for the numerous people who worked in the mills or on the edge of the textile industry.

Before masses of haulage vehicles ladened the roads, even before railways, canals were the route via which many materials and finished goods were sent or supplied. The need for waterways, man-made and natural, to accommodate such major industry meant the city is covered with an embroidery of canals and riverside paths for us runners to use.

Later, railways were used for haulage but the advent of cars meant the railways have been used less and many former train lines are now leisure paths and trails for us to pound.

On our doorsteps, however, we have the amazing sights of the Peak District National Park, the Cheshire Plains, Lancashire moorland. Manchester is one of the country's biggest cities yet we don't have to travel far to find solitude and untouched views which leave you in awe.

There are many runners who just want to tug their trainers on and go but for others the whole experience of being outdoors, of enjoying the peace and freedom of the country or city's green spaces adds to the fun.

You can do more to protect our spaces or make sure they are not forgotten by helping to get funds allocated to new projects or backing places to get Green Awards. Is there green land near you that needs saving. If so, why not surf to try and save it?

www.keepbritaintidy.org/GreenFlag

When you've had enough of surfing though, why not pant and pace, or grind and groan around monstrous hills and gentle plains and remember how lucky we are in this city to have the surroundings and scenes that we have.